PR RULES
THE PLAYBOOK

THE ENTREPRENEUR'S GUIDE
TO SUPERSIZING YOUR SMALL BUSINESS
WITH THE 8 STEPS TO PR SUCCESS

BY HOPE KATZ GIBBS

KATHLEEN McCARTHY

MICHAEL GIBBS ILLUSTRATION & DESIGN

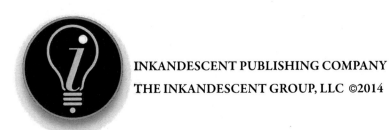

INKANDESCENT PUBLISHING COMPANY

THE INKANDESCENT GROUP, LLC ©2014

PR Rules: The Playbook

The Entrepreneur's Guide to Supersizing Your Small Business With the 8 Steps to PR Success

©2014 Inkandescent Rulebooks: Best Practices in Small Business

By Hope Katz Gibbs, President, InkandescentPR.com
Publisher, Be Inkandescent magazine
Founder, The Inkandescent Group, LLC

and Kathleen McCarthy, Managing Editor, Be Inkandescent magazine
Senior VP, The Inkandescent Group, LLC

Design and illustrations by Michael Glenwood Gibbs
Michael Gibbs Illustration & Design

Library of Congress Cataloging-in-Publishing Data
Gibbs, Hope Katz
PR Rules: The Playbook, 1st ed.
ISBN 978-0-9913016-8-3
Library of Congress Catalog Card No. 2013922264

Printed in the United States of America
First printing July 2014
10 9 8 7 6 5 4 3 2 1

Inkandescent Rulebooks are available at special discounts when purchased in bulk for team building and sales promotions, as well as for fundraising and educational use. Special editions or book excerpts also can be created to specification. For details, contact us at hope@inkandescentpr.com.

Inkandescent Publishing Company
The Inkandescent Group, LLC
Arlington, VA 22207
www.InkandescentPublishing.com

For the lights in our lives:

Anna Paige + Dylan Zane Glenwood Gibbs
Miranda, Kerry, Eleanor + Tony Reichhardt
and Anne P. Gibbs—who saw what we missed

May you always Be Inkandescent!

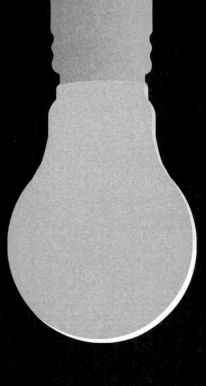

"Sometimes all you need is 20 seconds of insane courage—literally 20 seconds of embarrassing bravery. And I promise, something great will come of it."

— Benjamin Mee, *"We Bought a Zoo"*

Table of Contents

A Note From Hope

The Auspicious Power of the Number 8

Hope Katz Gibbs

8 IS THE MAGIC NUMBER IN "PR RULES: THE PLAYBOOK."
Our goal is to help you see your business from a new vantage point.
In this guide, you'll find advice in pieces of 8: 8 case studies, 8 hands-on exercises, 8 sets of 8 experts, 8 insights, 8 rules of thumb, 8 steps, 8 takeaways, 8 tips... 8cetera.

Here are 8 auspicious associations attached to the number 8:

■ An octave has 8 notes, and 8 planets circle our sun.

■ A byte is comprised of 8 bits, and 8 is the only positive Fibonacci number—aside from 1—that is a perfect cube.

■ Oxygen is number 8 on the periodic table of elements.

■ The number 8 has long been associated with wealth and prosperity, and business and financial success.

■ In fact, in Chinese, the word for 8 sounds similar to the words for prosper and wealth. And in China, the number 8 is believed to express the totality of the universe. In Buddhist beliefs, there are 8 elements on the path to enlightenment. The Olympic Games in Beijing honored 8 by beginning at 8:08 on 8/8/08.

■ In Indian mythology, the Earth is supported on the backs of 8 white elephants.

■ And, flipped on its side, the number 8 is the symbol for infinity.

■ But there's one 8 to be wary of: In the game of pool, being "behind the 8 ball" means to be in a difficult or baffling situation—exactly what this book is intended to help you avoid.

Our hope is that you'll use "PR Rules: The Playbook" to achieve the big dreams and ambitions that you have for your organization.

Here's to supersizing your small business! — Hope

Are You Suffering From the Trifecta of Small-Business Failure?

WHY DO SO MANY SMALL BUSINESSES FAIL? Because the very characteristics that make entrepreneurs want to start a business are the ones that cause them to stumble.

Sitting on our publicist's perch at Inkandescent PR, we have been privileged to work inside more than 100 companies—from solo-preneurs and start-ups to multimillion-dollar corporations. We have helped them create fireworks—and we have witnessed their trials and tribulations.

From these observations, we distilled the philosophy of the "Trifecta of Small-Business Failure." These three traits trip up the most experienced entrepreneurs. If your business is struggling, odds are good you are suffering from one or more aspects of the Trifecta. Not sure? Then see if any of these monikers describe you:

1. The Control Freak. When it comes to your business, have you ever thought this, or said aloud: "I want to do it all by myself," "You're not the boss of me," or, "The sky is falling!" If so, you aren't alone. Many entrepreneurs have a tendency to want to hold on tight to every single facet of their business. After all, being in control is why many people start their own companies. But beware: No one is good at everything. Even if you are, there aren't enough hours in the day to think of, perfect, and execute all the necessary tasks required to ensure a business succeeds. So let go—delegate and seek help from professionals. Collaboration is the key to success. Find partners you trust, and build your business.

2. The Small-Picture Person. Do you understand the icing-and-cake metaphor? If not, you may not be making the most of your core competencies—your *cake*—by leveraging them to make more money. Start by identifying your core competency, then step back and look at the big picture. Find the additional revenue streams that are available—your *icing*—and incorporate them into your business. For example, if you are a chef and you are only cooking for your restaurant, then you are leaving money on the table. Consider catering, and selling some of your products at local markets and online. Don't try just to break even. Aim to supersize.

3. The Win-Meister. In this scenario, the "win" comes only when you beat someone else at the game of business. In fact, for years this philosophy was a popular way to succeed in business. But that has changed. Today, if others have to lose for you to win, you are operating with an outmoded, inefficient model. To be effective, embrace the concept of the win-win-win—in which you win, and your customers, vendors, and colleagues win, too. Best of all, the world at large wins.

Many millennials work under this belief. If you don't, you could be missing out on the next generation of sales.

The good news is that a strategic PR and marketing campaign can help. Having a sophisticated strategy is the key. So is being patient about the timeline for your business success.

You'll know you are on the right path when:

■ Your sales exceed your expectations.

■ Reporters consider you to be an expert, and are eager to hear what you have to say.

■ Feedback from customers is glowing, and they want more of what you are selling—in ways that you may have never thought of. Open up to their ideas for innovation. It could take your company to a new place.

And that's the goal of this book. On the following pages, we encourage you to play with the ideas and exercises, and dive into the expert interviews. We hope the information will inspire you to think about your business, and yourself as an entrepreneur, in new and exciting ways. Go ahead—laugh out loud at yourself. We've all made the same rookie mistakes. After all, growth is an inside job. So be bold about discovering what holds you back, and find ways to leapfrog over the hurdles in your way.

Are you ready to supersize your small business? Turn the page, and get started. Here's to turning the Trifecta on its head! — **HKG**

"Find the fulcrum. Below the obvious, behind the superficial, under the excuses and facades, y ou will find the crux of the matter. Work from that point. Proper leverage gets a hell of a lot of work done."

— *Jessica Hagy, "How to Be Interesting (In 10 Simple Steps)"*

By Gene Weingarten

Flack Yourself

This just in:

Dear journalist: As a media-relations trade publication servicing public relations professionals, my job is to help ensure that my readers have accurate info about you so they can send you the best quality PR pitches. Please answer the following questions. Thanks! —Jim

Happy to oblige, Jim! I'll take 'em one at a time.

So...
you've got a great product or service. If you could just get a reporter's attention, the world would be clued in to why it needs what you're selling — and you'd make millions, right? Journalist Gene Weingarten has a slightly different take on the situation. His essay, "Flack Yourself," which originally ran in *The Washington Post Magazine,* will disabuse you of that notion. And not in a gentle way, as you might have already surmised from the title. Weingarten's humor column, *Below the Beltway,* has appeared weekly since July 2000. He also hosts a monthly humor chat. As a feature writer, he was awarded the Pulitzer Prize in both 2008 and 2010. Since 2010, he has co-authored the syndicated comic strip, *Barney & Clyde.* So what does it take to pique the interest of a high-profile reporter like Weingarten? In his deliciously acerbic style, "Flack Yourself" makes it clear why most reporters don't bother reading press releases—and why pitching your product to a reporter rarely works. Read it and weep. Then arm yourself with the tools in "PR Rules," wield them wisely, and get the visibility your business needs.

"Flack Yourself" is reprinted with permission from The Washington Post

1. Which specific beats and topic areas do you cover?

Poop, pee, and sex, mostly, with a subspecialty in character assassination. My favorite targets are public relations professionals, because they are a hoot. Their entire existence teeters on a ludicrous lie they tell their clients: that they are tight with the media. To most of the media, communications from PR people are as welcome as mosquitoes at a hemophiliacs' picnic. A PR pitch tends to be an enthusiastic description of a product or service that is so lame it actually needs the help of a PR professional. As pitches go, they're particularly slimy—not like spitballs so much as snotballs. Loogieballs. Sure, someone has to catch them, but we don't have to be happy about it.

2. What do the best PR people do to grab you, to get your attention and make you want to work with them?

Theoretically, I'd be willing to work with a PR person trying to sell me a story about the impending death of PR due to the sudden, simultaneous, slap-to-the-forehead realization by everyone in the entire world that PR is a silly waste of time and money. But that's, you know, unlikely.

Anyway, your question is predicated on an unsupportable thesis: that there is a "best" PR person. That's like asking what is the "best" crotch fungus. I'll pass.

3. What are some inappropriate pitches (i.e., material that PR people keep sending you that you don't cover, or pet peeves you may have about PR people)?

I already covered this a bit in Question 1, but it's a subject I never get tired of. I'm particularly appalled by "crisis management," which is a highly paid PR specialty involving extricating rich people and their avaricious corporations from humiliating situations, such as when the CEO has been caught stealing panties from laundromats or gnawing on a roasted human thigh. Usually the resulting campaign of rehabilitation through PR involves strategic subject-changing that's no less transparent than when a guy whom you've just caught in a lie gestures frantically behind you and says, "What's that?!"

4. Can you briefly tell me about a PR pitch that resulted in a story? What was it about the pitch or PR pro that sparked your interest?

Many years ago, I read a PR pitch that was describing a new line of decorative throw pillows as though they were the Bayeux Tapestry. You could smell the pungent stench of desperation. That gave me an idea: I started calling PR people and offering to write something favorable about their clients' products if the PR people would disclose humiliating things about themselves that I also would print. Not many declined this opportunity to snivel, to curry favor with a client by utterly debasing themselves. One PR professional told me how her husband had left her for a younger woman; another, how his butt was so big that he blew out his pants at a publicity event. One woman said that she was once so hungover in college that she accidentally appeared on a basketball court, for a game in which she was playing, naked from the waist down.

I'd hoped that column, as withering as it was, would convince PR people to stop sending me their crap. It worked for many years, but evidently has been forgotten. Maybe this one will do the trick!

Part 1: **The PR Playing Field**............................3

What is the difference between PR, marketing, advertising, social media, and sales? In each of these 5 chapters, you'll find insights from 8 experts, who provide you with tips that you can immediately put to work in order to better understand how to up your game. Don't miss the takeaways in each section to help you improve your outreach to customers and reporters, so that you can glow—and grow.

Part 2: **The 8 Steps to PR Success**.........53

In this section you'll learn what each step is, what it's not, why it's important—and learn how to play with each of the 8 Steps, including how to: create a stunning website (STEP 1); master the art of newsletter writing, utilize social media, and make advertising work to your advantage (STEP 2); write a column and host a radio show (STEP 3); get quoted in the news (STEP 4); network wisely (STEP 5); join a speakers bureau (STEP 6); write a book (STEP 7); and pay it forward (STEP 8). These 8 Steps to PR Success will help you create the most affordable, least time-consuming way to promote your business.

Part 3: **8 Case Studies**...117

Take a page from the playbooks of 8 of the country's top entrepreneurs in fields ranging from Conscious Capitalism and international relations—to being a best-selling author, Broadway show playwright, and candidate for governor of New Mexico. In this section you'll read their stories, learn from their advice, and gain Inkandescent Insights into how they have mastered the 8 Steps to PR Success.

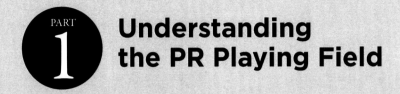

PART 1 Understanding the PR Playing Field

What is PR? 4

What is Marketing? 12

What is Advertising? 20

What is Social Media? 30

What is Sales? 40

The PR Playing Field: *Public Relations*

Y OU WANT TO BE FEATURED IN the news, right?

It can be a challenge, and here's why: Many journalists are wary of PR specialists, who sometimes act like pushy salespeople.

Reporters believe their job is to provide readers with legitimate news. Tension arises because reporters know that publicists are being paid to pitch a story—and that doesn't sit well with people who make a living sniffing out the truth, the whole truth, and nothing but the truth. Or, at least, to the best of their ability.

Having been reporters for decades, our team at The Inkandescent Group understands this well.

In fact, the reason we got into the PR business is the same reason we wrote this book—to help small-business owners figure out how to best spread the word about what they are doing so their companies will glow, and grow.

Time and again we have seen the blind spots that many small-business owners have about effectively promoting their companies. And often, they are simply so busy running their businesses (aka: working *in* them), that they don't have the time or energy to promote them fully (aka: working *on* them.)

What does it take to successfully pitch the nation's reporters—who have access to the eyes and ears of millions of potential customers?

We asked 8+ of our favorite PR professionals and journalists for ideas about how you can do that well—and you'll also find thoughts from clients whom we've helped get featured in some of the nation's top publications, including *The New York Times, The Wall Street Journal,* and on "The CBS Early Show."

Meet the experts:

■ **Lee Woodruff,** PR expert, journalist, and author of "Perfectly Imperfect," "In an Instant," and her first novel, "Those We Love Most"

■ **Jeremy Hazlehurst,** London-based writer, *Daily Telegraph* and *The Times*

■ **Tony Reichhardt,** senior editor of *Air&Space/Smithsonian* magazine

■ **Tom Shroder,** former *Washington Post Magazine* editor, and author of "Fire on the Horizon: The Untold Story of the Gulf Oil Disaster," "Old Souls," and "Seeing the Light"

■ **Meg Cox,** freelance writer, *The Wall Street Journal*

Check out these great PR hits from our Inkandescent PR clients:

■ **Sharon Armstrong,** author and human resources expert, on being featured in *CBS MoneyWatch*

■ **Sheldon Weiner,** financial advisor and partner of Egan, Berger & Weiner, LLC, on being featured in *The Wall Street Journal*

■ **Andy Hines, PhD,** futurist, and University of Houston professor of Futures Studies, on being featured in *The New York Times*

■ **Chris Carbone,** futurist and analyst for the Spike TV study, *The Future of Men,* on his "The CBS Early Show" interview

ESSENTIAL **3** **QUESTIONS**

Before you read tips from our experts, try this exercise—answer these three essential questions about you and your business:

1 **What do you do?** Summarize it in under 30 words (the fewer the better). If you can't, people will assume that you don't know what you do. So think it through.

> ***Example:*** *The Inkandescent Group is a PR and publishing company that helps entrepreneurs get more visibility using The 8 Steps to PR Success. (22 words)*

> ☛ **Your turn. What do you do?**

2 **Why do you do it?** Is your business your passion? Does it get you out of bed in the morning? If you didn't do this business, would it crush you? If you didn't answer yes to those questions—stop reading. You may not be doing what you're supposed to be doing.

But if you answered yes—then you are on the path to success. Passion is the key to every entrepreneur's success. It takes a whole lot more than that to be successful, of course—time, patience, capital, and human resources—and an amazing product or service. But if your business is not in your guts, like a child or a lover, then you'll never take it to the level you dream of.

So why do you do what you do? Your answer will be the difference between success and failure—and it will be what makes reporters want to call you, or not.

> ***Example:*** *Our team of journalists, PR experts, designers, photographers, and videographers love to tell stories. Our favorite stories are what inspired entrepreneurs to start and grow their businesses. The better the story, the more likely it is that reporters will call you for your expert opinion and advice.*
>
> *From authors and artists to restauranteurs, doctors, lawyers, financial advisors, insurance agents, management trainers, and self-help gurus—we find their energy and excitement about their work contagious. We have loved helping these creative, smart people build their websites, create monthly newsletters, get in the news, and shout their message from the rooftops. It makes us want to jump out of bed in the morning.*

> ☛ **Your turn. Why do you do what you do?**

3 **How do you do it?** Now for the nitty-gritty. The devil is in the details, especially when a reporter is quoting you, or, even better, writing a story about your company. So be sure your message about your business is clear, concise, and nailed down.

> ***Example:*** *At The Inkandescent Group, our mission is to promote, educate, and inspire entrepreneurs about best practices in small business. To walk that talk, our team provides a range of services that helps businesses get more visibility—from building websites and crafting monthly newsletters and magazine columns, to helping them host radio shows, network wisely, write books, and get out on the speakers circuit. We've developed those services to meet any and every need we've observed that will help them accomplish their goals.*

> ☛ **Your turn. How do you do what you do?**

Are you ready for more insights? Check out the tips from five experienced journalists and four experienced business owners who have struck publicity pay dirt.

Veteran PR expert, broadcast journalist, and author Lee Woodruff

Understand the Purpose of PR

Lee Woodruff has spent her career working in the news. A journalist, contributor to "CBS This Morning," and a New York Times best-selling author, she was also a senior VP at one of the nation's largest PR firms, Porter Novelli. Her clients included Fortune 500 companies, and she promoted everything from consumer goods to pharmaceutical companies. Then she had a baby. "My son's birth caused me to reconfigure my life," she recalls. Later, when her husband—ABC News anchor Bob Woodruff—decided to leave the practice of law and become a journalist, she started her own PR firm. Although the practice of PR has changed in the last decade, Woodruff says the same principles apply.

Lee Woodruff

What is the purpose of PR?

Lee Woodruff: To take a cause, product, or person and spread awareness about it. Whether you are talking about getting condoms to people in Ghana to keep HIV from spreading, or you are promoting Snooki's new book, PR is a way for people to access the best information about what you're selling, offering, or giving away.

Is it harder in the digital age?

Lee Woodruff: It's easier in some ways, because we all have access to information that was once available only from news outlets. But the landscape is also fractured. So targeting your message to the appropriate audience is even more critical. It used to be that the cover of *People* or *TIME* was the iconic client "ask," but the digital age and the power of social media have diminished the "big bang"

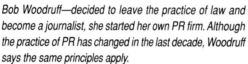

of a message in those places. Fortunately, the Internet has allowed us to focus on silos of information and better reach vertical audiences. Still, with so many options, it can be confusing to make budget decisions. That is why, first and foremost, you need a team you trust, and a solid PR plan that is realistic and achievable.

How can a company find the perfect PR fit?

Lee Woodruff: It's all about personality. You should *like* the person who's representing you, feel they understand what you are trying to accomplish, and they need to have the ability to share information and communicate well with reporters. You should also understand:

■ The rudimentary part of PR is the ability to put a clear message out on the news wires, update websites, and track where a client has been quoted. But that can be taught.

■ What's more important is to make sure your PR team is a good steward of your dollars. You want accountability; be sure you know what they are spending their time on.

How do you handle a client's expectations?

Lee Woodruff: A fundamental part of PR is to distill the crux of the message, and disseminate it on as many platforms as are relevant. In the end, the message/news has to be valid, and of interest, for PR to work effectively. Sometimes clients can have an over-inflated sense of the importance of their story. Naturally, everyone believes they have something valuable to say. But this is where a good PR partnership is critical. You need to trust and value your publicist's experience—and know when it's time to listen. That can be tough, because clients with inflated egos are always hard to manage. I have a friend who keeps switching PR people because he is convinced that given the right person to represent him, he'll get on the cover of the most popular news magazines. Really. It's what a person or company is doing that interests the public at large—that's what intrigues the nation's big media outlets.

How can you measure the success of a PR campaign?

Lee Woodruff: There are lots of ways to track sales and gather data, but in the end, the return on investment (ROI) on PR is elusive. You know you need PR when your business is not growing organically. And you know your PR campaign is working when everything is going well. Realize that PR is just one of the many tools an entrepreneur can use—including advertising, direct mail, and social media. Everything should work together.

Learn more at www.leewoodruff.com

International journalist Jeremy Hazlehurst

Appreciate the Tension Between Reporters and Publicists

British freelance writer Jeremy Hazlehurst says he is bombarded every day with email pitches from PR people hoping to entice him to write about their client or company.

"Most days you are working hard and trying to hit deadlines... and if you are an editor, too, you're dealing with picture editors, and commissioning writers and photo shoots," says Hazlehurst, who covers business and financial news and has written for the Daily Telegraph and The London Times. "If we don't respond to a pitch, often that's why."

Jeremy Hazlehurst

He certainly doesn't wish PR pitches would go away. "I like receiving them, because you never know what will spark an idea for a story." Here's his advice:

As a journalist who covers the public relations industry, how do you see PR?

Jeremy Hazlehurst: There are some bad PR reps who will lie to you—and worse. When I worked for a financial newspaper, I'd deal with PR reps who would simply threaten to sue if you published a (perfectly true) story about their client or employer misbehaving. Other times when I was on a tight deadline, I'd ask a PR rep a question, and they would get back to me at 6 p.m. with a 400-page document and say: "The answer's in there. You find it." That style of PR shows a total lack of ethics and competence. It stops the press from performing its legitimate function. In general, however, good PR reps realize that they can't behave like that—they have to face a bad story and deal with it. They help you with a story and understand that you have to be critical and ask questions. Journalists have a duty to ask the questions that their readers would ask if *they* had the time to investigate the story. If PR reps want an advertisement, they can buy one.

What type of PR pitches do you respond to?

Jeremy Hazlehurst: None, really. It's rare for PR people to really understand what works as a story, at a particular time, and for a particular publication. Interview offers might work. Too much detail is a turn-off. Give me in one line who is up for an interview, or what the idea is. Thousands of words of detail are a waste. I just don't have time.

Tell us about your article for *Management Today,* "Spin Masters: How PR Is Taking Over the World."

Jeremy Hazlehurst: I think that the days of spin are over.

The Internet means that people are better informed about businesses. You can't just tell lies and expect not to be found out. I hope that businesses will become better—in the sense of giving people what they want.

The other thing to remember is that the role of PR or communications professionals has widened. These days businesses interact with customers directly through Twitter, Tumblr, Facebook, and so on. If you are running all those things, then obviously you need more people in PR. If you have people at high levels in a business who understand how all this works, then it stands to reason that those businesses will be more innovative when it comes to communications.

Also, it's the PR people who... are the ones listening to what people want, and they are telling their company's board what customers like and don't like about the business. People know more about businesses these days, and they don't want to buy from businesses that use child-labor, pollute, or underpay their staff.

In your *Management Today* article, you quoted PR expert Tim Bell as saying, "Twitter is a sewer. The Internet is a sewer. If you want to live in a transparent world, then *someone* has to provide information about you. If you don't want someone else to, you have to do it yourself. That's what PR people do." Do you agree with Bell's comment?

Jeremy Hazlehurst: The problem with Twitter is that it is an echo-chamber for ill-thought-out, first-reaction ideas. And people follow a crowd. Take the release last year of a 30-minute video about Ugandan rebel leader Joseph Kony, which was crass and simplistic, but went around the world in no time at all. People who know about Africa despaired. This is a problem with social media—people are often ill-informed or don't understand what constitutes libel, and they don't realize that they can get in trouble for speaking their mind. Reputations can be trashed quickly and groundlessly. In the old days, newspapers stood between writers and readers. There are good and bad things about that, but one of the good things was that people didn't publish things without fact-checking them. On the Internet, anyone can say anything, so we need to be able to deal with that. For PR reps, that's about learning how to react to lies.

Learn more on Twitter @jhazlehurst

Three journalists and editors dole out advice

Find the Best Strategies to Get Featured in the News

1. Do your homework.

Air&Space/Smithsonian magazine senior editor Tony Reichhardt:

Tony Reichhardt

"My overall advice is to keep the pitches short—just long enough to clearly explain your idea and what makes it distinctive (an original angle, an unusual source)," Reichhardt explains.

"I can usually tell immediately if I want to follow up and ask for more information, which I usually do over the phone. If the writer is new to me, I'd want some links to other published stories, but the pitch itself should be only a couple of paragraphs. Don't agonize over a query so much that it ends up being half as long as the story you intend to write."

Keep this in mind:

- It may seem obvious, but before sending a pitch, first do a simple search of the website of your targeted publication to see if it has already covered your topic. Not only does that save you from wasting your time (and the editor's), it shows that you've taken enough initiative to understand something about the publication's needs.

If they have covered your topic, you could try suggesting a slightly different angle from a topic or an article that they have run before.

- Know the publication's target readership. For example, is it a trade newsletter or a popular magazine? A popular magazine won't have the slightest interest in that new subcomponent your company manufactures, no matter how important it is to your industry, unless you can explain how it can be turned into a story for a general audience.

- Press releases about personnel changes hardly ever get read. Again, unless it's a newsletter for industry insiders, why should anyone care that Joe Jones was just appointed vice president for international business? ■

2. Think like a journalist.

Veteran journalist and editor Tom Shroder, former editor of *The Washington Post Magazine*:

Tom Shroder

"You should approach your client's story as a journalist would approach it, which means you want to dig around until you find the most fascinating aspect of the story you are trying to tell," Shroder insists.

"Ask yourself what grabs *your* interest? If you pitch something that you genuinely find interesting or important—not because your job is to find it interesting, but because it *is* interesting—chances are, a journalist will think so, too." ■

3. Know when man bites dog.

Journalist and author Meg Cox, formerly a staff reporter for *The Wall Street Journal*, where she covered everything from culture to agriculture:

Meg Cox

"Two things would grab my attention when I was constantly bombarded with pitches at the *WSJ*—the unexpected 'man bites dog' story, and a truly fresh trend," Cox recalls.

"So, when a guy phoned me up in 1984 and said, 'You should profile the mogul of rap,' I was intrigued because that seemed like an absurd idea at the time, an oxymoron. He was talking about Russell Simmons, whom I did interview, for a front-page story that helped him get his first big record deal. I also said 'yes' when I had a chance to interview the guy who invented kitty litter.

"When I covered publishing, I listened most to the publicists who knew how my paper worked, and how I worked. They didn't just say, 'Write an article about this book,' but said, 'This book is part of a growing trend, and here are two other recent examples.'" ■

Learn more at airspacemag.com • tomshroder.com • megcox.com

HR expert and author Sharon Armstrong

Leverage Your Reporter Connections

Inkandescent Insight: Sharon Armstrong's two business books, "The Essential HR Handbook," and "The Essential Performance Review Handbook," have sold incredibly well, and not just because they are well-written guides. It's also because they provide content and advice that is easy to understand and crucial to implement. That's why it has been easy to get her quoted in the news—from *CBS MoneyWatch* and *The Wall Street Journal* to *Inc.* magazine and *American Express Open Forum.*

Keep this in mind: Having a great website on which to post press mentions is critical for all of our clients—especially authors. Armstrong's books have helped her leverage her company's visibility and build her reputation as an expert. Take a page from her playbook, and make sure your book website is not only aesthetically pleasing, but includes detailed information about the book, the author—and the business behind the book, which is what will actually generate the income.

Armstrong's Takeaway: "A website is your professional face that will be seen by all of your current and potential clients and customers. It has to be engaging and chock-full of good information and resources for visitors. It has to highlight your products and services and be easy to navigate. Having a strong online presence is also critical to getting speaking engagements. The challenge is to continue to keep it updated with strong material that changes regularly, and engages customers. While it's tempting not to spend a lot of money on it, hire a professional who is skilled in web design. And listen to them.

Sharon Armstrong

"My website helps me get press attention for my books, which in turn helps me reach the masses. I've been so fortunate to get my ideas into the hands of journalists who have a wide following.

"Every time one of my books is mentioned in an article, I see an uptick in my book sales. And building relationships with journalists—and responding to their queries with a substantive and timely response—paves the way for more requests and more exposure. It's a cycle that works." ■

Learn more at www.theessentialhrhandbook.com

Financial advisor Sheldon Weiner

Tell a Story That Can Help Others

Inkandescent Insight: Sheldon Weiner has been a financial advisor for nearly 40 years. Not only has he seen dramatic changes in the marketplace, he has tracked the trends that remain consistent.

He has a wealth of knowledge in many aspects of planning for retirement, and the case studies he's shared with us have been in-depth and revealing about best-case/worst-case scenarios for investors.

So when we saw that *The Wall Street Journal* had launched a new "Voices" column, we pitched Weiner's case study on "Utilizing a Client's Only Major Asset" to reporter Niki Reading, who thought it was a great story and wrote about it in March 2013.

Keep this in mind: To leverage the fact you are featured in a national publication like *The Wall Street Journal*, be sure to share it with your clients in your monthly newsletter, post a link to the article on your website, and brag about it on your social media pages.

Weiner's Takeaway: "I was pleased and proud to share the story of my work with a client, a 65-year-old woman who had recently lost her husband, along with a significant chunk of her monthly income. The husband's pension didn't include survivor benefits, and the widow's own Social Security and pension benefits provided just $2,000 in monthly income—far less than her $4,000 in monthly expenses.

"With only $35,000 in a bank account and a $25,000 annuity, she was on a pace to run out of money before she turned 80. She certainly

Sheldon Weiner

didn't have enough to last a normal lifetime, and she recognized that. We came up with an effective financial plan—and it helped the client accomplish her goals. Not only was it wonderful for us to tell that story, but our clients thought it was wonderful, too. Many of them called us after reading the article to say they learned a lot from the case study.

"Being featured in *The Wall Street Journal* was a big accomplishment, and we got the most bang for our buck by spreading the word among all of our outreach channels. I was amazed by how much additional visibility we got by taking that approach!" ■

Learn more at www.ebwfinancialnews.com

DEFINING PR

Futurist Andy Hines

Know Your Stuff—But It's OK
If You Don't Have a PhD in the Topic

Inkandescent Insight: It has never been hard to get futurist Andy Hines to speak to a reporter—nor is it hard to convince reporters to want to speak to him. And that was a rarity at the futurist think tank where he worked from 2006–2012. It was packed with 40 highly educated analysts and researchers who were tracking international business and consumer trends, and analyzing them for clients.

Despite this, they didn't have a lot of experience being interviewed by the media and were worried that they might not have enough information for reporters. Hines was always willing and able to step up—which got him national exposure when *New York Times* reporter Lisa Belkin called asking to interview him for her article, "You Won't Find Me in My Office, I'm Working." The article was about the new trend in the workplace—"white space"—in which workers find creative inspiration in spaces other than sitting at their desks.

Keep this in mind: Even if a reporter does know more than you do on a given topic, their job is to quote experts to prove their points. "It was great to talk about trends we were tracking in our own office,"

Hines says, "because—like all trends—these are things we often feel ourselves, and it's nice to know others feel the same. In this case I got to talk about white space, which is what we are looking for when we have thinking to do.

"I often start my lectures by asking my audience to name the place where they come up with their most creative ideas.

"The audiences vary, but the results are al-

Andy Hines

ways the same. The workplace is either not mentioned or is mentioned near the very end of the list, after all the other places have been exhausted. I do my best work while running or reclining in my favorite chair. Sharing that information through a giant media outlet like *The New York Times* amplified the message, and it gave me a platform to give readers insight into the work we do as futurists."

Hines' Takeaway: "What I learned from the experience is that the more visionary and higher-thinking the idea, the higher up in the article you'll be mentioned. I always seize the opportunity to spread the word about what I know because it allows me to share important trend information with the world." ■

Learn more at www.andyhinesight.com

Futurist Chris Carbone

Ignore the Butterflies:
Embrace the Spotlight

Inkandescent Insight: The futurist firm Social Technologies was tracking business and consumer trends, and we knew their work would be intriguing to producers at top news shows, including "The CBS Early Show." We first got on the producer's radar when futurist Kevin Osborn published a report on the topic of helicopter parenting.

The interview never made it on the air—but we didn't give up. When futurist Andy Hines headed up a study for MTV on the "Future of Youth Happiness," a call to the producer landed him a three-hour video shoot. The report got slightly over a minute of air time—a step in the right direction.

Then, when futurist Chris Carbone did research for Spike TV about the "Future of Men," we pulled out all the stops. At Philadelphia's Black Sheep Tavern, we gathered the men who participated in the primary research study. The stars aligned when the show's anchor, Maggie Rodriguez, came down from NYC to host. The segment aired for 3 minutes and 45 seconds.

Chris Carbone

Keep this in mind: When working with busy producers at big media outlets, be sure to help them do their job—and make them look great to their viewers and bosses. Give them as much information as they need, and be prompt with your response so you meet their deadline. Remember, they have a targeted audience and mission. So while they will likely be open to your ideas, they rarely deviate from the tried-and-true formula that works for them. Once the piece is produced, stay in touch with the team you worked with. TV and radio producers, and reporters in general, are always looking for great story ideas. As long as you and your expert advice are a direct hit for their target audience, they'll come back to you time and again. It's a win for everyone involved.

Carbone's Takeaway: "We leveraged the CBS media attention on our website, and in our printed newsletter. Admittedly, being on a national TV news show was a bit of a nerve-wracking experience, but it was well worth the butterflies." ■

Follow Carbone on Twitter @cwcarbone

PR TAKEAWAYS

1 Understand the purpose of PR. "The goal is to take a cause, product, or person and spread awareness about it. Whether you are talking about getting condoms to people in Ghana to keep HIV from spreading, or you are promoting Snooki's new book, PR is a way for people to access the best information about whatever it is you're selling, offering, or giving away." — *Lee Woodruff, former PR executive, and best-selling author of "In an Instant," "Perfectly Imperfect," and her most recent, "Those We Love Most"*

2 Appreciate the tension between reporters and publicists. There are some bad PR reps who will lie to you—and worse. The good PR reps realize that they can't behave like that—they help you with a story and understand that you have to be critical and ask questions. Journalists have a duty to ask the questions that their readers would ask if *they* had the time to investigate the story." — *Jeremy Hazlehurst, international freelance journalist, the Daily Telegraph and The London Times*

3 Think like a journalist. "Approach your client's story as a journalist would, which means you want to dig around until you find the most fascinating aspect of the story you are trying to tell. Ask yourself what grabs *your* interest? If you pitch something that you genuinely find interesting or important—not because your job is to find it interesting, but because it *is* interesting—then chances are, a journalist will think so, too." — *Tom Shroder, book author and former editor, The Washington Post Magazine*

4 Do your homework. "It may seem obvious, but before sending a pitch, first do a simple search of the website of your targeted publication to see if it has already covered your topic. Not only does that save you from wasting your time (and the editor's), it shows that you've taken enough initiative to understand something about the publication's needs. If they have covered your topic, try suggesting a slightly different angle from what they have done before. And keep the pitches short." — *Tony Reichhardt, senior editor, Air&Space/Smithsonian magazine*

5 Leverage your moment in the limelight. "Getting press attention for my books helps me reach the masses in a targeted way. Every time one of my books is mentioned in an article, there's a definite uptick in sales. Building relationships with journalists—and responding to their queries with a substantive and timely response—paves the way for more requests and more exposure. It's a cycle that works." — *Sharon Armstrong, HR expert and author, "The Essential HR Handbook," featured on "CBS MoneyWatch"*

6 Tell a great story that can help others. "When *The Wall Street Journal* featured my case study about a 65-year-old woman who had recently lost her husband and much of her monthly income, it was great to share information on how we helped keep her from going under. We got so many calls from our clients who read about it in our monthly newsletter. Getting in the news was a great accomplishment, but we got the most bang for our buck by spreading the word among all of our outreach channels." — *Financial Advisor Sheldon Weiner, featured in The Wall Street Journal*

7 Know your stuff. "It's okay if you don't have a PhD in a topic. As futurists we were always worried about being knowledgeable and academic enough to impress our clients—while keeping the message simple enough to share with the masses. Many of my colleagues were worried they weren't worthy of commenting on a trend they were tracking. I never felt that way. Even if a reporter knows more than I do on a given topic, I figure my job is to help them explain the trend they were describing to readers, viewers, and listeners." — *Futurist Andy Hines, featured in The New York Times*

8 Embrace the spotlight. "I have to admit that I was nervous about being featured on such a big news program, but I also knew that it was an important thing to do for my firm—and to spread the message about the findings we came up with on the "Future of Men" project we did for Spike TV. When all was said and done, I was proud to have overcome my fears—and even more psyched that we were able to spend 3 minutes and 45 seconds telling the world about what we do as a company. It was an incredible win." — *Futurist Chris Carbone, featured on "The CBS Early Show"*

The PR Playing Field: *Marketing*

"THE AIM OF MARKETING IS TO KNOW AND UNDERSTAND THE CUSTOMER SO WELL THE PRODUCT or service fits him and sells itself," business guru Peter Drucker famously said.

Most of us would agree with the American Marketing Association definition of marketing: "The process of communicating the value of a product or service to customers, for the purpose of selling that product or service."

But the key is to figure out the best campaigns in which to engage.

Award-winning branding consultant Simon Mainwaring offers this idea: "For a truly effective social campaign, a brand needs to embrace the first principle of marketing, which involves brand definition and consistent storytelling."

We couldn't agree more. At The Inkandescent Group, content is king—queen, prince, and princess, too. That's why we have our clients write regular articles and newsletters, which we turn into press releases, podcasts, videos, and any other media we can think of to leverage their message and increase their visibility.

And that takes work.

To help guide you through the process, in this chapter we glean 8 insights from four marketing masters and four entrepreneurs who have embraced the power of effective marketing campaigns.

Meet the experts:

- **Tara Palacios,** director of BizLaunch, Arlington Economic Development
- **Guy Kawasaki,** author, "Enchantment"
- **Carolyn Tate,** Australian marketing expert
- **Dave Farmer,** marketing expert, Washington, DC

Check out these examples of marketing campaigns from our Inkandescent PR clients:

- **Barbara Mitchell,** author, "The Essential HR Handbook" and "The Big Book of HR"
- **Alice Waagen, PhD,** founder, Workforce Learning
- **Peter Noonan, EdD,** former Assistant Superintendent, Fairfax County Public Schools
- **Janice Miller,** School Board Chairman, City of Fairfax Schools

BizLaunch director Tara Palacios

Forget Location, Location, Location. Think Strategy, Strategy, Strategy.

WITH MORE THAN 20 YEARS OF private-sector and public-sector experience in marketing and sales, Tara Palacios—director of Arlington Economic Development's BizLaunch program—has four essential "Do's" for entrepreneurs:

■ **Be strategic in how you spend your marketing dollars.** In marketing, time and effort is money. If you budget $2,000 for a marketing campaign, spend it!

■ **Understand your clients/ customers as well as they understand themselves.** Provide goods and services based on actual customer needs versus what you think or believe those customer needs are. Do market research and find out where the opportunities are before you launch a marketing campaign.

■ **Embrace competition.** If you are the only one doing what you're doing, there is a reason why. Competition means there's a demand for the goods or services you're providing.

■ **Know when you need to hire a professional.** This is critical because you can't do all the work yourself. So budget for a professional to help you.

What is your biggest marketing "Don't"?

Tara Palacios: One of the most common mistakes is throwing money into an advertising campaign without giving it careful thought. Whether it's print ads, social media, daily deals, or on TV, this can happen easily, because ad sales execs can be so persuasive.

And entrepreneurs can be incredibly stubborn.

When they get an idea, it's tough to change their minds. In fact, we know one entrepreneur who gave away $15 coupons to all customers who signed up for his company's birthday club. This attracted several new customers, but only on their birthdays. The rest of the year, there was no profit to be seen—even when family accompanied the birthday celebrant.

The business owner wasn't happy, and understandably so. But it took him years to figure out that he wasn't spending his money wisely. Ultimately, he went out of business. If he had had a little more insight, that might not have happened.

How can entrepreneurs avoid this mistake?

Tara Palacios: A marketing campaign that has not been fully researched, and is done purely based on instinct, often produces a negative effect—such as not generating new or repeat customers. Be careful to avoid diving in before you test the waters. A campaign that fails to help improve sales and depletes your cash flow is one that needs to be aborted sooner rather than later. It is imperative that business owners fully understand how their customers access information— and how best to utilize those lines of communication to quantify and qualify the endeavor that they seek to launch.

How important is social media?

Tara Palacios: Social media campaigns are cheap to launch and easier to track in terms of sales generated and online analytics that prove where the interest is coming from. We worked with one business owner who was able to skillfully craft a social media campaign based on primary and secondary market research. They were able to launch their product via Twitter because they understood what motivated their customers (quick and fast turnaround responses), and they were able to customize a campaign based on those interests. Think twice before you throw money into marketing. And ensure that the marketing tool you use is one that will motivate your potential clients so you can turn opportunities into sales.

Have you taken the BizQuiz?

Tara Palacios is the director of Arlington Economic Development's successful small-business program, BizLaunch, which serves more than 10,000 entrepreneurs a year, and has won numerous awards. Palacios is the mastermind behind BizQuiz, a business assessment tool designed for entrepreneurs (both start-ups and existing businesses) that helps them evaluate how well their business performs across seven managerial best-practice areas, and how well it compares to other entrepreneurs who have taken the BizQuiz.

Tara Palacios

Take the BizQuiz at bizlaunchblog.com

DEFINING MARKETING

Marketing guru Guy Kawasaki

"Enchantment" Is the Key to Marketing Success

If *you haven't read Guy Kawasaki's books, you are missing out on some of the greatest guides on how to launch a successful, effective marketing campaign.*

Top of the list is his 2011 tome, "Enchantment: The Art of Changing Hearts, Minds, and Actions." In it he explains: "Enchantment transforms situations and relationships. It converts hostility into civility and civility into affinity. It changes skeptics and cynics into believers, and the undecided into the loyal."

Not surprisingly, "Enchantment" charmed millions and hit three bestseller lists: The New York Times, The Wall Street Journal, and Publisher's Weekly. So we were keen to share his insights with our readers, and thrilled when Kawasaki agreed to be our Entrepreneur of the Month in the August 2011 issue of BeInkandescent.com, our national business magazine for entrepreneurs.

Another winner is, "Reality Check: The Irreverent Guide to Outsmarting, Outmanaging, and Outmarketing Your Competition," which he published in 2008.

So we couldn't think of a better guru to talk to when it comes to teaching us all how to master the art of marketing.

Guy Kawasaki

How do you define good marketing?

Guy Kawasaki: Marketing is the creation or fulfillment of demand for a product or service that people usually are not aware of. Ultimately, it is about anticipating or creating a need. Take Apple, where I worked earlier in my career.

The key to Apple's marketing success is not marketing, per se, as much as the fact that it makes great things, and so Apple's path is, "If we make great things, we do well and the marketing works. If you make crappy things, it doesn't work." It's kind of simple that way.

Your book, "Reality Check," which is an encyclopedia of essential marketing information and business tactics, offers a 10-step checklist that includes important questions for business owners to ask themselves, including, "Do you have a mantra for what you do?" What do you mean by that?

Guy Kawasaki: I think that many companies create a mantra that is much too complex. My recommendation is that you limit yourself to about two, three, maybe four words to describe why your product or service should exist, and I call this a mantra. So the mantra for Nike could be "authentic athletic performance"; the mantra for FedEx is "peace of mind"; my personal mantra is "empower people."

I think that if companies had something as simple as that, it would really make their lives much better, because employees could remember what they are doing, and consumers could understand what they're doing. It leads to a certain clarity when you are limited to such a small number of words.

Your goal is to empower people.

Guy Kawasaki: I hope I can empower people with my writing and my speaking. My latest book is called, "APE: Author, Publisher, Entrepreneur," and I'm trying to empower people who want to write a book. So with my investments and my writing and speaking, I try to empower entrepreneurs, and now I am trying to empower writers.

Publishers may not be happy with what I teach, but arguably those people should be ticked off. Traditional publishers are trying to maintain the status quo where only a few companies pick the winners and losers.

If you have that kind of power you don't want to see your power being eclipsed, I understand that, but you know, life goes on. So this book is about how people who are interested in writing a book can do it. There are three stages: authoring, which is writing; publishing, which is producing; and entrepreneuring, which is marketing.

My best tip is to get off your butt and start building your social media platform the moment you decide you're going to be shipping something, whether it is a book or a piece of software or a website or a service, because you're going to need a social media platform. Don't wait to start the platform once your product or service or book is done.

You have more than 1 million followers on Twitter. How do you wield your power in the social media sphere?

Guy Kawasaki: I have about 1.2 million followers, and there are people with many more. But many of those people got their high number of followers by being on the Twitter "suggested user" list. I was never on that list, so mine is more organic. And organic marketing is more powerful than

DEFINING MARKETING

spending $100 million on Super Bowl commercials. While at a certain point, money does buy marketing, for the reasonable range that we are discussing, organic marketing rules.

Truly, the best way to make your marketing great is to have a great product. It sounds like an evasive answer, but I've tried to enchant people with great stuff and I've tried to enchant people with crap, and it is a lot easier to enchant people with great stuff than it is with crap.

So, that's step one. Step two is to keep an empathetic perspective—don't ask people to buy, say, register, or do anything that you wouldn't do. Assuming you're not a psychopath, that will keep you on the straight and narrow in what you ask people to do in your marketing.

When it comes to marketing, what do you advise entrepreneurs to avoid at all costs?

Guy Kawasaki: I advise people to avoid things that insult people's intelligence, things that are too "in your face." I like marketing that assumes that the person is intelligent and is providing information, and then enables a person to make a free-will decision. I don't like marketing that insults people.

In fact, I think it's good for ethics and karma that you maintain those kinds of principles. I'm a big believer in karma, and those are some of the principles that guide me.

At the end of the day, yes, you would of course like to close a sale, but the real question for a marketer is not so much, "Can you close the sale?"—which is good, don't get me wrong—as much as, "Will the person that you've just closed the sale with then tell other people to buy the same thing?"

That's the test. Yes, it's hard to close a sale, but once you close the sale, truly, if you are doing things right—great product, great marketing—then that person will become your evangelist. That's a good test.

What's your favorite example of guerrilla marketing?

Guy Kawasaki: It is a story of a pizza chain that was coming to I think Denver for the first time, and what it did was it ran a promotion in which if you brought in the Yellow Pages ad of its competitor, you would get two pizzas for the price of one. They effectively removed their competitors from the Yellow Pages for a year! So that's an example of guerrilla marketing. I think that's a very cute example.

Another example is a Costco/Price Club kind of store opened up next to a small independent, and the independent didn't know what to do, since it was up against, you know, a bigger store, bigger selection, cheaper prices. What it did was, it renamed its store Main Entrance, and it was right next to the big box store, so that's also kind of a cute idea. Things like that show you're using your brains, and your humor, instead of your ego and your wallet.

That goes back to what you advise in "Reality Check," where you offer ways to get your product to market with no budget.

Guy Kawasaki: I think the key to taking your product to market with no or low budget is social media. Using the book as an example, I had about 1,500 people read it before it was shipped, and that yielded, I don't know about hundreds, but certainly dozens of great reviews on Amazon. It's a perfect example of no-budget marketing.

First of all, you have to get over your paranoia that people are going to get your book electronically and then give it away to everybody so then no one will buy your book. You need to trust people. And secondly, you need to be willing to take that kind of risk, and I think it pays off. I have never been screwed by doing something like that.

So you advise coming from your heart, and doing the right thing when it comes to all aspects of marketing—and business—in general.

Guy Kawasaki: Yes, along with thinking like a guerrilla as opposed to being a gorilla. It's also one of the essential elements to building a sound business.

The key is to hire people who are better than you in any given skill area, because if you are better than they are, then why do you need them at all? If you are the engineering person, you should hire a better finance person, a better marketing person, a better PR person, a better ops person.

If you're the ops person, you sure as hell should hire a better marketing person and a better finance person, and a better engineering person. So if everybody hired people who are better than they are, the level of quality of employee just keeps rising. I think losers hire people who are worse than they are so that they can always feel superior.

You also advise entrepreneurs to "give to get."

Guy Kawasaki: Absolutely. One last marketing tip would be, to the greatest extent possible, enable people to test drive your product or service. If it's a book, give them excerpts; if it's a website, let them use much of the service until some time period expires or you go over a certain storage limit or number of records or something.

Basically you're saying, "I think you're smart. I'm going to give you the experience—then you decide."

Learn more at www.guykawasaki.com

DEFINING MARKETING

Aussie marketer Carolyn Tate
Conscious Marketing Is the Future

The business of business is no longer business, insists Australian marketing expert and author Carolyn Tate. "The business of business is to leave the world a better place," she believes, even though she concedes that sometimes even the best intentions aren't enough.

"Marketing a small business on a limited budget is tough," Tate says. And that's why small business owners need to think less about promotions and more about purpose.

"Creating a product or service that is so compelling that people simply want to join your tribe and tell others about you is the best way to grow your business through word of mouth," writes Tate in "The Conscious Marketing Revolution: Marketing for the 21st Century."

"Spending more time on the principles of Conscious Marketing will mean less time, money, and energy spent on promotional tactics that might grab attention, but may not engage your audience or encourage them to buy," she says.

"It's too easy to adopt a 'spray and pray' approach, to attempt to get to as many people as possible with as many marketing tactics and messages as possible. A conscious, inside-out, less-is-more approach is required."

Carolyn Tate

Here are the basic principles of Conscious Marketing:

■ Build something fundamentally good into the heart of your business so people want to become your advocates.

■ Ensure all activities of the company are aligned with your higher purpose—the "why" behind what you do. Your product (or service) then becomes the finest manifestation of your purpose so that it truly serves all people involved in the production, delivery, and use of your product, from the smallest supplier to your largest customer.

■ And finally, Conscious Marketing is all about promoting your offering with honesty, transparency, and congruency, and with messages of joy, hope, love, and humanity. It's about taking a "cause leadership" approach and bringing your industry along with you in a spirit of collaboration rather than competition.

"A conscious approach to marketing is the cornerstone on which to reinvent and build your business," explains Tate. ■

Learn more at carolyntate.co

Communications expert Dave Farmer
Don't Boil the Ocean

Dave Farmer

When it comes to launching a successful marketing campaign, Dave Farmer, VP of the communications firm Environics, advises his clients to take their time and have realistic expectations.

"The ocean is enormous, and so is the full spectrum of marketing options that small businesses face," insists Farmer. "So take your time and start out boiling one pot of water at a time."

His advice:

■ "By understanding your target markets, how you satisfy their needs, and how they want to receive your message—you will be empowered to make wise decisions on investing marketing dollars."

■ That likely means not trying to be everywhere at the same time. Farmer adds: "You may find that media relations outreach is more ef-

fective than advertising, or that a social media campaign gets you more bang for the buck. What's important is to focus your effort and grow your marketing program as you learn what works best." ■

Learn more at environicspr.com

HR author Barbara Mitchell
Create a Campaign to Build Your Credibility

Barbara Mitchell

Inkandescent Insight: When Barbara Mitchell and her co-author, Sharon Armstrong, approached The Inkandescent Group to help promote their book, "The Essential HR Handbook" in 2008, they weren't convinced that using digital media to promote a printed book made sense. "When we first published the "HR Handbook," I wasn't sure how a website could be helpful in selling books," Mitchell admits. "But my doubts have certainly been erased."

What's the benefit? Here's Mitchell's perspective: "Five years later, the book is still selling extremely well in a very competitive market of business publications. The website keeps us in front of potential readers and buyers, and for that, it was well worth the investment."

Keep this in mind: "Having a well-crafted website is critical to establishing credibility—and it is also critical to keep it fresh and 'living,'" believes Mitchell, who is also the author of "The Big Book of HR," with Cornelia Gamlem. "It needs to be informational, creative, colorful, and inviting, as well as easy to navigate. Having a website to market your book is especially important in publishing," Mitchell adds.

"When I found out that the publisher really wasn't going to market my books, I was astonished. After all, they are the ones who make the lion's share of the money from sales of the book. But, once I knew the marketing was our responsibility, having the website was critical, along with getting speaking engagements, as well as radio and print interviews."

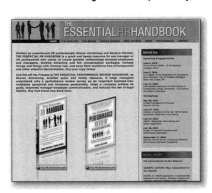

Mitchell's Takeaway: "Find good PR and marketing partners to work with—people who know how to get you publicity, and how to market your book, product, or service." ■

Learn more at www.theessentialhrhandbook.com • thebigbookofhr.com

Management expert Alice Waagen, PhD
Make Sure Your Marketing Is Consistent and Reinforces Your Brand

Inkandescent Insight: Management training expert Alice Waagen began working with The Inkandescent Group in 2008. She told us that she was unhappy with the website she had launched five years earlier—and she wasn't sure what to do with the hundreds of business cards she'd collected over the years. Should she write white papers, she wondered? She knew that the management

Alice Waagen

training workshops she offered to Fortune 500 companies, nonprofits, and government agencies were effective and successful, but she wanted a bigger slice of the market share. And she knew instinctively that she needed to pull together her marketing strategy. We started with a photo shoot that helped brand her firm around its biggest asset: Alice Waagen, PhD. Soon after, we rolled out a new website and an educational monthly newsletter in which she authored articles that showed off her experience and expertise. Then we leveraged those articles into pitches to reporters. In the years since, Waagen has been quoted in *The Philadelphia Inquirer*, in *Inc.* magazine, and on Monster.com.

Keep this in mind: The importance of branding yourself well cannot be underestimated. The goal for your marketing plan should be to take control of your message, as elegantly, seamlessly, and consistently as possible.

Waagen's Takeaway: "The time it takes to manage my branding and outreach efforts is considerable, don't get me wrong. But the payoff is well worth the investment. I never imagined I'd get into the publications that I have, and I credit it to the fact that my online presence accurately represents the work I do as an expert in workforce management." ■

Learn more at www.workforcelearning.com

DEFINING MARKETING

School Board Chairman Janice Miller
Educate Your Community

Inkandescent Insight: We started working with the City of Fairfax Schools in 2001, when the School Board—led by Chairman Janice Miller—was working to pass an $86 million bond to rebuild Fairfax High and Lanier Middle School. Nearly 80 percent of the voting residents were part of an aging population that didn't have students in the schools. Using a newsletter created by our journalist,

designer, and photographer, and mailed to every City household, the City was able to tell the community about what the schools were accomplishing. Those efforts helped convince voters that the bond was worthy of passing. It did, with 81 percent of the vote. In the next decade, we won nearly a dozen awards for the newsletter, *City School Close-Up*. Starting in 2006, the newsletter was published online. It was branded to mirror a website that featured educational issues that were important to residents.

Keep this in mind: Whenever you are working in a political environment, which is often emotionally charged, it's crucial to tell the truth, stick to the facts, and celebrate your successes. *Close-Up* provided a forum to feature the No Child Left Behind Act and the impact of SOLs on student achievement.

Feature stories such as a graduation address by former Secretary of State Colin Powell, and a visit to Fairfax High by then Education Secretary Margaret Spellings, highlighted the importance of our students and our schools.

Janice Miller

Miller's Takeaway: "All of our marketing and PR efforts were focused on sharing the good we were doing.

"That's never easy, but having a consistent, beautiful campaign that focused on educating the community about what we were doing was the key to our growth and success.

"While it's always challenging to be effective communicators through changing times, we were successful because we took the approach of a journalist—be honest, and forthcoming. This was our instinct, and it was good to have a strong communications team working with us to ensure we stayed on track." ■

Learn more at cityoffairfaxschools.org

Superintendent Peter Noonan, EdD
Be Smart About Walking Your Talk

Inkandescent Insight: When City of Fairfax Schools Superintendent Peter Noonan was the assistant superintendent of the Instructional Services Department (ISD) in Fairfax County Public Schools, he needed to communicate to hundreds of principals and teachers information about best practices in the curriculum. He knew there was no more efficient, effective way to spread the word than with a

quarterly newsletter. He commissioned us to create *Inside ISD*, a multi-page newsletter that discussed topics ranging from digital textbooks to how to close the achievement gap.

Keep this in mind: "*Inside ISD* was a beautiful publication that helped me tell the story of what we were doing at an administrative level in easy-to-understand terms," says Noonan. "We educators sometimes have a tough time getting our message across as clearly as we'd like to, because we love our jargon.

By hiring a team of journalists to help out, we didn't suffer from that problem—and the impact of the newsletter was incredibly effective.

"When dealing with layers of smart, dedicated professionals who have similar but slightly different goals, it's important to keep the message clear and concise—and to give the leaders in the community the opportunity to speak for themselves. We worked closely

Peter Noonan

with as many educators in each issue as possible, and simply helped them tell their stories."

Noonan's Takeaway: "There's no getting away from the fact that the ability to interpret and understand what others are trying to communicate is critical to spreading your message well," explains Noonan, who is now the Superintendent of the City of Fairfax Schools. "Being creative and having a good imagination doesn't hurt, either. My goal is always to find people who have an intrinsic understanding of what I'm trying to accomplish—then have them help me translate it so as many people as possible understand the message. That's what we do for the children we educate, after all. It's important to do that for every audience—including teachers, other educators, and parents." ■

Follow Noonan on Twitter @peternoonan

8

MARKETING TAKEAWAYS

 ❶ Master the art of enchantment. "Marketing is about anticipating or creating a need. Keep it simple. I think that many companies create a mantra that is much too complex. My recommendation is that you limit yourself to about two, three, maybe four words to describe why your product or service should exist. I call this a mantra." — *Guy Kawasaki, author, "Enchantment"*

 **❷ Engage in Conscious Marketing.** "Creating a product or service that is so compelling that people simply want to join your tribe and tell others about you is the best way to grow your business through word of mouth. Spending more time using Conscious Marketing principles will mean less time, money, and energy spent on promotional tactics that might grab attention, but may not engage your audience or encourage them to buy. It's too easy to adopt a 'spray and pray' approach, to attempt to get to as many people as possible with as many marketing tactics and messages as possible. A conscious, inside-out, less-is-more approach is required." — *Carolyn Tate, author, "The Conscious Marketing Revolution"*

 **❸ It's all about strategy, strategy, strategy.** "Forget, 'location, location, location.' One of the most common mistakes entrepreneurs make is throwing money into a marketing campaign without giving it careful thought. Whether it's print ads, social media, daily deals, or on TV, this can happen because ad sales execs can be so persuasive. A marketing campaign that has not been fully researched, and is done purely based on instinct, produces a negative effect—such as not generating new or repeat customers." — *Tara Palacios, director of Arlington Economic Development's BizLaunch*

 ❹ Don't try to boil the ocean. "Start out boiling one pot of water at a time. The ocean is enormous and so is the full spectrum of marketing options that small businesses face. By understanding your target markets, how you satisfy their needs, and how they want to receive your message, you will be empowered to make wise decision about how to invest your marketing dollars." — *Dave Farmer, vice president, Environics*

 ❺ Build a website that increases credibility. "When we first published 'The Essential HR Handbook,' I wasn't sure a website would be helpful in selling books. I have certainly been proven wrong. Five years after publishing it, the book is still selling extremely well and our website keeps us in front of potential readers and buyers. It was well worth the investment." — *Barbara Mitchell, HR expert, author, "The Essential HR Handbook," and "The Big Book of HR"*

 ❻ Make sure your website, newsletter, and media outreach reinforce your brand. "Before I started working with The Inkandescent Group, my marketing and PR efforts consisted of a lot of disjointed activities. I now have a co-ordinated plan that includes a new website, a bi-monthly newsletter, and press mentions. I am proud to say that I am viewed as a credible, reliable source. The approach of the Inkandescent team helped me accomplish in six months what I had not been able to do in five years—which is why we kept our contract going." — *Alice Waagen, HR and management expert, and founder, Workforce Learning*

 **❼ Educate your community.** "The key with all of our marketing and PR efforts was to share the good we were doing, and that's never easy. While it's challenging to be effective communicators through changing times, we were successful because we took the approach of a journalist—be honest, and forthcoming. This was our instinct, and it was good to have a strong communications team working with us to explain what we were doing and why we were doing it. That helped us stay on track." — *Janice Miller, chairman, City of Fairfax School Board, Fairfax, VA*

 **❽ Be smart about walking your talk.** "There's no getting away from the fact that the ability to interpret and understand what others are trying to communicate is critical to spreading your message well. Being creative and having a good plan is key. My goal is to find people who have an intrinsic understanding of what I'm trying to accomplish—then have them help me translate it so as many people as possible understand the message. That's what we do for the children we educate, after all." — *Peter Noonan, EdD, superintendent, City of Fairfax Schools*

The PR Playing Field: *Advertising*

W HICH OF THESE PERSPECTIVES ON ADVERTISING DO YOU SUBSCRIBE TO?
"Many a small thing has been made large by the right kind of advertising," said Mark Twain.

The dystopian novelist George Orwell thought otherwise: *"Advertising is the rattling of a stick inside a swill bucket."*

If you are an entrepreneur in a small business, you'll want to take a page from Twain's playbook.

Learn how to put down the stick and pick up the tricks that will flip the switch that brings customers through your door.

How much should you spend on an ad campaign, and what do entrepreneurs of small and mid-size businesses need to know about crafting an ideal ad campaign for their budgets?

In this chapter, you'll find 8+ insights from seven advertising execs and five entrepreneurs who have executed excellent ad campaigns:

Meet the experts:

- **Derek Woodgate,** founder, The Futures Lab

- **Sam Barry,** co-author with Kathi Kamen Goldmark, "Write That Book Already!"

- **Erin Hood,** producer at ABC7 WJLA-TV and News Channel 8, Washington, DC

- **Michael McGinn and Sharon Gresh,** NYC award-winning ad designers, Standard Issue

- **Darren Slaughter,** advertising executive focused on the construction industry

- **Andrew Smith,** founder of the ad firm Initiate-It

Check out these examples of ad campaigns from our Inkandescent PR clients:

- **Judy and Matt Curry,** founders, Curry's Auto Service

- **Dr. John Maguire and Dr. John Jones,** founders, Simplicity Urgent Care

- **Chef Stephen Sands,** founder, Culinaria Cooking School

Futurist Derek Woodgate, president, The Futures Lab, Inc.

The Future of Advertising: To 2020

ADVERTISING IS EXPERIENCING A huge disruption in every aspect of the industry. The revolution is certainly creating considerable concern among those comfortable with traditional industry structures and approaches. Yet this shift will open new opportunities in terms of media and advertising formats, and consumer reach and engagement—not to mention cross-disciplinary collaborations, specializations, and the ways in which technologies will be delivered.

As Internet technology guru Clay Shirky recently stated:

"It is the people who work out how to work simply in the present, rather than the people who mastered the complexities of the past, who get to say what happens in the future."

As I see it, four very distinct but interacting layers will provide the strategic architecture for the coming revolution in advertising:

1. The changing human;
2. The blending of, or moving across, the four consumer touch spheres (the public sphere, the social sphere, the tribal sphere, and the psychological sphere);
3. New media and advertising formats and technologies; and
4. New effectiveness criteria and metrics.

These four layers will be supported by a number of critical overlays:
■ Changing business models/financial structures (predominantly subscription, bundling, pay-as-you-use, even fan-funded programming);
■ Types of agencies/players;
■ New creative tools and production techniques; and
■ New content providers.

❶ THE CHANGING HUMAN: Behaviors, Attitudes, Lifestyle, Identity, Archetypes

Even though we may still see the remnants of mass advertising campaigns, the thrust of future advertising will be micro-personalized and largely experiential, leveraging the consumer's subjective experience and perceived relevance by:
■ Building and extending brand citizenship.
■ Providing information that is personalized and relevant.
■ Understanding the consumer's deepest needs through research and continuous dialog.

Having intelligent tools to achieve this level of personalization will not be the issue.

It will be relatively easy to create in-depth individual consumer profiles by:
■ Analyzing purchase or "interest" behavior or hits (such as retail behavior monitoring of a customer's reaction to an advertisement, product, retail display, etc. via facial expressions, voice, and gesture); or
■ Analyzing a potential customer's social media and online interests, their conversations, and behavior; or
■ Monitoring physical movement or specific touch points with individual "friends" within one's social group or special interest group.

However, dealing with the intercrossing of multiple, often interacting, non-coherent identities of an individual will be more difficult. The continuing shift towards "remix lifestyles," with their unrestricted canvas of choices, often means the consumer takes up a very subjective, short-lived position or behavior that does not represent the person's typical behavior.

For advertisers, understanding emerging status markers, social signals, and identifiers—and how they will be expressed and what they actually mean or represent—will be crucial. They will need to take an agile approach, even adapting in real time.

Delivering "messages" will reinforce saliency. This is true whether the message is delivered on a mobile device, a wearable computer, as a projection on one's hand, or in the midst of an in-store product display as one walks down the aisle. As a counter to extreme personalization, advertisers will also need to understand the grow-

Derek Woodgate

ing power and intercommunication of the "crowd" and the problem of transient collective personality that it brings. This is different from a traditional, more easily defined cohort.

How will "the changing human" affect advertising by 2020?
■ By 2020, advertisers may be paying attention to the whims of persuasive digital avatars and personal assistants or artificially intelligent trendsetters and tastemakers—but it is the changing human who will be more difficult to cajole.

DEFINING ADVERTISING

■ Message development will be particularly difficult for the 18-24-year-old demographic in 2020 (in 2014, those are the 12-18 year olds), whom Keith Blanchard, chief content officer of storyworldwide.com, considers to be: "The grossly entitled, helicopter-parented, permanently ear-budded, pre-diabetic, super-brat generation. This includes blissfully ignorant walking babies born with fingertip access to all the world's information who can't find Texas on a map, and cyborg-wired superslackers who spend their days texting, illegally downloading *One Direction* remixes, and YouTube-chronicling the nonstop party that is their lives."

■ 2020 advertisers will have to take into account the entitlement attitude of consumers, since it will likely provide a shield against reality. In particular, the 18-24-year-old demographic (which will no longer be referred to as a cohort) may well expect their lives—as well as the imagery and sensations that surround them—to be a kaleidoscope of ever-changing, interplaying possibilities.

is here that advertisers can help create and bind the brand's and consumers' identification with specific groups.

■ **The psychological sphere** is the realm in which affect is not only deeply experienced, but also given a purpose—such as new ways to articulate ideas, engender habit formation, guide reasoning, and elicit emotion.

There will be multiple ways in which consumers interact and experience the media delivered across these four spheres.

Consider experiential retail, where we are beginning to see the blending of online and offline worlds, as well as socially integrated, interactive experiences, personally tailored and very much part of our everyday lives. For example, we can expect to see personalized life-games in which one's world and everything we do in it becomes game-ified. Whether we are talking about loyalty points or even big-prize draws when we enter retail, we will be stepping into a parallel, participatory social gaming world.

Equally, the advent of augmented-reality storytelling, which will involve immersive, digitally layered worlds, will allow us to experience new realms of reality, blending media, information, and story by providing contextual entertainment anywhere and everywhere we go.

② THE BLENDING OF THE 4 CONSUMER SPHERES: Public, Social, Tribal, Psychological

The lifestyle sphere is the cradle for experiential advertising and marketing. When developed and blended across the four spheres—public, social, tribal, and psychological—advertising moves from a media-centric approach to a more customer-centric approach.

Instead of focusing first on which media to emphasize in a campaign—outdoor displays, smart media carts, mobile TV, 3D walls, etc.—brands would be better served by establishing how to leverage the spheres to best infiltrate and integrate into consumers' lives in a way that optimizes meaning, context, relevance, and engagement.

What do advertisers need to know about the "lifestyle spheres"?

■ **The public sphere** traditionally has been one in which brands endeavor to connect with consumers during "idle time." However, with the advent of experiential or interactive advertising, that idle time is being transformed into "active time"—through the ability to win either enhanced experiences or actual material benefits.

■ **The social sphere** provides the opportunity for advertisers to migrate messages across multiple media platforms through social interaction.

■ **The tribal sphere** is about more-focused social engagement. It

③ THE EMERGENCE OF NEW MEDIA AND ADVERTISING FORMATS AND TECHNOLOGIES

The convergence of communications, media, data, and entertainment is revolutionizing everything from content and delivery, to location, device, and reception.

■ The average person spends 90 percent of his or her life indoors, but advances in mobile computing have meant that media and advertising are just as likely to be viewed on a mobile device as they are on "fixed" equipment.

■ Meeting this changing landscape will require considerable thought on behalf of the consumer, producer, and advertiser as to which content, device, and delivery mechanism will achieve optimized effect and affect.

■ The Internet and mobile devices are central to many of these developments, enabling anywhere, anytime access, as well as incredible choice in deciding which and how such media will be delivered and consumed.

Together, the Internet and new modes of mobility will enable multiplatform, multi-device, and multi-screen reception simultaneously across various media. Physical media formats of the past are being replaced or supplemented by direct replacements on the web. We are beginning to see direct customer advertising opportunities in multi-purpose apps—with the Cloud playing a prominent role—that provide news and social media management to mobile entertainment.

In parallel, advances in transmedia, cross-media, and blended media are requiring advertisers to develop multiple and new media-specific advertising formats that best leverage the medium.

For example, we will see advertising as 3D projection mapping on buildings and storefronts (even in the sky), with added 4D components such as smell-a-vision, locative advergames, and annotated, augmented environments.

These will include interactive billboards and transportation, integrated social media at every turn, even opportunities to project ourselves into the advertisements themselves, especially as telepresence technologies expand and become ubiquitous.

Advancement and learning from 3D world and game developments will lead to new levels of immersion, sensation, and ambient experiences. The addition of augmented reality and sensory enhancement will make these experiences more compelling, believable, and desirable, and will increase retention.

NEW EFFECTIVENESS CRITERIA AND METRICS

One of the biggest changes we can expect in the near future (and we are already witnessing its impact in a lower form) is the move towards more one-to-one advertising, or interactive and responsive personalized advertising.

Supported by bots and artificial intelligence, which are continuing to provide more in-depth consumer profiles, advertisers will be able to discern levels of engagement in real time.

Our ability to quickly collate, analyze, and react to "big data" will make this personalization even more relevant to the consumer. However, more importantly, as we see substantial meaningful progress in the field of neuroscience and its relationship with advertising, we will also be able to better understand and substantiate the power and truth of advertising messages and claims.

A good example of this development is the UK chocolate brand Beyond Dark, which is using scientific evidence to determine the pleasure coefficient of various cocoa levels in its chocolate. The company has been collaborating with neuroscientists to study a group of users' brain waves to measure how eating its dark chocolate ranks against other pleasurable activities such as finding money or stroking a puppy.

Such approaches, which have arisen from the growing field of neuromarketing, go way beyond traditional focus groups by tapping into consumers' subconscious using biometric indicators (heart rate, brain wave activities, respiratory rate, for example).

Similar mirror technologies that read gesture, touch, facial muscle reaction (environmental psychophysics), etc., are being introduced into interactive window displays, virtual walls, physical and virtual 3D pop-up ads, smart kiosks, interactive shelving, and smart media trolleys in order to enable advertisers to explore, analyze, and react in real time to consumer behavior.

As this field expands, we will see a broad introduction of sensory analysis to measure consumer perception. Accordingly, advertisers will be able to better understand how consumers identify, discriminate, and perceive the quality of a brand or offering.

About Derek Woodgate

Futurist and author Derek Woodgate is the CEO of The Futures Lab, a futures-based consultancy headquartered in Austin, with seven offices around the world. The firm specializes in creating future potential for major corporations and institutions, especially in the fields of entertainment, media, culture, communications, and new communities.

He spent nine years as a British diplomat, and 13 years as a corporate executive. He is an authority on the application of emerging and immersive technologies and the changing human in the design and production of experiential entertainment with his creation of what are termed "Sense Events."

His books include: "Future Flow" (2013), with a preface by DJ Spooky; and "Future Frequencies" (2004).

Learn more at www.futures-lab.com

DEFINING ADVERTISING

TV producer Erin Hood

Are You Ready to Start Advertising on TV?

SHOULD YOU ADVERTISE ON TV? COMMERCIAL PRODUCTION MANAGER ERIN Hood is an Emmy Award winning producer, writer, and director who has been at ABC7 WJLA-TV & News Channel 8 in Washington, DC, since 2003. Before you invest in advertising, Hood insists:

1. Understand the purpose of advertising. Your goal is to let people know your business exists. It's essential to growth, and it shouldn't be overlooked—even if your budget is small.

2. Be confident and strategic. I have to admit that I'm a little biased toward TV, but I am convinced that all advertising works! It just takes time to see the results, and that can be tough for small-business owners struggling with where to get the best value for their dollars.

Keep these tips in mind:

■ **Advertise your business where your potential customers are watching.** Just because a TV ad seems affordable doesn't necessarily make it so. It's only affordable if it brings you more business.

Erin Hood

■ **Don't waste your money advertising to people who are already your customers.** The point of advertising is to get new customers.

■ **Invest in high-quality, creative ads.** The more professional your ad, the more likely it is that customers will take your company seriously.

■ **The more platforms your ads can span, the bigger your campaign will appear,** but don't spread yourself too thin. In terms of TV ads especially, depth is more important than breadth.

3. Remember the Rule of 3s. Generally, someone needs to see something three times to really process it. It can be three times in the same medium (such as TV), or three times across different media. For example: The new client got a direct mailer, saw your ad on TV, then happened to drive by your shop. Boom. That's the magic number. If they need what you are selling, odds are good they'll stop in and shop. If the customer experience is a good one—you'll have a new customer.

4. Be smart about measuring your success. Of course, the advertiser needs to measure success—but this can be tricky. You have to give an ad campaign time to work. Think of advertising as a giant snowball. The longer you push it, the more snow it will accumulate.

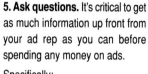

News Channel 8 reporter Sonya Gavankar interviews Egan, Berger & Weiner partner Bryan Beatty on the noon news show, "Let's Talk Live."

Likewise, the more people you reach and the more times they see your ad, the more effective and successful your campaign will be. So pick a reasonable window of time to track your effectiveness (for example, year to year), and factor in possibilities like a recession, a big shift in your business plan or staff, etc. If you sold more products or services this year than last—you'll know the campaign is working.

5. Ask questions. It's critical to get as much information up front from your ad rep as you can before spending any money on ads.

Specifically:

■ Know how many people you'll reach and what the cost is to reach each person.

■ Find out who the audience is (number of households, demographics, etc.) and decide if this audience is your ideal customer.

■ Now, based on the cost to reach each customer, calculate how many sales you need to make to recoup what you've spent on ads.

6. Know what makes a TV commercial successful. For most small businesses, a direct-response approach is best. Be sure to look professional, give people a reason to shop today (such as a sale or special offer), and try to appeal to the widest audience possible.

7. Have a plan. For your advertising campaign to succeed, you need a plan and a reasonable budget. It's a new twist on an old saying. Instead of, "You gotta spend money to make money," think of it as, "You gotta get new customers to make money." Advertising is an investment in your business. Think it through before you spend your advertising dollars. Do your homework, study your finances, and invest wisely!

8. Back up your ads with a beautiful website. Advertising is but one of the tools at your disposal that can help you increase the visibility of your company. Step 1, which is outlined in The 8 Steps to PR Success in this book (page 57), is to have a professional website! This is without question the most important thing any small business can do, because it works hand in hand with your advertising campaign: A customer who sees your ad on TV will want to check you out online. Whether you are a bricks-and-mortar company or not, your website is your storefront—and no one wants to walk into a sketchy-looking store.

Learn more at www.wjla.com

Ad execs Darren Slaughter and Andrew Smith

How Much Should You Spend on Your Ad Campaign?

Darren Slaughter

Darren Slaughter gets the money question a lot. "Small-business owners want guidelines to follow, but the only person able to answer this question is the one writing the check," says the founder of a boutique digital ad agency that focuses on website design, social media management, and reputation management in the home improvement industry.

A great place to start, Slaughter believes, is by figuring out how much you want to make. "If you want to just get by, then a minimal marketing budget with a solid referral business will do. If you have bigger ambitions, like being the industry leader in your market, then you're going to need to spend a lot more than the guy who just wants to get by. Either option requires a budget."

So what are the numbers?

1. While it's estimated that two-thirds of small businesses close their doors within five years, that number is even higher in the home improvement industry. "Most contractors start out with some business cards, tools, and a desire to do great work. But many don't set aside any cash to tell the world about how great of a plumber or electrician they are."

2. Most small businesses can get away with spending 5% to 10% of gross sales on advertising; the construction industry is no different.

3. Know that many of the high-fliers in the trades spend 12% to 15% of gross sales on marketing their businesses.

4. There are contractors out there who will tell you they haven't spent a dime on marketing in years, getting new business solely from referrals. Well, that's great for them, but bad advice for you—especially if your contracting company is less than five years old.

5. New businesses need more care and feeding. If your business is five years old or less, you are still a start-up in the trades. Take a page from the high fliers and for the next three years, plan on spending 15% of gross sales on advertising.

6. If you think that 15% of gross sales is too much, you have to re-think that and understand that your budget can't be too limited if you want to make an impact.

7. The closer you are to the five-year mark, the more important it is that you keep getting your name out there. This is especially true if the economy is shaky and you're in a business—like contracting—that is dependent on a strong economy.

8. Know the cardinal rule. One thing I know for sure is that the more you put into marketing efforts for your company, the more money you *will* make. Just be sure your ad campaign is done properly. ■

Learn more at www.darrenslaughter.com

When Andrew Smith launched his Richmond-based ad agency, Initiate-It, in 2012, he'd already spent decades in the ad business. And he knew all too well why entrepreneurs have such a hard time investing in advertising.

Andrew Smith

"Every business owner I have met is confused about advertising," he says. "Each year, they are typically approached by ad representatives from local newspapers, outdoor advertising companies, magazines, and radio stations—and each makes a case on how they are the leader in the market and that they will get you the best results in sales or brand awareness for your business. To say this can be overwhelming is clearly an understatement."

To get the most bang for your advertising dollars, Smith advises:

1. Sit down and determine exactly how much you are willing to invest. Be realistic, and know that what you want to spend initially might change as you define your short-term needs and long-term goals.

2. Don't be cheap. Realize that one ad will get you nowhere. If you are only going to run your ad once, then you might as well save your money and not run it at all. Repetition is what counts in the ad game.

3. Determine what you hope to get back in return (notoriety, sales, or both). Having a grip on your goals is as important as knowing your budget. Without it, you won't know how to track return on investment.

4. Realize that advertising on TV and radio during prime time is ideal. This is when you'll reach the most potential customers. It's also the most expensive time to run your ad. Decide how valuable that is to your business.

5. Quality ads are key. Hire a professional to help you. Trust their opinion, but trust your gut more.

6. Provide your ad team with as much information as possible. Are you a T-shirt-and-jeans kind of company, or a black-tie outfit? Be sure your ads reflect your business.

7. Think ahead. Get out your calendar and map out your ad plan for an entire year. Coordinate ads with specials, holidays, and other highlights that will drive customers to your business.

8. Test your ad with a group of people who are your target customers, and take their feedback to heart. If the majority of the test group hates the ad, consider scrapping it. But ask them for ideas on what they'd like to see. And if 100 percent of them love it, be dubious—and ask a handful more for their opinion. ■

Learn more at www.initiate-it.com

DEFINING ADVERTISING

Author Sam Barry

Write That Book Already—But Don't Spend Money on Ads

Author, editor, and all-around funnyman Sam Barry has been in the book business for decades, and has seen authors struggle with selling their books. In fact, his 2011 book, "Write That Book Already! The Tough Love You Need to Get Published Now," co-written with

his beloved wife Kathi Kamen Goldmark (who passed away in May 2012), offers some of the best tips on writing books that we've seen. And it's no surprise. Being a good writer runs in the family—Sam's brother is award-winning author Dave Barry.

Here are Sam Barry's 8 tips that authors can take to the bank:

1. Buyer beware. Authors, especially with their first books, shouldn't spend a lot of money on advertising. There are better ways to get the word out. Keep reading...

2. Newbie alert. Books written by lesser-known authors sell either by word of mouth, or are lucky enough to attract great media coverage—or a combination of the two.

3. Be about the buzz. The goal is to get some buzz going among readers. This means you need to go to where the readers live. (Not literally. I mean, don't go to their homes. Or if you do, don't say I sent you.)

4. Make social media your best friend. Learn how to use social media effectively; the publishing house Wiley has an excellent line of books on effective online marketing. And Goodreads.com, a giant online book group, has a giveaway program for authors. Consider offering copies of your book as a prize to drive book sales and garner reviews.

Sam Barry

5. Stay sane. Don't drive yourself crazy by trying to do every social media site—focus on a few big ones, such as Facebook, Twitter, Tumblr, or Twaddle.

6. Bibliophiles win. Become active in the book world. Join discussion forums, offer to be a guest blogger, comment intelligently on other people's blogs, and start a blog of your own.

7. Be a joiner. Participate in the local, regional, and national writing and reading community to become a bigger booster of other authors, especially those who, like you, are aspiring to greatness.

8. Don't be cheap. Send review copies of your book to reporters at your local newspaper and other media outlets in your area, and volunteer to speak at libraries and writers groups.

"Remember to have fun, because it may take years (and numerous books) to build a following," insists Barry, who writes the "Author Enabler" column for *BookPage.com*. "If you aren't having fun, why are you doing this? It would be far easier to get a real job. Good luck!" ■

Learn more at www.bookpage.com

Designers
Michael McGinn
and Sharon Gresh

Clean Lines
+ Clever Copy
+ Dynamic Design
+ Elegant Execution
= Awesome Ads

Award-winning advertising designers Michael McGinn and Sharon Gresh founded their Brooklyn firm, Standard Issue, in 2005 with one simple idea: "We believe in collaboration led by experienced vision."

Each member of their six-person team has worked with brand leaders at cultural and aesthetically driven companies—including Herman Miller and Kenneth Cole.

"Our mission is to be a model for collaboration, facilitating the contributions of our designers and collaborators," says McGinn.

Clean lines, clever copy, dynamic design, and elegant execution are the keys to this firm's success.

Take a page from McGinn and Gresh's playbook:

1. Keep it clear. Sure, the cost of an ad may be more than you'd like to spend, but that's not a reason to jam it so full of messages that it confuses or bores readers to death.

Michael McGinn
and Sharon Gresh

2. Keep it clean. Resist the temptation to fill the ad with everything you sell.

3. Keep it focused. Focus on the one thing you want your customers to know today. They'll learn all the other good things you have to offer as they get to know you.

4. Keep it simple. That way it works best in print, radio, TV, and online.

5. Less is more. A few very carefully chosen words and perhaps a memorable image can be very powerful.

6. Smart sells. Work with the best professionals you can afford.

7. Beware of asking creative friends for favors. Sure, creating good ads will cost you money, but you don't want to waste your investment in the ad space you're buying by using someone other than a professional. Advertising pros may not know your business (yet), but they know more than you do about advertising. You're paying them for their expertise, advice, and guidance.

8. Listen to them. ■

Learn more at www.standardissuedesign.com

Curry's Auto Service owners Judy + Matt Curry
Track Your Success

Matt and Judy Curry

Inkandescent Insight: When Judy and Matt Curry approached Inkandescent PR to assist with an ad campaign featuring coupons to increase spring sales, Inkandescent's Art Director Michael Gibbs revved into action. He began creating six ads, including three with the pithy tag line, "Regular Car Maintenance Makes Lots of Cents," that featured a wrench turning a shiny, hexagon-shaped penny.

Knowing the clients he'd cultivated for a decade well, Matt Curry provided ad copy he felt they would respond to, as well as draw in new ones.

"Our goal was to show the reader that Curry's Auto was not only the best car maintenance option in town, but also the most affordable—and that regular maintenance would save owners money in the long run," says Gibbs. When Curry's wanted to coordinate the February opening of a new shop in Leesburg, VA, with the February birthday of Dr. Seuss, their ad featured Matt Curry in a "Cat in the Hat" hat, and Gibbs penned an original Seuss-style poem (at right).

"Matt and Judy were great to work with," says Gibbs, "because they had clear ideas of what they wanted in the ads, based on their in-depth knowledge of how their customers think, and what makes them laugh."

Keep this in mind: Knowing what you want from your ad and letting the design team work its magic are the best ways to engage advertising and marketing professionals. The Curry's didn't micromanage, but provided great guidance to ensure their customers would respond to the ads. It was a win-win-win for everyone.

Curry's Takeaway: "'Be creative and be brilliant.' Those were our instructions to Inkandescent PR. We knew the Inkandescent team would hit both goals because we'd seen the work they had done for some of their other clients. They exceeded our expectations." ∎

Learn more at www.currysauto.com and www.thehybridshop.com

---

*Curry's Opens
in Leesburg, VA*

*Oh boy, said the car,
I am so out of tune!
If I'm going to hum
I need Curry's—and soon!*

*My oil is too low,
and I might have a leak.
My pads are worn out,
so my brakes tend to squeak.*

*My tires are wearing
and could use a rotation.
My battery is weak
and needs charge-ification.*

*My innards are clogged
'cause my filters are dirty.
My wipers are shot,
so my vision is blurry.*

*I know of some guys
who can fix all my worries.
They've got a garage
and they call themselves Curry's!*

Curry's Ads: Designed to Rev Readers' Engines

Keep It Simple: Simplicity Urgent Care

Inkandescent Insight: When Drs. John Jones and John Maguire opened the doors of Simplicity Urgent Care in November 2010, they wanted to make a healthy impression. The experienced ER docs sought

to reach patients they saw year after year who came to the ER when they really didn't need that level of care.

Keep this in mind: The first step was to send out 1,000 postcards to the zip codes in the five-mile area around the Arlington, VA, clinic. The postcard re-

Drs. Jones and Maguire

flected the elegant lines of the company's logo, as well as images of happy, healthy people.

Refrigerator magnets with the clinic's contact information were given to patients to refer to in case an urgent-care issue came up.

Advertising in local publications was the next step, and included regular ads in *The Connection* newspaper, *YourHealth* magazine (an opportunity that came with a monthly article), *The Hill Rag* (which reached moms living on nearby Capitol Hill), and a handful of newsletters in surrounding neighborhoods. Simplicity's docs also took booths at local festivals and events where neighborhood families could meet the staff in person.

Simplicity's ad: Short and sweet

Simplicity's Takeaway: "The key to our advertising outreach was to hit specific marks of growing our patient roster, while building our brand, and staying within our budget. We hit all the marks we'd hoped for within 18 months, and now we are able to grow by word-of-mouth referrals as well. This kind of organic growth wouldn't have been possible without the initial advertising push. It worked like a charm." ■

Learn more at www.simplicityurgentcare.com

Use Good Taste: Culinaria Cooking School

Inkandescent Insight: Opening a cooking school was Chef Stephen Sands' dream. He spent 10 years planning and preparing to make that a reality when he retired from his job as a nuclear physicist at the Nuclear Regulatory Commission. He bought a commercial building on a high-traffic street in the Washington, DC suburb of Vienna, VA. He gutted it and renovated it to feature an elegant work space featuring two kitchens with seating areas for students.

The challenge? The opening took six months longer to happen than Chef Sands had anticipated. Undaunted, he primed DC-area residents

Culinaria's Ad for *Washingtonian*

for the grand opening by buying a series of ads in regional magazines and newspapers like *Washingtonian*. Hundreds of people flocked to the school the day the doors opened. Thereafter, Sands regularly took out

ads to remind customers of upcoming classes. The ads, like the weekly newsletter that Inkandescent PR helped Sands craft, always included the calendar of classes. The multi-page newsletter also functioned as a mini-cookbook in which customers could find delicious recipes. And regular appearances on DC-area TV shows raised Culinaria's pro-

Stephen Sands

file, helping it become the go-to cooking school where any aspiring cook can learn to prepare dishes like Parsnip Soup With Truffle Oil and Rack of Lamb Stuffed With Brandied Apricots.

Keep this in mind: The Inkandescent PR team couldn't have asked for better visuals to work with than the beautiful fresh ingredients and amazing dishes prepared by Culinaria Cooking School's chefs. The images contributed greatly to the success of the ads. Using a professional photographer was essential, and DC photog Steve Barrett did a great job capturing the essence of Culinaria's high-quality brand.

Culinaria's Takeaway: "Our classes teach the fundamentals of cooking, and appeal to novice cooks as well as seasoned chefs," Chef Sands says. "So, our ad campaign had to target this audience. The newsletter was a fantastic tool. Our reputation spread, and today thousands of people have come through our doors to learn how to cook like a professional chef in their own kitchen." ■

Learn more at www.culinariacookingschool.com

8

ADVERTISING TAKEAWAYS

❶ When planning an ad campaign—look to the future. "Advertising is experiencing a huge disruption in every aspect of the industry. As I see it, four very distinct but interacting layers will provide the strategic architecture for the coming revolution in the world of advertising: The changing human; the blending of, or moving across, the four consumer touch spheres (the public sphere, the social sphere, the tribal sphere, and the psychological sphere); new media and advertising formats and technologies; and new effectiveness criteria and metrics."
— *Futurist Derek Woodgate, president, The Futures Lab, Inc.*

❷ Be confident and strategic. "I am convinced that all advertising can work if done right! It just takes time to see the results, which can be tough for a small-business owner who struggles with where to get the best value for their dollar. The point of advertising should be to get new customers, so advertise your business where potential customers are looking. Know, too, that while advertising on multiple platforms can help spread your message, don't spread yourself too thin. Most importantly, spend money on high quality, creative ads. It'll pay off in the long run." — *Commercial production manager Erin Hood, ABC7 WJLA-TV, Washington, DC*

❸ Get the most bang for your advertising dollars. "Since buying ads can be overwhelming, the key to being efficient is to think clearly. Sit down and determine exactly how much you are willing to invest. Don't be cheap—if you are only going to run one ad one time, then you might as well save your money. After you determine what you hope to get back in return (notoriety, sales, or both), then you can decide what to buy." — *Andrew Smith, Founder, Initiate-It*

❹ Book authors take note: Don't advertise. Use social media. "After you write a great book (don't forget this important step), your goal is to get some buzz going among readers. This means you need to go to where the readers live. (Not literally. I mean, don't go to their homes. Or if you do, don't say I sent you.) Goodreads.com has a giveaway program for authors—offer copies of your book as a prize to drive book sales and garner reviews."
— *Author Sam Barry, "Write That Book Already!"*

❺ Clear, clever, and concise ads sell products. "Sure, the cost of an ad may be more than you'd like to spend, but that's not a reason to jam it so full of messages that it confuses or bores readers to death. Resist the temptation to fill all the space with everything you're selling. Make the main idea the one thing you want your customers to know today. They'll learn all the other good things you have to offer as they get to know you." — *Michael McGinn and Sharon Gresh, founders, Standard Issue*

❻ Keep it simple. "We wanted to get as much bang as we could for the limited ad budget we had, so we loved the approach of spreading the word to the community within a five-mile radius of the clinic. We started with a giant postcard mailing to the three zip codes closest to our clinic, then we expanded out from there with more mailings, and ads in local newspapers and neighborhood newsletters. Plus, we showed up at local festivals and events to introduce ourselves personally to the community. Today, we get most of our clients by word-of-mouth, but this first layer of advertising outreach was critical to our launch." — *Drs. John Jones and John Maguire, founders, Simplicity Urgent Care*

❼ Use ads to get your party started. "Our classes appeal to novice cooks as well as seasoned chefs, so we needed to make sure our ad campaign reached that target audience. It didn't take long for our reputation—and our message about the art of cooking well—to spread. Our advertising and PR efforts definitely helped us get the party started. Thousands of people have come through our doors."
— *Chef Stephen Sands, founder, Culinaria Cooking School*

❽ Track Your Success. "'Be creative and be brilliant.' Those were our instructions to Inkandescent PR when we hired them to create a series of six ads for us. Whomever you hire to help you craft your ads, make sure they hit both goals because that's how you'll impress your clients. And to see how effective the ads are, include a tracking code so that you know which offers the customers are taking advantage of." — *Matt Curry and Judy Curry, founders and owners, Curry's Auto Service, 10 locations in the metro DC area*

The PR Playing Field: *Social Media*

WHAT IS SOCIAL MEDIA? AH, THE MILLION-DOLLAR QUESTION, AND ONE WITH SEVERAL ANSWERS.
■ According to Google.com, it is "websites and applications used for social networking."

■ Wikipedia says it's "the interaction among people in which they create, share, and exchange information and ideas."

■ Experience tells us social media platforms are useful places where we can chat, post status updates, and connect with friends—old and new.

■ As a business development tool, social media can lead to finding potential clients, vendors, and employees, as well as future employers, if used properly.

■ But beware. Playing with social media can become a habit that consumes hours of your day with no clear way to measure your return on investment.

Small-business owners know they need to have a social media presence. They know they need to maintain their online pages, and spread the word about what they are doing on a regular basis. And they throw up their hands in frustration when they can't manage the medium.

On the following pages, 8+ experts and entrepreneurs aim to give you information that will let you move ahead with refreshing ideas about how to use social media to help your brand sizzle.

Meet the experts:
■ **Simeon Spearman,** on the future of social media
■ **Jennifer Abernethy,** author of "The Complete Idiot's Guide to Social Media Marketing"
■ **Sonya Gavankar,** former Miss DC, reporter, and the "Face of the Newseum" in Washington, DC
■ **Ronnie Bincer,** virtual conference expert
■ **Kristine Carlson,** creator of the 2013 Mom's Virtual Conference

Check out examples of social media-savvy companies profiled in *Be Inkandescent* magazine:
■ **Caroline Leavitt,** best-selling author, on the art of using Facebook to market your books
■ **Sonja Kristiansen,** co-owner of Blo San Francisco, on using Twitter to blow out your business
■ **Michael Radparvar,** co-founder of Holstee.com, on going viral with the Holstee Manifesto
■ **Charles Best,** founder of DonorsChoose.org, on the power of crowd funding

Futurist Simeon Spearman

The Future of Social Media

SOCIAL MEDIA HAS QUICKLY BECOME ONE OF THE MOST POPular methods of communication.

Every day, people of all ages begin using social media for the first time, and signing up for social networks has become a rite of passage. According to the Pew Internet & American Life Project, 72 percent of online adults in the United States use social networking sites.

Here's what you need to know:
Facebook, Twitter, and YouTube have emerged as leaders in the social networking space and will remain so for the foreseeable future due to the size of their audiences.

 Facebook currently has more than 1 billion Internet users, representing the largest reach of any social network. It will continue to be the largest platform, but its transition to a media company will require PR professionals to figure out how paid and earned media work together.

 Twitter also continues to grow and is becoming more like a media company. The ease and simplicity of the service, as well as its more public nature, means that Twitter will serve as a global water cooler for years to come. Twitter's incorporation into the larger media ecosystem underscores its future importance. The simplicity with which tweets can be included in mainstream press coverage means that its influence will remain strong.

Facebook and Twitter represent "traditional" social networks built on connections to friends and family with a large focus on status updates, but a shift to visual communication will shape the future use of social media. These two sites have also made it easier than ever to share photos and videos, but a new generation is turning to other platforms more suited for content-sharing.

 YouTube is currently the best example of a social network built on visual content. In June 2013, 82.5 percent of the US Internet population viewed online video, with YouTube a large portion of that. By simplifying the production and sharing of video content, YouTube is making it easier for video to become an affordable communications strategy. Consumption of online video is set to grow as more of the world gains access to high-speed mobile Internet and also to smartphones capable of reliably streaming video content.

YouTube's growing importance is also coinciding with other strongly visual social networks, such as Instagram, Tumblr, and Pinterest, all of which present new ways to communicate through photographs, animations, and images.

The popularity of these networks is reflected in their rapid growth up to this point. Instagram alone has grown to more than 130 million users worldwide since launching in 2010, rapidly becoming the de facto mobile social network for sharing photos.

Spearman

The Bottom Line

■ Over the next few years, consumer technology will continue to evolve toward supporting visual communication.

■ Smartphones are evolving into "smart cameras," focusing more on the quality of photography and video recording than on voice chat and text messaging.

■ Wearable technology such as Google Glass demonstrates that photography and video will become core to how people communicate moving forward.

Learn more at www.simeonspearman.com

DEFINING SOCIAL MEDIA

Social media marketing author Jennifer Abernethy

Why Should You Use Social Media?

ARE YOU LOSING MONEY AND MARKETSHARE IF YOU AREN'T using Social Media? When Jennifer Abernethy wrote the 2nd edition of her "The Complete Idiot's Guide to Social Media Marketing" in 2012, there were 525 million active daily users, 900 million active monthly users, and over 4 million status updates each day in the world's largest social network.

By January 2014, Facebook.com reported more than 1 billion active users; 4.5 billion "likes" generated by the 699 million people who log on every day; with five new profiles being created every second.

Jennifer Abernethy

So we asked the author 8 questions about the essentials that you need to know about social media marketing.

1. If you aren't on Facebook—or the other top social media sites—are you losing money, and marketshare?

Jennifer Abernethy: For most people, yes. For one target segment, however, I would say no. The industries that typically don't do well on Facebook are those that are targeting senior executive men, because these guys aren't logging on to Facebook.

2. With more than 1 billion users, Facebook is the biggest social media site. But LinkedIn provides value for businesses and Twitter has its place. Should entrepreneurs be active on all three?

Jennifer Abernethy: Yes, on all three—and I would add Instagram, videos on YouTube, and perhaps Pinterest, too.

3. Not all Internet users seem to realize they should be following "Internet social netiquette," let alone that there is such a thing. In your book, you talk about the "Unwritten Rules of Engagement." What are they, and why are they so important?

Jennifer Abernethy: The rules are:

- If you don't want what you write appearing on the front page of *The New York Times*, don't write it on social media. It stays there forever.

- Don't talk politics or religion. You have a 50 percent chance of offending a possible customer.

- Keep your updates roughly 80 percent business, 20 percent personal. You are there for business connections and networking.

- No bad-mouthing competitors. No over-automating. If everyone automated their updates, no one would be reading them.

- Post different updates on different sites. Each site has its own vibe. Facebook is not LinkedIn, therefore you wouldn't want to post the same thing in both places.

4. Video has become an essential element of many people's social media and website presence. What do small-business owners need to be aware of when it comes to shooting video?

Jennifer Abernethy: Use your webcam or iPhone, and start getting comfortable communicating via video. Experts predict by 2016, a substantial portion of our communication will be via video—like it or not.

5. Having a strategy about what you post online every day is essential. What do you advise business owners to do to get started—and to keep their social media campaigns fresh?

Jennifer Abernethy: Start talking (writing) to your potential customer. Keep it conversational and share great content.

6. If you are new to the social media sphere, how do you determine who your target market is?

Jennifer Abernethy: Well, if you have a business, you must know your target market. Take that same target market and find it online.

For example, if you are targeting executives, then you know you need to be on LinkedIn. If you are targeting entrepreneurs, then you must be on Twitter and Facebook. And if you are marketing to moms, then you need to be on Facebook and Pinterest.

7. If you and your company already have a social media presence, how can you increase your base?

Jennifer Abernethy: Stay consistent. Show up daily. Begin experimenting with social marketing and different sites.

You'll find new audiences and prospects on Instagram that you won't find on Facebook and vice versa.

8. What do you see as the future of social media? Will Pinterest overtake Facebook?

Jennifer Abernethy: It's our entire social media footprint that will be important—all of the sites when combined together. What we post is more important now than ever before.

The future is wearables—Google Glassware and digitally fit clothing. Our wearables will search the digital footprint of our online networks and we will be able to search people via their influence or digital clout or by content.

When I walk into a room wearing smartwear, I will want to know who the influencers are, who their following is, and what they are interested in. And my glasses or digital wristband will tell me!

Learn more at www.thesaleslounge.com

Media personality Sonya Gavankar

How to Maximize Social Media

WHAT DO YOU NEED TO KNOW TO HARNESS THE power of social media?

When Sonya Gavankar was crowned Miss District of Columbia while in college at American University, she understood the power of reaching the masses with a great smile, a sense of humor, and a poised walk down the runway.

Today, as the "Face of the Newseum," local TV reporter, and a sought-after MC, Gavankar has mastered the art and science of using social media to build trust with consumers by using her voice and honesty to brand herself.

"Social media platforms let you show your company's personality and use it to your advantage," she says. "But that means you have to be captivating."

Here's Gavankar's advice on how to shine in the social media sphere.

How do you know which social media sites to pay attention to?

Sonya Gavankar: It's so hard to know which new social media site will take off. I suggest joining them all early so that your brand has first choice of name.

Sonya Gavankar

Also play around on the sites. You'll quickly learn which work best for you and which grab your attention. Those are the sites others are also likely to gravitate to.

Remember to ask young people to help you craft messages for these sites. Interns, for example, are a great resource to find new and interesting sites to amplify your corporate voice.

What are the elements of a great social media campaign?

Sonya Gavankar: Staying true to your company and its brand is key. There is nothing wrong with being serious and buttoned-down if that is who you are. Think of it like a first date. You don't want to lie to your date with a personality you cannot maintain.

When you are honest in tone and message, you win over everyone. Consumers who use social media can quickly tell when you are trying too hard. Also, don't try to be funny if your company isn't. The jokes will always fall flat when you try too hard.

How do you measure success in terms of return on investment?

Sonya Gavankar: ROI is something you should consider early. Before crafting your message, think about the impact you want to have. For example, do you want your site to be easily found? Or is it more important to offer your customer base a taste of what makes you special? Doing this advance thinking will keep you from throwing too many possible options at the wall to see what sticks. Then tailor your message to the outcome you expect.

What are some no-nos about social media campaigns that you have seen people learn the hard way?

Sonya Gavankar: Low-quality content is still low-quality content. There was a time when you could get away with poorly lit video from your cell phone, because online video was new and different. But those days are numbered. While your iPad or iPhone is capable of recording high-quality video, it still won't look like it was shot by a professional. It's better to spend the money to have high production values in your visual content.

If you don't have the budget for video, just go with audio podcasts. Folks can focus on hearing your message if you don't have the resources to make it look good. Garbage in, garbage out.

Should the social media campaign change depending on what you are selling?

Sonya Gavankar: I don't think the campaign should change. The voice needs to be consistent regardless of the message.

In your opinion, what are the key things entrepreneurs should keep in mind when crafting their social media program?

Sonya Gavankar: First and foremost, you should have a core group of people review your campaign before it launches. These should be people who know your brand and who have institutional knowledge, but there should also be some who are new since they can give an objective view from the outside.

Also, spend the money to do it right! That doesn't mean you have to outsource all your social media, but you should ask experts for their insight.

It will quickly become clear who "gets" you and who doesn't, and you might discover you can learn all you need to know to be able to do it yourself. Social media and traditional media are the same at the end of the day. If the content isn't worth listening to, no one will.

Learn more at www.sonyagavankar.com

Online meeting expert Ronnie Bincer

The Rise of Virtual Conferences

HAVE YOU BEEN TO A VIRTUAL CONFERENCE? IF NOT, ODDS are good you'll be attending one in the near future.

According to Market Research Media, the virtual conference marketplace is expected grow to $18.6 billion by 2015. One of the big players in the field, ON24, said its survey of 10,000 executives showed that 87 percent were ready to go virtual.

The reason is simple: virtual conferences can save a company a bundle.

Ronnie Bincer

"From hotel rooms and airfares to conference room rentals and food, companies can spend a fraction of the cost when they take their conferences online," says Google+ Hangout expert Ronnie Bincer, who offers the 8 insights that follow.

1. Are virtual conferences the new thing?

Ronnie Bincer: I see the rise of the virtual conference as a natural progression in existing online activity. More and more of our connections are being made online, so adding a conference to this type of activity is a logical next step.

2. The biggest benefit for many conference hosts and corporations is that virtual conferences are cheaper than the real world version. What are some of the other benefits?

Ronnie Bincer: Not only are VCs beneficial because of cost savings, they increase the likelihood of getting "exclusive" speakers to appear. If the hosting organization can offer a better fee to the speaker because of lower overhead elsewhere, or a shorter time commitment, then the organization has a better chance of getting that awesome speaker from anywhere in the world to participate in the conference.

3. One of the biggest downsides to virtual conferences is the inability to network spontaneously. Is there a workaround?

Ronnie Bincer: The ability to meet face to face and shake a hand is certainly what we're used to. But I've seen virtual networking take place among those who are comfortable enough using the tools to say that the future is moving quickly in this direction. And those who get comfortable with the tools will quickly have an advantage. In fact, the ability to network after the event remains—and many find it easier to come back "later" and spend quality time at their own convenience after picking through the discussions. This way, we identify the proper contacts more efficiently.

4. What do virtual conference planners need to know?

Ronnie Bincer: Make sure communication is clear and repeated often. Just like at a "real event," people can get lost and become unsure of where they want to go or need to go next. Offering virtual assistance to those with a question is essential. Have a chat room open (or multiple chat rooms) so that anyone at any time can ask a question and be guided to the answer via links or other info. Coordinators should also create a "virtual lobby space" for those who want to meet and debrief about the session they just attended.

5. What should virtual conference planners avoid?

Ronnie Bincer: Do not assume attendees know what to do. I would also suggest that they try to avoid being a tech support department for any and all computer-related issues.

6. What should attendees of virtual conferences be aware of?

Ronnie Bincer: Attendees will need to feel comfortable using the tools:

- Take the simple tutorials that tell you how to "attend" and interact with the chosen conference tools.

- Move away from normal working environments so you are not distracted by day-to-day phone calls or interruptions—which you would be missing anyway, if you were out of the office attending a conference.

- Have tools ready to take notes on the information that is important to you. Just because you are attending via a virtual connection does not mean you have "become one" with the information—you will still need to find ways to remind yourself later of what you felt was important when you were hearing the conference presentations.

7. Do you honestly think real-life conferences will go away in the coming years?

Ronnie Bincer: I do not think that real-life conferences will totally go away, but I do feel that they will take place less often. There will still be valid reasons to physically be at a conference, but the number of those reasons will be fewer and fewer moving forward. I do see the rise of hybrid real-life conferences—those that have a panel of experts, with some physically there and others appearing on-screen. Eventually, I expect future conferences to feature a holograph of a speaker, but for now, most people will settle for expert panel members from all over the world gathering together virtually with real-life counterparts on a physical stage.

8. What are some of your favorite virtual conferences?

Ronnie Bincer: I have been part of speaker panels in virtual conferences, and I have participated in many live interviews and discussions that might be considered mini-virtual conferences. But only a few to date were billed as such. Those involved with the cooking/food industry seem to be taking the lead on the virtual conferences that I've been involved with to date. 💡

Learn more at www.thehangouthelper.com

DEFINING SOCIAL MEDIA

Author Kristine Carlson

Mom Knows Best When It Comes to Virtual Conferences

One of our favorite virtual conferences was created in 2013 by Kristine Carlson, co-founder of the "Don't Sweat the Small Stuff" series—and one of our speakers bureau stars on InkandescentSpeakers.com.

To celebrate Mother's Day 2013, and commemorate her newest book, "Don't Sweat the Small Stuff for Moms," she hosted a Mom's Virtual Conference. More than 50 best-selling mom-focused authors and speakers came together online to talk about the keys to stressing less and enjoying their family more.

Kristine Carlson

Why did Carlson decide to go virtual?

"In the past two years, I have been looking for ways to increase our brand presence on the Internet, and I knew a virtual conference would help identify my market, and be a great list-building tool," she explains.

"Plus, moms are busy. So it is very convenient and cost-effective for them, since they don't have to physically go somewhere to attend. And, it was a perfect venue to promote my book for Mother's Day."

Obviously, planning a virtual conference is much easier than planning a traditional "in-person" conference, because there are fewer components to manage, but Carlson found she still had to tackle a mountain of scheduling and email correspondence to book the speakers and plan the interviews. "To make that easier, I partnered with a strong team of mommy bloggers and enlisted a savvy technical support team," she says.

The biggest downside to offering a virtual conference, she says, is that there is no real profit in it, unless you have a monster list.

"The back-end marketing eats up most of the profit," she admits. "Although the conference exceeded my expectations in terms of how well it was received and attended online, I don't think you can replace the value of the one-on-one interaction that transpires live."

Still, she believes that she'll do another virtual conference. "But it's going to be a new topic," she says. "I like to change things up, and keep them lively." ■

Read more about Kristine Carlson's work in Part 3, page 129

Best-selling author Caroline Leavitt

How to Be a Social Media Queen

Caroline Leavitt is the author of 10 novels. Her latest, "Is This Tomorrow," is an Indie Bookstore Pick, a *San Francisco Chronicle* Lit Pick, a Jewish Book Council Pick, a Women's National Book Association Great Group Reads, and the winner of an Audiofile Earphones Award.

Her 2010 hit, "Pictures of You," is a *New York Times* and *USA Today* best seller, a Costco Pennie's Pick, and on the *San Francisco Chronicle's* Best Books of 2011.

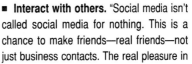

Leavitt's essays, stories, and articles have appeared in *Salon, New York Magazine, The New York Times, Real Simple, Psychology Today, New York Magazine, Parenting, The San Francisco Chronicle,* and *Redbook.*

Impressive, right? So when it comes to receiving recognition for her work, and developing a community of fans and followers in the social media sphere, Leavitt has gotten equal amounts of traction.

Here's how she uses social media to her advantage:

■ **Don't promote just your work—** because no one wants to read that. "Talk about your cat. Your dinner. Your best friend. And do it in a very honest way. If you want to promote, personalize it. Instead of writing, 'My novel is

on a big best-seller list,' make it a story. Say something like: 'I came home from a movie weeping—and wept even harder when I heard the news that I made the *NYT* list!' Be real. Share your joy—and your pain."

■ **Interact with others.** "Social media isn't called social media for nothing. This is a chance to make friends—real friends—not just business contacts. The real pleasure in

Caroline Leavitt

social media is getting to meet offline if you can, too. The more you widen your circles, the better the experience. If people know and like you, they will want to come to your readings and buy your books and, even better—meet you for coffee."

■ **Let people know you.** "Communicate on social media the same way you would in real life. Be warm, and be yourself."

These tricks of the trade are certainly working for Leavitt, who is at work on her 11th novel, "Cruel Beautiful World." She is sharing her experience on social media.

"People know when I am wrestling with a chapter, and when I feel a glimmer of hope. I always ask for research help," she shares. "This particular novel is set in the early 70s, and I put a call out to talk to people, and already I have a back-to-the-land person, someone who interacted with the Manson Girls, and much more. It's invaluable to me. And oh yes, fun." ■

Learn more at www.carolineleavitt.com

DEFINING SOCIAL MEDIA

Sonja and Merete Kristiansen, Blo franchise owners

Good Hair Cures Everything

SONJA KRISTIANSEN'S LOVE STORY WITH THE HAIR salon Blo began in her hometown of Vancouver. No one else could tame her thick Scandinavian mane. In 2012, the 20something (aka, "Blonde, James Blonde"), put down the puck at her marketing position with the Vancouver Canucks to take over Blo Union Street in San Francisco with her sister, Merete.

Their mantra: Good hair cures everything.

Here's our Q&A with Sonja, one half of the sister team that is rocking the world of entrepreneurialism—one blow-dry at a time.

Sonja and Merete Kristiansen

Tell us about Blo.

Sonja Kristiansen: Blo is North America's original blow-dry bar. Scissors are verboten. Dye, ditto. No cuts, no color: Just wash, blow, and go. Hair Cadets (clients) choose from seven styles featured in the Blo Hair Menu, from the razor-straight "Executive Sweet" to the runway-inspired "Pillow Talk." It all started with a vital question: "Why isn't there a place for quick, affordable catwalk-quality blowouts?" We've been coiffing ever since. Currently, Blo has 28 locations across North America and Asia, with more opening soon.

What are your ambitions for the company?

Sonja Kristiansen: We would love to open two or three more locations in the USA, starting with another in the Bay Area. There are plenty of markets that are starving for a business of this nature, which is why Blo is expanding so rapidly into other states (and continents)!

We love your marketing materials—especially the hot-pink signature color, which is the same signature shade as InkandescentPR.com. Tell us about some of your promotions, such as our favorite—"frequent dryer miles."

Sonja Kristiansen: The Blo tab is a package we offer to our clients who rack up "frequent dryer miles": in other words, you get eight blowouts for the price of seven ($245), and we keep a running tab on how many you have left. With the Blo tab, there's no reason to ever have to wash your own hair.

What can we look forward to seeing at Blo in 2014 and beyond?

Sonja Kristiansen: Blo as a franchise is rapidly expanding around the country and opening in some exciting new locations, such as Manhattan, Beverly Hills, Moscow, and London (and many more). As the North American pioneer of the blow-dry bar concept, we can't wait to see where Blo will go.

What are the three things you do in the social media sphere to dazzle current and potential customers?

Sonja Kristiansen: If you are a B2C company, especially one that focuses on the fashion and beauty market, this is a page from our playbook.

1. Use Twitter as your front-line customer service touchpoint. Engage directly and immediately with any unhappy customers, and turn their experience around. If they're tweeting about you, this means they're socially savvy. You will want these guys on your side.

2. Social media also provides you with a way to connect with potential employees. While most companies use Instagram as a branding tool, be sure to use it as a staff recruiting tool, too. Post photos of your team outings and behind-the-scenes fun. This will advertise to your followers how great it is to work for you (and it will boost your brand, too).

3. Make friends with your industry's blogger community. Host an event or execute a promotion strictly for this audience (and sweeten the pot with freebies and partner offerings). This will encourage this influential group to follow you on social media platforms, engage with you in a personal way, and ultimately promote you and your company to their friends and followers. 💡

Learn more at www.blomedry.com

Entrepreneurial philosopher Michael Radparvar, co-founder of Holstee

Using Social Media to Change the World

WHAT HAPPENS WHEN THREE 20SOMETHINGS, EACH WITH a social conscience and desire to make a difference in the world, sit down and write a manifesto about the change they want to see?

The Holstee Manifesto.

We found it (while on a Wiki-trip, of course), and reached out to co-author Michael Radparvar, a graphic designer who in 2009 co-founded the Brooklyn design studio, Holstee, with his brother Dave, and their buddy Fabian.

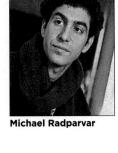

Michael Radparvar

We wanted to learn what life at Holstee has been like since their manifesto went viral, and millions have dubbed Radparvar and his co-authors the entrepreneurial philosophers of their generation. And, we wanted to learn what these millennials know about the power of social media.

You started Holstee in 2009, during the Great Recession.

Michael Radparvar: We did, and it turned out to be a good business move because we figured that we weren't likely to get jobs somewhere else. In addition to creating cool clothes, we wanted to create a lifestyle company that made a difference.

Six months into it, after a huge learning curve, we launched a line of T-shirts made of 100 percent recycled plastic bottles that were milled, cut, and sewn within 150 miles of each other in North Carolina.

And, we lent 10 percent of all sales to entrepreneurs in extreme poverty through nonprofit micro-lending organizations like Kiva.org. It's a tradition we still embrace.

What were you doing pre-Holstee?

Michael Radparvar: My life pre- versus post-Holstee has been distinctly different. I was working in a job that started off well, but ultimately, my work and life weren't in harmony.

That is what we became obsessed with at Holstee. It's a company that complements our lives, rather than vice versa.

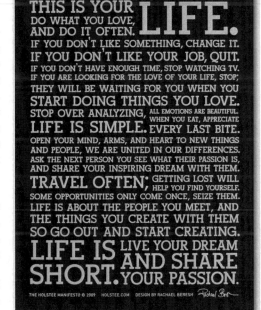

What is core to your company DNA? What makes you tick?

Michael Radparvar: Holstee is on the edge of a lot of amazing change—from a website redesign, to new partnerships, to some awesome product launches on the horizon.

Our company DNA is a vital part of our process. We strive for transparency, intentional design, and products that simplify life. If something

can be made in a more sustainable, ethical, and beautiful way, we want to know how and we want to be a part of it.

Our mission is to be proud of everything that Holstee creates, whether it's online social initiatives or the products that we promote. The Holstee Manifesto is a great example of what we want to put out into the world—not just for ourselves, but for everyone.

Tell us about the power of social media and share three tips other entrepreneurs can use to harness that power.

Michael Radparvar: It's pretty basic and logical.

1. Build relationships with like-minded organizations. The opportunity is incredible when similar organizations work together.

2. Become a destination for something spectacular. Whether it's music, culture, or inspiration, try to maintain a consistent messaging that will allow you to become a reliable destination for it.

3. Select your channel and focus. There are a growing number of social channels that organizations can use. Pick the ones that make the most sense for you. Be prepared to be active, and give more than you ever plan to ask for from that community.

What are your plans for the future of Holstee? Will social media be a big part of your marketing strategy?

Michael Radparvar: Our goal now is to focus on Holstee Print. We want it to be the first place that people go to when looking for artful prints to put up in their home, office, studio, or cafe. We have a growing range of designs in our Holstee shop now, and they all share a common thread: They inspire mindful living. Our hope is to make these designs easily shareable both online and offline. To date, social media has helped our designs to be viewed more than 80 million times around the world. Our hope is to one day reach 1 billion.

Learn more at www.holstee.com

Educator and philanthropist Charles Best, founder of Donors Choose

Crowdsourcing at Its Best

EDUCATOR CHARLES BEST CAME UP WITH A VERY BIG IDEA one day back in 1999 while eating lunch with his fellow high-school teachers in the Bronx.

"My colleagues and I were talking about books that we wanted the students to read, field trips we wanted to take them on, and art supplies that we needed—but we all knew these ideas wouldn't go beyond the teacher lunchroom because of funding issues," explains the founder of *www.DonorsChoose.org*, one of the nation's first peer-to-peer philanthropic websites. Best spent $2,000 to get the beta site up and running—and several platters of his mom's famous roasted pears with orange-rind dessert to bribe his colleagues to post those projects.

Charles Best

Determined, the man who grew up in Greenwich Village and graduated from Yale with a degree in history was on a mission.

"I knew there were people from all walks of life around the country who would want to help improve our public schools," says Best, noting that 11 teachers posted projects, and Best—with help from his aunt, Phoebe Devenish—anonymously funded them.

It didn't take long for the word to spread to the other boroughs of New York City, and within weeks, dozens of teachers began posting everything from requests for a library cart and dry-erase boards to clever programs that teach desktop publishing, metamorphosis, and Western expansion. Determined to get more donors involved, Best's students helped him address 2,000 letters to potential funders; $30,000 in donations rolled in.

In the 15 years since, close to 1.4 million citizen philanthropists have risen to the occasion. So far, they have donated more than $240 million to fund 455,559 classroom projects posted by 186,044 public school teachers. The average project costs about $650 to fund. Many are $150, but ideas for bigger-ticket items, like new playgrounds, can hit $30,000.

This simple, yet powerful crowdsourcing tool has caught the attention of some of the nation's most famous celebrities and business leaders—including TV talk show hosts Oprah Winfrey and Stephen Colbert, *Newsweek* editor and author Jonathan Alter, actor Zac Efron, and Craigslist founder Craig Newmark—who are all on the board or are vocal endorsers of DonorsChoose.org.

Even first lady Michelle Obama gave a thumbs up to Best's organization at *TIME* magazine's "100 Most Influential People Awards" in 2009.

In her speech at the *TIME* party, Obama said: "Through Donors Choose.org, ordinary citizens directly fund projects initiated by public school teachers. An art class in the Bronx had no paintbrushes, and now every single student has a set. This is exactly the kind of social innovation that we should be encouraging."

Part of the charm of the website is that it is so simple to use—and therefore, to participate. Donors scan the projects posted, and then click on the ones they want to help fund and check out with a credit card. At the end of the transaction, donors also have the option to choose to support the organization's overhead with a 15 percent allocation. Best is proud to say that for years, donors have generously funded all of that overhead—including payroll and rent for the offices in New York City and San Francisco.

Transparency and integrity are critical to the organization's continued success. The "How it Works" page of the site clearly states: "We vet every request submitted by teachers, process donor transactions using the most secure and trusted technology available, and purchase classroom materials and ship items directly to the school—alerting the principal when the materials are on their way."

Plus, donors who contribute $50 or more receive thank-you notes from students, photographs of the project, and a letter of appreciation from the teacher. While keeping in close touch with the donors is important, Best believes the real magic of the micro-funding process is helping classroom teachers unleash their innovative ideas.

"Our nation's teachers know their kids better than anyone else in the system," Best insists. "The projects they ask us to help fund aren't wish lists of stuff that they want—but from horseback riding lessons for disabled students to cooking equipment for middle schoolers to teach them the real-life benefits of understanding math—these are creative ideas that will clearly benefit the students."

Here are his three best tips on how other teachers and entrepreneurs can harness the power of social media:

1. Keep it simple. Social media can consume you or your team if you don't keep it in check. We map out our content on a calendar and use online tools to help schedule posts in advance.

2. Empower your followers. Give them tools and content to spread your message and keep them coming back. When donors give to a project, we offer them a preformatted Facebook post and tweet to share on their networks if they don't want to write an original message.

3. View social media as a business tool. Allowing teachers to sign up for automated Facebook posts during key points in the project process has helped us raise more than $1 million for classrooms over the past two years.

Learn more at www.donorschoose.org

8

SOCIAL MEDIA TAKEAWAYS

 1 Social media will continue to gain traction. "According to the Pew Internet & American Life Project, 72 percent of online adults in the United States use social networking sites— and those numbers are likely to grow in the coming years. Consumer technology will also continue to evolve toward supporting visual communication. Items such as smartphones are evolving into smart cameras, and wearable technology, like Google Glass, demonstrates that photography and video will become core to how people communicate." — *Futurist Simeon Spearman*

 **2 Know the rules.** "If you don't want what you write appearing on the front page of *The New York Times,* don't write it on social media. It stays there forever. Don't talk politics or religion. Keep your updates 80 percent business, 20 percent personal. No bad-mouthing competitors. No over-automating. Post different updates on different sites." — *Jennifer Abernethy, author, "The Complete Idiot's Guide to Social Media Marketing"*

 **3 Stay true to your brand.** "There is nothing wrong with being serious and buttoned-down if that is who you are. Consumers who use social media can quickly tell when you are trying too hard. Think of it like a first date. You don't want to lie to your date with a personality you cannot maintain. When you are honest in tone and message, you win over everyone. Don't try to be funny if your company isn't. Jokes will fall flat when you try too hard."—*Sonya Gavankar, former Miss District of Columbia, who is now "The Face of the Newseum"*

 4 Try a virtual conference—but know its limits. "The biggest downside to the 2013 Mom's Virtual Conference was that there was no real profit in a virtual conference. Unless you have a monster list, it's hard to make money because the back-end marketing eats up most of the profit. I don't think you can replace the value of the one-on-one interaction that transpires live." — *Kristine Carlson, best-selling author of "Don't Sweat the Small Stuff for Moms," and creator of the 2013 Mom's Virtual Conference*

 **5 View social media as the business tool it is—and empower your followers.** "Give your social media contacts the tools and content they need to spread your message. When donors give to a project, we offer them a pre-formatted Facebook post and tweet to share on their networks if they don't want to write an original message. Allowing teachers to sign up for automated Facebook posts has helped us raise more than $1 million for classrooms over the past two years." — *Charles Best, former teacher, and founder of DonorsChoose.org*

 6 Don't promote just your work. "Talk about your cat. Your dinner. Your best friend, and do it in a very honest way. If you want to promote, personalize it. Instead of writing, 'My novel is on the best-seller list,' make it a story. Say something along the lines of: 'I came home from a movie weeping —and wept even harder when I heard the news: I made the *New York Times* best-seller list!'" — *Best-selling author Caroline Leavitt*

 7 Select your favorite social media channel and focus on it. "There is a growing number of social media channels that organizations can choose from. So pick the ones that you like to use best—the ones that make the most sense to you. Be prepared to be active, and give more than you ever plan to ask for from that community, including useful information, insight, and free giveaways." — *Michael Radparvar, co-author, The Holstee Manifesto, and co-founder of Holstee.com*

 8 Make friends with your industry's blogger community. "Host an event or execute a promotion strictly for this audience (and sweeten the pot with freebies and partner offerings). This will encourage this influential group to follow you on social media platforms, and also to engage with you and promote you to their own large following. Friends don't want friends to have a bad hair day, so this helps us spread the word about the great service we offer at Blo." — *Sonja Kristiansen, Blo hair salon, San Francisco*

The PR Playing Field: *Sales*

WHAT IS SALES?
It's the way to get to the bottom line, and the reason that a company invests and engages in PR, marketing, advertising, and social media. It's the return on investment, and the financial goal of any self-sustaining corporation.

But more importantly, perhaps, is the question: What is the purpose of selling something?

"If you sell based on a deep mission and purpose, revenue will follow," insists the best-selling author of "StrengthsFinder 2.0," Tom Rath. "You have to start with how to change another life, then work back from that purpose."

In that spirit, this section of "PR Rules: The Playbook" brings you insights from 8+ sales experts who have been in the trenches for decades. Their expertise derives from owning a chain of hardware stores, to running presidential ad campaigns, to being a reformed Mafia don. All come to the same conclusion: If you are going to sell something—make it matter.

Meet the experts:

- **Gina Schaefer,** CEO of nine Ace Hardware stores in Washington, DC and Baltimore, MD

- **Lisa Earle McLeod,** author of "Selling With Noble Purpose: How to drive revenue and do work that makes you proud," and owner of McLeod and More, Inc.

- **Roy M. Spence,** author of "It's Not What You Sell, It's What You Stand For: Why every extraordinary business is driven by purpose," and CEO of the ad agency GSD&M Idea City

- **Buddy Teaster,** president and CEO of the nonprofit, Soles4Souls

- **Amy Elizabeth Fox,** president of Mobius Executive Leadership

- **Louis Ferrante,** author of "Mob Rules: What the Mafia can teach the legitimate businessman"

- **David Mattson,** CEO of the global training organization, Sandler Training

- **Gene B. Reynolds,** CPA, and founder of Reynolds & Associates, PLLC

- **Stefani Cuschnir,** business development manager

- **Lisa DuBois Farrell,** account executive

Entrepreneur Gina Schaefer, owner, nine Ace Hardware stores

Don't Let Your Lack of Experience Stand in the Way of Your Success

GINA SCHAEFER AND HER HUSBAND MARC FRIEDMAN OWN NINE ACE Hardware stores in Washington, DC, and Baltimore, MD. As a member of the Ace Hardware Cooperative, Schaefer has access to a large buying entity, which enables small, independent hardware stores to thrive in an era of big boxes.

Gina Schaefer

"When I am speaking about my business, people inevitably ask what kind of hardware experience I had prior to opening Ace Logan Hardware," Schaefer says. "The answer is easy—almost none. I did not inherit the business or buy it from someone. More importantly, I had very little retail experience, which I think probably would have helped me more than knowing how to change a flapper or use a hammer drill."

With hindsight being 20/20, Schaefer now realizes that not giving in to the fear of being inexperienced turned out to be valuable when she started down the path to business ownership.

How have you mastered the sales cycle?

Gina Schaefer: We have been fortunate in most cases to reach our goals pretty quickly in the lifespan of our locations. We have been challenged with a very slow location as well as a new model that hasn't performed quite as quickly as we had hoped. These experiences keep us on our toes though, and they have helped ultimately to make us better at what we do. We are currently rethinking our merchandising mix at these two locations and increasing our training efforts. We also did a postcard mailing, which is rare for us, to the surrounding residents. That really bumped up sales for the month.

Do you panic when sales are down?

Gina Schaefer: Modern-day hardware stores are often more like old-fashioned general stores in the sense that we can sell just about anything. We have the ability to customize each location based on the neighborhood, and that helps us stay relevant despite what the economy is doing. We do have some months that are slower than others and we use this time to do more training, freshen up the stores, and bring in new products for when the new season kicks in.

What's your philosophy of having a "sale" to bump up sales?

Gina Schaefer: Our co-op, Ace Hardware, has experimented in the number of national sales it holds each year. They have also tested a variety of advertising methods for these sales, including number of pages in a sales flier, number of days the sale runs, number of non-stocked items in a sale. There have been many changes in how sales are marketed, and we do our best to keep up with the latest trends, for example, in social media. When we first opened our business we held very few sales. It's difficult as a small business to plan a good sale and to get the word out. We have steadily increased options to include an annual sidewalk sale, events, and monthly "red-hot buys."

We know that when people shop, they want to get in and get out of

the store. They often want help but they want it fast. Customers flock to big-box stores, but soon return to our stores because they like the personal attention we provide.

What are the most essential elements of a powerful sales effort?

Gina Schaefer: Hands down, the hardest part is picking the right products. Once you've determined those, a host of activities kicks off. These include any point-of-sale needs related to the sale (such as making sure items ring up properly at the register), staff education, social media, and print and in-store marketing. And finally, doing a good post-sale recap to see what you might want to change in the future.

In terms of the process of selling—the essential elements start with the right team. And many would say the right atmosphere. Ask yourself, what message are you trying to convey to your audience? How does the store look, feel, smell, and operate? If you were a customer in your shop, would you be pleased? These are the key elements to think about.

Should a campaign change, depending on what you're selling?

Gina Schaefer: Not necessarily. Going back to my point of having the right team, installing a consistent sales model that can handle minor tweaks is the most important way to run a campaign. For example, we have a fantastic woman in the paint department. If there is a sale going on one day, having her add a line to her greeting—something like, "Have you seen the items on sale today?" is important. It changes the dynamic of the conversation and the rest of the interaction.

Learn more at www.acehardwaredc.com

DEFINING SALES

Sales expert and author Lisa Earle McLeod
Selling With Noble Purpose

WHAT DOES IT MEAN TO SELL WITH NOBLE PURPOSE? That's the question that author Lisa Earle McLeod answers in her book by the same title, which encourages business leaders to drive revenue by doing work that makes them proud.

"Most people believe that money is the primary motivator for top salespeople, and that doing good by the world runs a distant second. That belief is wrong."

McLeod wrote the book because of an experience she had in 2006, when she was part of a consulting team that was asked by a major biotech firm to conduct a six-months-long, double-blind study of its sales force.

Lisa Earle McLeod

"The purpose of the study was to determine what behaviors separated the top salespeople from the average ones, and it revealed something no one expected: the top performers all had a far more pronounced sense of purpose than their average counterparts did," McLeod explains. "The salespeople who sold with noble purpose—who truly wanted to make a difference to customers—consistently outsold the salespeople who were focused on sales goals and money."

It was a startling discovery that McLeod says she might have missed had it not been for a curbside conversation at the Phoenix airport.

Tell us about that curbside conversation.

Lisa Earle McLeod: It was a double-blind study, meaning my team and I didn't know who the top performers were, or who the average performers were. Near the end of the study, I was finishing a two-day ride-along with a sales rep. As she dropped me off at the airport, I asked her a question I hadn't asked the other reps: "What do you think about when you go on sales calls? What's going on in your head?"

"I don't tell this to many people," she confessed, looking around the car as though someone was going to hear her secret. "When I go on sales calls, I always think about this particular patient who came up to me one day during a call on a doctor's office.

"I was standing in the hallway talking to one of the doctors, wearing my company name badge, so I stood out. Suddenly, an elderly woman tapped me on the shoulder.

"Excuse me, Miss," she said. "Are you from the company that makes drug X?"

"Yes, ma'am," I answered.

"I just want to thank you," she said. "Before my doctor prescribed your drug, I barely had enough energy to leave the house. But now I can visit my grandkids; I can get down on the floor to play with them. I can travel. So thank you. You gave me back my life."

The sales rep told me, "I think about that woman every day. If it's 4:30 on a rainy Friday afternoon, other sales reps go home. I don't. I make the extra sales call because I know I'm not just pitching a product. I'm saving people's lives. That grandmother is my higher purpose."

Sitting in that blistering Phoenix heat, I realized the sales rep had revealed something incredibly important. I thought about that conversation during the entire flight back to Atlanta. Our consulting team had spent months shadowing salespeople all over the country. We'd conducted in-depth interviews and analyzed every aspect of the sales calls. But this was the first time anyone had spoken so openly and dramatically about their mindset.

Was the big differentiator between top performers and average performers really a sense of purpose?

What Lack of Purpose Costs a Sales Force

"When the customer becomes nothing more than a number to you, you become nothing more than a number to the customer—and your entire organization suffers," explains sales expert Lisa Earle McLeod, noting that the problem doesn't stop there, but has a ripple effect on salespeople, who:

- Start thinking only about the short-term.
- Fail to understand the customer's environment.
- Cannot connect the dots between their products and the customers' goals.

Then the problem escalates, McLeod observes:

- Customers view you as a commodity.
- You have little or no collaboration with them.
- Customers place undue emphasis on minor problems.
- Customer "churn" increases.
- Contracts are constantly in jeopardy over small dollar amounts.
- A salesperson's default response is to lower the price.

- The rest of the organization perceives the sales force negatively.
- There is little or no product innovation.
- Sales force turnover increases.
- Salespeople try to game the comp plan.
- Top performers become mid-level performers.
- Salespeople view their fellow salespeople as competitors.
- Sales force morale declines. ☼

DEFINING SALES

Lisa Earle McLeod: I went back to the transcripts of the interviews looking for references to "purpose," and there it was—the rep who said, "My dad was a doctor. Doctors have an even harder job than most people realize. I want to make it easier for them."

At the end of project, the client asked us to look across all the reps and identify who we thought were the top performers. It was a double-blind study, so the other consultants and I didn't know who was at the top and who was just average when reviewing the interviews. I found seven reps who had talked about having a sense of purpose. I told the client, "I think these seven are top-performing salespeople."

And I was 100 percent right.

You cite a study revealing companies that center on improving peoples' lives have a growth rate triple that of competitors. Why?

Lisa Earle McLeod: When you have a strong sense of purpose, beyond making money, it changes the way you approach customers. Instead of customers being just a target, your job is to help them. Many companies say that they do this, but in reality it's often just lip service. When you look at the way organizations talk about customers, they're viewed as just numbers and targets. The primary purpose in business is to make money. But customers can tell the difference between someone who wants "to close them" versus someone who truly wants to help them. It all starts with the purpose.

When it comes to being noble, does that mean creating world peace—or can it be something slightly less transcendent?

Lisa Earle McLeod: I believe that making a living for your family and improving life for your customers is a noble endeavor. In both cases, it's about doing something outside of yourself. It's been said that small-business owners are the backbone of our economy, but they're also the backbone of our communities. My father once told me that when you become someone's boss, you become the second most important person in their life. Next to your spouse, your boss has the power to make your life miserable or to make your life wonderful. Being a good boss is a noble endeavor. If you show up every day as the person who is only there to squeeze your customers and employees for all they're worth, your business is going to suffer, and you'll find yourself lonely and unhappy. But if you show up, most days, with the true purpose of improving lives for others, you're going to make more money, and you're going to be happier.

In the box on page 42, you explain what lack of purpose can cost a sales force. Tell us why this is.

Lisa Earle McLeod: Lack of purpose erodes employee morale and customer trust. Organizations are embracing noble purpose because:

■ It works. The data clearly demonstrate that organizations with a noble purpose make more money.

   ■ It helps you attract and retain higher-performing employees.

   ■ People want their lives and their work to count for something.

You talk about the dirty little secret of sales training.

Lisa Earle McLeod: Most sales training is a waste of money. Companies spend millions teaching their salespeople how to better connect with customers, but then every single day leaders only talk about sales targets. The internal conversation becomes the external conversation. If you treat your customers like a number, they'll return the favor.

The back of your book is filled with brass-tacks advice.

Lisa Earle McLeod: Most companies start their sales proposals with benefits, or worse, product features. We train our clients to start proposals with the customers' objectives, and then demonstrate how they're going to help meet them in a very specific way. In terms of preparation, the number one thing you should be thinking about—whether it's 10 hours, 10 minutes, or 10 seconds before the sales call—is, "How will this customer be different as a result of doing business with us."

How can you use your noble sales purpose in negotiations?

Lisa Earle McLeod: Most negotiations start from the place of what you want. This is actually a terrible starting point, because it puts you and the other side on the defensive. A better starting point is what you want to accomplish. A sales person might be tempted to say, "I want to close this deal," but again, that's about you, not the customer. Instead, start with your noble sales purpose. With pricing issues, you can say, "If we cut the price, we are going to have to compromise safety, or potential reliability, and we've agreed that those are our primary goals." A noble sales purpose doesn't make pricing issues go away, it provides a framework for you to see pricing in the context of value.

Once you embrace these ideas, how can you keep your noble sales purpose from being just a tagline?

Lisa Earle McLeod: It's tempting to turn it into something that marketing talks about. But a noble sales purpose is supposed to be something that the sales force embraces. For example, the noble sales purpose of one client is, "We bring health and hope into the lives of patients."

It would be easy just to put that on the sales collateral and a signature line, and forget it. But then they'd be like every other company.

Instead, salespeople with a strong sense of purpose ask themselves before each sales call, "How can we bring health and hope today into the lives of the patients at this practice?" They also ask the question in strategy meetings, or when facing important decisions.

A tagline is something you say; a noble sales purpose is something you do.

Learn more at www.lisaearlemcleod.com

DEFINING SALES

Ad executive and author Roy Spence

It's Not What You Sell, It's What You Stand For

WHAT DOES YOUR COMPANY STAND FOR? HELPING CLIENTS IDENTIFY and articulate their purpose has long driven Roy Spence, CEO of GSD&M Idea City, an ad agency he founded in 1971 whose client list includes Southwest Airlines, BMW, John Deere, the PGA Tour, and MasterCard.

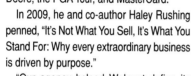

In 2009, he and co-author Haley Rushing penned, "It's Not What You Sell, It's What You Stand For: Why every extraordinary business is driven by purpose."

"Our agency helped Walmart define its purpose—saving people money to live better—and helped Southwest Airlines realize its true purpose of democratizing the skies," Spence explains. "Purpose-driven compa-

Roy Spence

nies like these are the ones that can survive and thrive in any economy, because they have a reason for being that their customers can't live without."

Spence believes a company with purpose is a deeply satisfying place to work. "You can sense it in the assuredness of front-line employees, the passion of leaders, and the satisfaction of customers. Innovation became easier, and there's stability even in tough times."

What's wrong with simply having a company that makes money, but doesn't strive to have a purpose?

Spence and Rushing: In a company without purpose, people have no idea what they're really doing there. They often look to the competition to decide what to do rather than navigate by their own sense of what's right. With a purpose in place, an organization knows its reason for being and is driven to perform and innovate. Purpose sets you apart from the competition, authenticates your brand, inspires passion in your people, and helps you achieve the impossible.

Is a lack of purpose part of the reason why so many companies have been failing during the recent financial crisis?

Spence and Rushing: We're all paying the price right now for companies that stood for nothing but emptying our pockets. This led to their inevitable downfall and should sound an alarm to all of us in business about the importance of purpose. Those companies that have it will survive and thrive, and those that don't will inevitably fail.

How and why can purpose help companies survive a downturn?

Spence and Rushing: During a downturn it is critical that your workforce be united toward a common goal and motivated by a common ideal. Without that they'll inevitably suffer from high anxiety and low morale. When you have purpose, even your most budget-conscious customers will stand by you if they believe in what you are doing and

---

Take a Page From Roy Spence's Playbook

Five Steps to Developing Your Organization's Purpose

Step 1: Revisit your heritage. Talk to the founding fathers of your organization, review the founding documents, and find the motivation that's been present since the inception. For example: Sam Walton founded Walmart to save his customers an extra dollar, the foundation of today's "Save Money. Live Better." campaign.

Step 2: Ask why. Look at the major initiatives under way at your organization and start asking: "To what end?" "For what purpose?" "To make what difference?" Also ask what you won't do. For example: A founding document of Southwest Airlines insisted that it was not going to fly anything but 737s, and it was not going to issue conventional tickets or seat assignments.

Step 3: Find the thrill. Consider what you and your employees are already genuinely passionate about and what you can be the best in the world at. For example: AARP discovered that its passion comes not from giving out discounts on car rentals, but on championing positive social change that will enhance the quality of life for all of us as we age.

Step 4: Talk to your customers. Find out why you are essential to them. For example: BMW researched its customers and found that they valued ideas and creativity over conspicuous consumption and driving fast. So BMW changed its branding strategy to emphasize ideas by celebrating the world-class architecture of its manufacturing plants, and by sponsoring a TED conference.

Step 5: Articulate your purpose. Don't just write a mission statement. Instead, create a clear and simple purpose statement that will guide every decision your organization makes. For example: The American Legacy Foundation was able to communicate both of its missions—to help teenagers reject tobacco and to help smokers kick the habit—with one wonderfully simple purpose statement: "To build a world where young people reject tobacco, and anyone can quit."

find it important instead of expendable. To get through a recession, we think identifying your company's purpose is far more important than cutting your expenses, or any other strategy.

How do you know if your organization has purpose?

Spence and Rushing: The best way to answer that question is to ask yourself a few more questions. Would your customers mind if you ceased to exist? Do you feel like your work matters? Do you have a North Star that guides you on what to innovate and how to make important decisions? If you don't, then it's time to start finding your organization's purpose and transforming everything you do around this—from your branding to management to human resources.

What do you say to entrepreneurs who need help discovering their company's purpose?

Spence and Rushing: Look to your organization's heritage and the reasons why it was founded. Ask yourself why you do what you do.

Why does your organization matter? What are you passionate about? What can you be best at in the world—something that your competitors can't?

Also ask yourself what you are not willing to do. Southwest Airlines was founded with a document that listed seven items they were not going to do—they would not fly anything but 737s, they were not to going to issue conventional tickets or seat assignments, etc. What you would never do can help you discover your values and priorities.

Lastly, talk to your employees, your customers, and your heart. If you listen carefully, you will find your organization's purpose. [For more help articulating your organization's purpose, see the box on page 44.]

How is articulating your organization's purpose different from and more effective than writing a mission statement?

Spence and Rushing: Most mission statements don't provide a mission, let alone a purpose. A purpose statement is a definitive statement about the difference you are trying to make in the world. It is not a tagline. It's for internal guidance. When you try to get too clever or creative with your purpose statement, you risk minimizing the clarity that's necessary for it to be truly meaningful and effective. So keep it simple and stay focused. And aim high, but don't end up in the ether.

Why do you say organizations have to find "the thrill"?

Spence and Rushing: Purpose-based companies feel "the thrill" because they are passionate about making a difference. Whether they were born that way, stumbled into it, or had an awakening along the way, the drive to make a difference is what fuels the company. It's the thrill of being in business.

> "Roy Spence is a brilliant, sparkling gem. Dedicated to the idea that true greatness comes in direct proportion to passionate pursuit of a purpose beyond money, he has inspired and changed leaders in every sector."
> —JIM COLLINS, author of *Good to Great*, co-author, *Built to Last*

IT'S NOT WHAT YOU SELL, IT'S WHAT YOU STAND FOR

Why Every Extraordinary Business Is Driven By Purpose

Roy M. Spence, Jr.
with Haley Rushing

To find "the thrill" at your organization, you can look for signs of fanaticism in your employees, for new market opportunities unnoticed by others, for a noble cause, or most often, a unique way to improve the lives of your customers.

How does purpose help guide decisions?

Spence and Rushing: Leaders driven to fulfill a purpose will make decisions to ensure that the purpose is never violated. For example, if a decision comes to the table and it violates the core purpose of Southwest Airlines' ability to keep costs down and fares low, it's thrown out. If a piece of automotive technology is presented to BMW that does not support the core purpose of enabling people to experience the joy of driving, they discard it. If some idea is put forward at John Deere that might compromise their quality, commitment, innovation, or integrity, it will be passed over. If any compromise on design is put on the table at Kohler, it is ignored.

What's the goal of your book?

Spence and Rushing: It's the job of CEOs, boards, and senior managers to steer companies in the right direction and guide decisions. Nothing can do this better than purpose. Marketing and branding executives will find much to learn about how to articulate their organization's purpose to their customers. HR professionals need to motivate employees and make "people decisions" with purpose. We've also included chapters and many case studies for executives at nonprofits and higher-education institutions. While not in the business of making money, these organizations depend on effectively communicating their purpose to drive fundraising, awareness, motivation, and achievement. Whatever your job is, choose and evaluate it by asking yourself if it matters and gives you a sense that you are making a difference.

How did you first discover your own company's purpose?

Spence and Rushing: We were talking to author Jim Collins about the concept of purpose, which he touched on in his book, "Built to Last." We asked him what he thought we could be the best in the world at. He helped us articulate what we have been doing for 35 years, but we didn't have a name for—delivering visionary ideas for companies that actually have a purpose. Ever since, that conversation has shaped everything we do as a company, including our founding in 2002 of the think tank called the Purpose Institute, and the writing of our book.

Learn more at www.itsnotwhatyousell.com

Soles4Souls president and CEO Buddy Teaster

The Power of the Soft Sell

BUDDY TEASTER IS WEARING OUT POVERTY, ONE SHOE—OR PIECE OF clothing—at a time. Consider how he marked the 43rd annual Earth Day, an American creation that Wikipedia reports is now the largest secular holiday in the world, celebrated by more than 1 billion people each year in 192 countries.

He headed to an event in White Plains, NY, organized by his high-school friend, Jill Iannetta. The goal was to collect 20,000 pairs of new or gently used shoes for his nonprofit, Soles4Souls, Inc.

"Engaging so many people on any social good has to matter because of the difference it makes in our collective consciousness about these issues," says Teaster, who notes that Americans every year throw away one billion pounds of clothes and shoes. "If we went back in time one minute for each pound, we would be in the middle of the Roman Empire."

Here's the good news: Thanks to Soles4Souls, Goodwill, the Salvation Army, and thousands of other philanthropic groups, countless pairs of shoes and millions of pieces of clothing make their way to needy people worldwide.

The bad news, says Teaster, is that a lot of perfectly good items get chucked.

At the same time, the demand for used products like these, especially in the developing world, is practically unlimited.

"It makes me wonder if the problem is not so much a 'stuff' problem as it is an information problem," Teaster adds. "Anytime there is a mismatch in the market, you can be sure that a lack of information is the cause of most of the distortion."

Sure there are logistical issues, big ones, Teaster knows, but he believes that most Americans, whether they're celebrating Earth Day or not, would like to do better than just throw things away.

And that's where Soles4Souls steps in.

Last year, the organization kept more than three million pounds of shoes and clothes out of landfills. That is only one-third of 1 percent of what might be put to good use.

Plus, the effort could support micro-enterprise merchants in Haiti or Honduras where so many live on $2 a day. Or, it could distribute footwear in Africa to keep villagers there from contracting an inflam-

Buddy Teaster

matory skin disease known as "jiggers," which can be prevented by wearing shoes.

"Using this soft sell, we do our part to keep useful goods out of the landfills—that's a great cause in and of itself," Teaster says. "But if you want to do something to celebrate Earth Day—and every day—then take the things you can't wear or don't want to wear and give them to people who do. You'll be making the world a better place in more ways than you can imagine."

Become a traveling ambassador.

Travel4Souls is a Soles4Souls program whose mission is to create lifelong change by providing opportunities for caring people to travel and distribute shoes in developing countries.

"Through distribution trips to Haiti, Costa Rica, Honduras, India, Jamaica, and Tanzania, we see a world of sustainable development achieved through building relationships," Teaster explains. "Your transformation is carried back into your daily life. Traveling ambassadors report feeling a sense of connectness that sets the foundation for a continued journey of service. It starts in the simple yet profound act of handing out a pair of shoes, and it builds into a lifelong love of service to others that can reverberate and touch thousands of people."

Watch Soles4Souls videos and you will see the impact firsthand.

"Also, spend a few minutes reading the stories, looking at the photos, and enjoying our tweets. All of these sources give tremendous insight into what we're all about. You can do this, too, and we make it easy," adds Teaster.

And here's the soft sell: "We take care of all the details when you donate, or fundraise. And, all payments and donations made are tax-deductible. Join the movement," Teaster concludes. "Share your spirit by sparing your soles."

Learn more at www.soles4souls.org

Leadership expert Amy Elizabeth Fox

Why Being Generous Sells

Amy Elizabeth Fox

WHEN IT COMES TO TEACHING COMPANIES TO BE MORE effective—not just in sales, but in all aspects of their business—including training, executive coaching, and organizational strategy—Amy Elizabeth Fox has experience consulting for corporations and nonprofit organizations around the country and around the world.

Since 2004, she has been heading Mobius Executive Leadership, a boutique firm specializing in large-scale work on changing an organization's culture, capability building, and leadership development.

Communication, team building, adaptive leadership, and organizational health are the essential elements of her effective approach for clients that include Fortune 500 companies, and public-sector organizations and NGOs.

"These are times when there's a lot of change, a lot of stress, and a need to help senior leaders and others who are going to be involved in the change-management process cultivate qualities of discernment, calm, and collaboration," Fox knows.

"We help leaders foster an attitude and mindset of learning to aid high performance. We work on the human capital dimension of large-scale change—the people part."

Fox's leadership programs center on four aspects of change:

- **Leading Self:** This includes cultivating emotional intelligence, being able to manage reactivity, and being able to bring an optimism and positivity to daily interactions, team meetings, and projects.

- **Leading Others:** Interpersonal skills are the focus here. The goal is to help facilitate the business-critical conversations people have every day so that they happen as skillfully and productively as possible, but with greater candor and tolerance for diversity of perspective.

- **Creating High-Performing Teams:** In this third dimension, Fox looks at what behaviors and team norms enable people to think effectively together when they're trying to work collaboratively.

- **Systems Thinking and Organizational Learning:** This last dimension focuses on how to help people lead in the face of uncertainty. "We work on managing organizational resistance, which is inevitable in a large change process. This way, new mindsets and behaviors get embedded in the organizational fabric."

> *"Generosity is very closely related to the stance of gratitude. Having gratitude for small things and large gifts enables you to be openhanded rather than grasping."*

Being generous is the key to Fox's training workshops—and her business philosophy.

What advice does she have for others about the impact of generosity on sales?

"I am certain that generosity is the essential business skill that makes companies successful. I believe the universe works on a principle of reciprocity.

"If you give generously in openhanded faith, and you believe that there isn't a scarcity of resources—or a scarcity of customers, or a scarcity of love—your business will grow faster and bigger than you ever imagined."

Plus, Fox knows that when you lead with love, and live in a culture that is loving and abundant, success will follow.

"I think it's a self-fulfilling prophesy and that the mindset of generosity begets that in others. It's certainly the kind of world I would prefer to live in," she believes. "Generosity is very closely related to the stance of gratitude.

"Having gratitude for small things and large gifts enables you to be openhanded rather than grasping. Best of all, it leaves you feeling optimistic about the future."

In turn, Fox believes, your company will reap a windfall of opportunities.

The stance of openhandedness enables you then to look constantly for:
- opportunities to serve others,
- opportunities to be of help,
- opportunities to include others in the work that you are doing, and
- opportunities to lift up the efforts of others in your industry—those who might otherwise appear as competitors.

The bottom line: "It's important that leaders lead not just by their level of technical knowledge," Fox explains, "but with their ability to intuit, to scan the environment for early signals, and to encourage a culture of imagination."

Learn more at www.mobiusleadership.com

DEFINING SALES

Former Mafia don, author, and entrepreneur Louis Ferrante

What Can the Mafia Teach You? Here's Wisdom From a Wise Guy

WHO SAYS CRIME DOESN'T PAY? NOT LOUIS FERRANTE, A FORMER associate of the Gambino family, who by age 21 had netted millions for his employers. "My natural talent for management led Mafia bosses to rely on me," explains the man who went on to pay a big price for the crimes he committed—more than eight years in prison.

While in prison, Ferrante realized there was more to life than what he knew, and he decided to go straight. He also realized that the Mob's most valuable business lessons would allow him to survive—and thrive—in the real world.

He was right. In the years since, he's written "Unlocked," a memoir of his criminal life and his time in prison, and "Mob Rules," a bestseller that offers dozens of insights into what the Mafia can teach the legitimate businessman. Millions around the world have read the books, which landed him a TV show: "Inside the Gangster's Code," which airs in 217 countries on Discovery Network International.

Here are three of our favorite sales tips.

Lessons for a Soldier (Employee)
Turn Garbage Into Gold:
Learn to Sniff Out Opportunity

Mob Rules: "Business-minded mobsters aren't wild and reckless. They prefer the shadows and dress like Mister Rogers. But they're street-smart and know how to give people what they want. It's a different side of mobsters, one we're not used to seeing, and they're quite happy not to be seen," says Ferrante. "They're sated with money, power, and success; who needs notoriety?"

Ferrante's Takeaway: "Look around your current business for areas of untapped profits—jobs others turn their noses up at, markets people don't bother trying to appeal to; there's opportunity everywhere."

Take This to the Bank: "If the Mafia had been in ancient Egypt, they would have supplied the stone for the pyramids, unionized the slave labor, put up a sausage and pepper stand, and turned the Sphinx into a casino. (They also would have robbed the gold from the pharaoh's tombs; Napoleon later did.)"

Lessons for a Capo (Middle Manager)
Toss the Dice: Deal With Unreasonable Ultimatums

Mob Rules: When John Gotti was a capo, his brother Gene, and close friend Angelo Ruggiero, were members of Gotti's crew. The authorities recorded tapes of Angelo making drug deals, and the tapes also implicated Gene. As part of discovery in their upcoming trial, copies of the tapes were given to Gene and Angelo. Gambino boss Paul Castellano demanded Gotti get the tapes so he could pass judgment—leaving Gotti with an unpalatable ultimatum: Deny his boss' request and die for his disobedience, or hand over the tapes, which would lead to the murders of his brother and friend. Ferrante asks: What would you do?

Louis Ferrante

Ferrante's Takeaway: "Gotti took a page from Caesar's playbook and executed the hit of the century—he killed the boss and underboss in a hail of gunfire, thus decapitating the Gambino family in one night. None of us likes to take such big gambles with our livelihoods, but sometimes your only option is to toss the dice and see where they land."

Take This to the Bank: "Often, the loss of your job means a better one awaits. If you're a person with little faith in destiny, this may seem outrageous," Ferrante admits. "But I assure you, everyone has a destiny. Don't let cowardice interfere with yours."

Lessons for a Don (the Boss)
Don't Build Yankee Stadium,
Just Supply the Concrete

Mob Rules: "Yesterday's Mafia wore pinstriped suits and fedoras. Today's Mafia can be seen wearing T-shirts and Levis. Considering the original business approach of Levi Strauss, founder of Levi Strauss & Company, his blue jeans are an apt metaphor for the Mafia's methods because he could spot a hidden nugget. Strauss never sought the glitter of gold. Instead, he sought to clothe the men mining it," Ferrante notes. "Smart mobsters use the same principle. They may not get a big contract to build Yankee Stadium, but they set themselves up to supply a million ancillary needs."

Ferrante's Takeaway: "Think about Yankee Stadium for a few minutes and let your mind open up to the profit possibilities. Sod. Dirt. Plastic seats. Electronic boards. Flagpoles. This list is long, and we're just getting started. And, construction can take years."

Take This to the Bank: "Like Levi Strass, the Mafia can spot gold that doesn't glitter. Today the Mafia operates worldwide in more than 40 countries. Levi Strauss & Company still sells blue jeans, now in more than 60 countries. Essentially, Strauss outdid the Mob 3 to 2."

Learn more at www.louisferrante.com

DEFINING SALES

Sales expert David Mattson, CEO and president, Sandler Training

Talk to Strangers

SANDLER TRAINING IS A GLOBAL TRAINING ORGANIZATION based in Baltimore, MD, with more than three decades of experience and proven results.

From 225 locations worldwide, Sandler's trainers spend more than 92,000 hours each year teaching "against-the-grain" sales principles to small, mid-sized, and Fortune 1000 companies.

Standing at the helm is president and CEO David Mattson. Since 1986, he has been a trainer and business consultant for management, sales, interpersonal communication, corporate team-building and strategic planning throughout the United States and Europe.

David Mattson

We sat down with Mattson to talk about how small-business owners can improve their sales techniques and help their businesses grow.

What is the goal of sales—and how does sales differ from PR, marketing, and advertising?

David Mattson: The goal of sales is to find a need for a product or service and then sell for a profit. Ultimately, sales is the result of marketing communications initiatives, as the goal is to close the leads that come in from firsthand promotions (marketing and advertising) and third-party endorsements (PR). Sales has more of a one-to-one messaging strategy, with the others focused on a one-to-many approach.

What makes so many people uncomfortable about doing sales—even when they are passionate about their business product or service?

David Mattson: One part of sales that many people have a hard time coming to terms with is "talking to strangers." After a lifetime of society telling us not to talk to strangers, sales insists you power through your discomfort. Start by scripting out hypothetical conversations and prepare yourself to answer dreaded and more challenging questions.

Another reason people often don't like doing sales could be that salespeople have earned some unfortunate adjectives, like "slimy" and "pushy." The best way to gain confidence is to change that negative perception by viewing your role as that of being a problem solver rather than simply pushing your message or product. By asking questions and understanding the problem, you'll find a solution.

How do you measure success in sales? Is it as straightforward as the number at the bottom of the "product sold" ledger?

David Mattson: Not everyone believes that success in sales should be measured only by the number of products sold. Another, and possibly more effective way to measure sales success is by measuring behaviors. Are we doing the best we can? Indeed, this is the only thing we really can control.

What can salespeople do to generate sales leads?

David Mattson: With the help of technology, sales leads can be generated in a variety of both active and passive ways. Social media (including LinkedIn and Twitter) has changed the prospecting game for many sales professionals, as those platforms can help target potential customers.

Other more classic examples include cold-calling, email outreach, and requesting referrals. Though many salespeople are timid about asking for referrals, they're a great way to drum up new business since they serve as a strong third-party endorsement of a company's service and product.

What is the best way to overcome customer resistance?

David Mattson: A case of customer resistance likely stems from past experiences with pushy salespeople. As a salesperson, the best way to disarm your customer and to be treated differently is to *act* differently.

Check your ego at the door and focus on the customer—and not the product or service you're selling. People buy emotionally, so the best approach to sales is to build a genuine relationship with the customer that's focused on providing solutions.

What the biggest mistake you see salespeople making?

David Mattson: Giving away too much information too soon. In the early stages of your customer-seller relationship, it's important to ask questions and fact-find, not educate or show off your knowledge.

What is the most important trait of successful salespeople?

David Mattson: Successful salespeople listen more than they talk. To truly understand the needs of a customer, salespeople need to listen.

What advice do you have for firms about closing a deal?

David Mattson: The best advice for firms is to know their strengths and point of differentiation. Then create an activity plan, and practice their "selling."

Learn more at www.sandler.com

Gene B. Reynolds, CPA

Accounting Rules: How to Track Your Sales Progress

Here's the fact: Only 47 percent of retail start-ups are still operating after four years in business. Why? Quite often, it's a lack of financial planning, little knowledge of finance, little or no experience in record keeping, and poor credit-granting policies. How can you keep your business from becoming a statistic? By keeping in mind four ratios to use as a guide, says CPA Gene Reynolds. "These key performance indicators will help you monitor your business on a monthly basis so you stay on a positive track."

1. Gross Profit Ratio. This ratio is an indication of pricing strategy. The gross profit ratio reveals the average amount of money made per sales dollar. For example, if sales are $10,000 for the month and it cost you $6,000 to purchase those items you sold, then your gross profit is $4,000. Divide the gross profit by sales for the month. Your gross profit ratio is 40 percent. The recommended gross profit ratio is 50 percent for product-oriented companies.

2. Operating Expense Ratio. Operating expenses are not just merchandise purchases, they include rent, utilities, payroll, and office supplies. To calculate the operating expense ratio, divide your total operating expenses by sales. The performance target for product-oriented companies should be 25-35 percent of sales.

3. Inventory Turnover Ratio. This ratio tells a retailer how often it is necessary to replenish the stock. Too high a turnover ratio signals sales may be hurt by limited selections in the store. Too low a turnover

ratio signals too much money is being tied up in inventory. Note: Retailers should turn over their inventory three or four times per year.

4. Current Ratio. The purpose of this ratio is to calculate your ability to meet short-term obligations. You begin by calculating the current assets from your balance sheet (cash, accounts receivable, inventory). Then you calculate your current liabilities (accounts payable, short-term portion of long-term debt). Divide current assets by current liabilities. Note: The recommended ratio is 2 to 1: Current assets should be double the amount of current liabilities.

Next steps:

■ Ask your accountant to teach you how to monitor these performance indicators. The more consistent you are in hitting them, the more financially successful your business will likely be.

■ To find a good accountant, the best source is your banker, who can refer you to someone who is experienced in your industry.

■ Budget in the range of $300-$500 per month for your accountant, especially for the first three years of your business.

■ Accounting fees range from $65/hour for clerical and bookkeeping assistance, to $250/hour for tax planning and business strategy consulting. ■

Learn more at www.gbrcpas.com

Business development manager Stefani Cuschnir

People Don't Buy Products: They Buy You

Stefani F. Cuschnir

"For the last 20 years, I've sold everything from diamond bracelets to innovative software, and through it all my philosophy has been the same: People don't buy products—they buy you. Through the sales process, which ends with closing the deal, the key is to maintain your integrity, be honest, and develop trust. If you don't communicate these values to your prospective customers, you may make the sale once—but that's probably it. A better approach is to set a strong foundation for years of sales to come. Customer service, open communication, and a consistent and reliable follow-up will ensure that your clients come back to you for advice, and more help." ■

Account executive Lisa DuBois Farrell

Stop Talking: Listen for What Your Customer Needs

Lisa DuBois Farrell

"Really hear your customer—not just what they say, but what they mean. The long-term relationships I have developed and retained in my three decades as a business development professional were achieved due to my ability to truly listen to what a customer wants and needs. I use my intuition to accomplish this. It is a skill as well as an art, and this approach to sales is one that I have trained dozens of junior sales-team members to cultivate. The key is not just to focus on the immediate business opportunity, but to understand the customer's long-term goals. Try it the next time you meet with a new prospect. I guarantee this personal approach to business will propel your business relationship to the next level." ■

⑧

SALES TAKEAWAYS

 ❶ Have a great sales team. "In terms of the process of selling—the essential elements start with the right team. And many would say the right atmosphere. Ask yourself, what message are you trying to convey to your audience? How does the store look, feel, smell, and operate? If you were a customer in your shop, would you be pleased? These are the key elements to think about." — *Gina Schaefer, owner of nine Ace Hardware stores in Washington, DC, and Baltimore*

 **❺ When it comes to doing sales successfully, people don't just buy products—they buy you.** "The sales process ends with closing the deal, so the key is to maintain your integrity, be honest, and develop trust. If you don't communicate these values to your prospective client, you may make the sale once—but that's probably it. Consistent follow-up will ensure that your clients come back to you for more." — *Stefani F. Cuschnir, business development manager*

 **❷ Sell with noble purpose.** "Most people believe that money is the primary motivator for top salespeople and that doing good by the world runs a distant second. That belief is wrong. If the customer becomes nothing more than a number to you, you become nothing more than a number to the customer—and your entire organization will suffer." — *Lisa Earle McLeod, author of "Selling With Noble Purpose: How to drive revenue and do work that makes you proud"*

 ❻ Spot new rackets. "Yesterday's Mafia wore pinstriped suits and fedoras. Today's Mafia can be seen wearing T-shirts and Levi's. Consider the business approach of Levi Strauss, who never sought the glitter of the actual gold. Smart mobsters use the same principle. They may not get a big contract to build Yankee Stadium, but they set themselves up to supply a million ancillary needs." — *Louis Ferrante, former Mafia don, author of, "Mob Rules: What the Mafia can teach the legitimate businessman"*

 **❸ It's not what you sell, it's what you stand for.** "In a company without purpose, people have no idea what they're really doing there. They often look to the competition to decide what to do rather than navigate by their own sense of what's right. With a purpose in place, an organization knows its reason for being and is driven to perform and innovate. Purpose sets you apart from the competition, authenticates your brand, inspires passion in your people, and helps you achieve the impossible." — *Roy Spence, author, "It's Not What You Sell, It's What You Stand For"*

 ❼ Be generous—it sells. "I am certain that generosity is the essential business skill that makes companies, and people, incredibly successful. That's because I believe the universe works on the principle of reciprocity. If you give out generously in openhanded faith, and you believe that there isn't a scarcity of resources—or a scarcity of customers, or a scarcity of love—your business will grow faster and bigger than you ever imagined." — *Amy Elizabeth Fox, CEO and co-founder, Mobius Executive Leadership*

 ❹ Talk to strangers. "One part of sales that many people have a hard time coming to terms with is talking to strangers. After a lifetime of society telling us not to talk to strangers, when you do sales you need to talk to anyone who is your target market—so you must power through your discomfort. Ease your way into it by scripting out hypothetical conversations and prepare yourself to answer challenging questions. Salespeople have earned some unfortunate adjectives like 'slimy' and 'pushy.' Gain confidence by changing that negative image." — *David Mattson, CEO, Sandler Training*

 ❽ Go for the soulful soft sell. "At our shoe-collecting nonprofit, we know that Americans throw away one billion pounds of clothes and shoes annually. If you want to do something to celebrate Earth Day, take the things you can't wear, or don't want to wear, and give them to people in need. You'll be making the world a better place in a million ways that you can't even imagine. Whatever you do, engage as many people as possible on any social good. At the very least, it will make a difference in the collective consciousness." — *Buddy Teaster, president and CEO, Soles4Souls*

PART 2 The 8 Steps to PR Success

Get Ready to Supersize Your Small Business

The 8 Steps in Action:
The Entrepreneur's Guide

What is the best, most affordable, least time-consuming way to promote a business?

That's the question that every entrepreneur wants the answer to.

They also want to know:

- How do we get into the news?

- We got into the news—why isn't that driving sales?

- Why should we publish a monthly newsletter?

- Is anyone besides my mother really going to read it?

- How do we use Twitter to get the word out about what we're doing?

- Why do we need to deal with Twitter?—And LinkedIn, Facebook, Google+, Pinterest, and Instagram?

The options for promoting your business are endless, and it's too easy to spend every waking hour trying to tell the world about what you are doing—and never make a penny from all of your efforts.

So why do it?

Because if you don't, no one will know you are there. And if you don't continue to market your business, all your past marketing efforts will become a distant memory—just like those pretty fireworks from the 4th of July.

It's a conundrum, we realize. But take solace in knowing that you aren't alone. Every entrepreneur feels the same way. Too much to do; too little time and money to do it.

But the sky isn't falling. There is a solution, and it's right here in Part 2 of "The Playbook": The 8 Steps to PR Success.

The reason we call this section "The Entrepreneur's Guide" is simple. It gives you a big-picture look at the landscape of what is possible for you to engage in, so that you can cherry-pick which of these tools makes the most sense. Then you can design a strategy that will help you make smarter decisions about where to spend your time and money. This section also shows you *how* to promote your business, and why each of the 8 steps is important.

By using The 8 Steps to PR Success, you can decide when you can go it alone, when you need to bring in reinforcements—additional employees, outside professionals—and when you should ramp up the next phase of your PR plan.

Take a deep breath, suit up, and remember what Aesop said: "Slow and steady wins the race."

Create a Stunning Website

What it is:

■ Your website is your little black dress. Your Brooks Brothers suit. Or—depending on your business—your coolest T-shirt and jeans. You want it to look as fantastic as you do. And this is why it's often a painful process to create it. You are looking at your business, and yourself, in the mirror. You know it will be viewed, potentially, by the entire world. And that can make you feel vulnerable. Don't let it. Let this process be exciting—just like dressing up for an important event.

■ Your website is the place to answer the 3 essential questions that you responded to on page 5: What do you do? Why do you do it? And, how do you do it?

■ Your website is the spot where you flesh out the answers to those questions in clever, informative, and educational ways. The goal is to make customers and reporters want to do business with you. As you're creating it, the phrase to keep in mind is: "What's in it for the reader?"

What it's not:

■ Your website is not the hamper into which you toss everything your company has ever done.

■ It's not the place to feature your favorite songs. Tempting as it is, please don't put music on your site. Not everyone shares the same taste in tunes, and you don't want your visitors to tune out!

■ It's not the place to cut loose in your use of Flash animation. Be restrained! If potential customers are taking the time to visit your site, they want to access information immediately. On the other hand, *videos* are increasingly important to have on your site, because they let readers learn more about you—when they are ready. But be sure to use them judiciously.

Why it's important:

■ Did you wear your high school prom dress or powder-blue tux to this year's big office party? We hope not. Just as fashions continually change, websites have to keep up with the times. Clearly, these online portals have evolved tremendously in the last decade. Your business needs to stay current with trends in your industry—and your website must do the same. Additionally, if your site functions as little more than an online version of a printed brochure, you are missing an opportunity.

■ How much time do you spend visiting a web page that is poorly designed, dysfunctional, poorly written, or filled with irrelevant content? Exactly. Us, too. Even in the best of cases, users often leave web pages in 10-20 seconds, according to website usability expert Jakob Nielsen. His observation: "Pages with a clear value proposition can hold people's attention for much longer."

■ Do you have a tough time ending a dysfunctional relationship? (That's a topic for another book.) If so, please don't carry that behavior into your website—or your business. Unfortunately, too many entrepreneurs refuse to break up with their dysfunctional websites. Why? Because they don't know if something new will actually be better. They don't want to spend the money. And, even if they are ready to take the leap, they don't know where to turn for guidance and good design—or which content management system to use to make managing the site easy and efficient. While the frustration is understandable, it's a bad excuse for staying in a bad relationship with your online presence.

Inkandescent Rule of Thumb: Having a stunning website that is easy to navigate is not a luxury—it is a necessity.

PLAY WITH IT!

Here's how:

It's easy to get so close to your website that you can't be objective about it. To ensure customers understand your business in the way that you want them to:

■ Ask someone (or more than one someone) who doesn't know your business to give you feedback. If they aren't immediately engaged, it's time to rethink what you've posted online.

■ Think logically through the structure of your site. Building a website is like building a house. No matter how many options you may have, every house needs to have a kitchen, a bathroom, and somewhere to sleep. Likewise, all websites share a handful of common architectural elements. See "The Nitty Gritty" section on the next page for suggestions on how to structure your site.

■ Understand that people learn in different ways. When the Inkandescent team builds a website, we use psychologist Howard Gardner's theory of multiple intelligences to help guide our site designs, and we know from his research that most people are "picture smart." Since two thirds of people learn best from pictures, be sure your site has plenty of high quality, relevant images—and incorporate as many of the "intelligences" into your site as you can.

How Are You Smart?

Use Howard Gardner's Multiple Intelligences to Maximize the Effectiveness of Your Website

Are you "picture smart"?

Most people are. That's why the best websites are chock full of photos and artwork. Picture-smart people like to draw, build, create things, and daydream. They are good at imagining things, sensing changes, solving puzzles, and reading maps. And they learn best by visualizing, working with colors and pictures.

To capture this audience:

■ *Whether it's in the banner, homepage, or inside pages, be sure to include great photos and illustrative graphics (as needed) throughout your site.*

■ *Stock images are acceptable, but original photos are better.*

■ *Be sure to set up a photo shoot with a professional photographer—especially for photos of your team—so that your public image is as attractive as the website you are building.*

■ *If you can't afford to have a professional photographer take pictures to sprinkle throughout your site, affordable images are available on a variety of stock photo websites. One favorite is www.shutterstock.com.*

Are you "word smart"?

These are people who like to read, write, and tell stories. Word-smart people are good at memorizing names, places, and trivia. And they learn best by saying, hearing, and seeing words.

To capture this audience:

■ *Make sure that everything on your site is well-written, and has substantial content—ideas that educate your clients about your products and services.*

■ *Obviously, the entire site should be free of typographical errors, and be grammatically correct.*

■ *We encourage you to hire a good copy editor and/or proofreader to make sure you look as smart as you are (or smarter).*

Are you "logic smart"?

These people like to do experiments, figure things out, and work with numbers. They are good at math, reasoning, logic, and problem-solving. And they learn best by categorizing and classifying abstract patterns.

To capture this audience:

■ *Be sure to offer a lot of information on the site—with options to mine down for more.*

■ *Provide facts, data, and any statistics you have to make your points.*

Are you "people smart"?

This group likes to have lots of friends, they like to talk, and join groups. They are good at leading others, communicating, and mediating conflict. Plus, they learn best by sharing, comparing, relating, and cooperating.

To capture this audience:

■ *Engage the reader as much as possible.*

■ *Provide areas for feedback, interactive Q&As, and opportunities where readers can participate in your social media network.*

■ *Host annual networking events where you can bring even more people to the party that is your business.*

For more on Howard Gardner's theory of multiple intelligences, see "Smart Stuff: How is your child intelligent?" in the January 2010 issue of *Be Inkandescent* magazine.

The Nitty Gritty

Most websites only require about 10 pages of content and two sets of navigation.

The **top navigation bar** offers information that is static and tends not to change:

> Home • About Us • Contact Us / Directions to Your Firm • In the News • Testimonials

The secondary **sidebar navigation**—whether it's actually along the side of your site or in a secondary menu, drop-down menus, or boxes—allows you to get creative:

- This is a good place to show off your products, services, and what sets your business apart from the competition.

- If you offer several products or services, this is a great place to outline them for your customers.

- If your customers have diverse needs (some buy products, some want information), this is an opportunity to provide specific content for each audience.

- Sidebar navigation also gives you the opportunity to showcase your videos, highlight secondary offerings (books or CDs for sale), and demonstrate your value proposition.

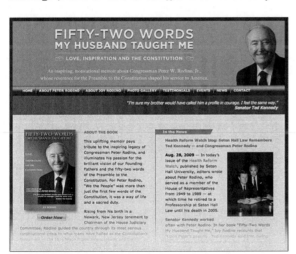

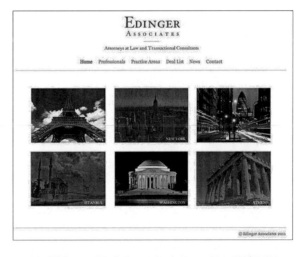

Grab your markers.

The **content area** is the bulk of your website's real estate—the place where you tell your story.

■ Ask yourself: "What do I want people to know about my company?" List your answers below.

■ Now, get creative and find interesting ways to describe your products and services, and the details of your business that set you apart from your competition.

■ Remember: Content is king when it comes to search engine optimization (SEO)—the term for what makes your website rank high when someone searches for terms relating to you, your company, and industry. Be sure to create a place on the homepage of your site where you can regularly update the content.

■ Make another list on the next page of all the articles you'd like to write, or have written, that should be posted on your site. Think big! Then prioritize the list so you can see what you can realistically tackle, especially if you have several articles to write before you take the site live. Three articles should suffice.

■ Give yourself homework. You are the expert, so be sure to share your wisdom. Try to write one article each month to add to your site.

■ Be realistic about what you have time to accomplish—and accomplish well. The articles on your site don't have to be long. Sometimes a short-and-sweet article that provides useful action items to your customers is more valuable than a 1,000-word essay.

What do you want people to know? Describe your business, and what sets it apart:

Make sure the look of your site matches what you do.

■ The sky is the limit when it comes to design approach. For the main content area, think beyond text! Photos can be a great way to make a homepage dynamic, especially for businesses such as restaurants that want to tempt customers with mouth-watering entrees, and retailers that want to showcase top products or sale items.

■ Mine down into the essence of what you do, and choose the proper images to reflect that. No nature scenes for financial planners. No stock photos of people rushing to conferences for brain researchers.

■ Slideshows are also a great feature to place on the homepage—or any page—of a website. Case in point: ITShows is a company that works with the needy in developing countries. So on their website, www.itshowsinc.com, we included a slideshow of 15 images that highlights the population their services support. It proved to be a dynamic way to get the message across about what they do, because a picture **really is worth a thousand wor**ds.

Grab your mouse and scissors:

■ Surf the Internet to find websites that grab your eye. Bookmark them, print them out, and then pick your three favorites to show your designer and website developer what appeals to you.

■ To get ideas for photos for your website, search your favorite industry-related magazines for images that grab your attention. If you like them, chances are your customers will, too. This is the kind of imagery that you should seek for *your* website.

■ Also surf the web for articles and themes that capture your imagination. Let these spark your own ideas about how to incorporate information and style into your site.

List topics for 10 articles you'd like to write:	

Develop an Explosive PR and Marketing Campaign

What it is:

■ When it comes to creating your PR and marketing campaign, this is the time to play with all the different ways to tell the world about your business. This is where it is necessary to understand the playing field, and that involves knowing the difference between PR, marketing, advertising, social media, and sales (see Part 1 of "The Playbook")—and how these tools should be coordinated to provide maximum visibility.

■ PR and marketing campaigns shout out why your products and services are the best in the business—and the ones your customers must buy. These campaigns should be as creative as your business is. And there should be a coordinated strategy around all of your campaigns, including press releases, e-newsletters, ads, and your social media efforts.

■ Your PR and marketing campaign is a fantastic way to display your understanding of the icing-and-cake metaphor that we talked about in "The Trifecta of Small-Business Failure" (page vii). Your cake may be financial services, home-improvement services, or a line of tasty tacos—but what other revenue streams could you be adding? Whatever you decide, make sure your PR and marketing campaign shows off everything you can do for customers.

What it's not:

■ PR and marketing is not direct sales. It's information-sharing, story-telling, relationship-building, and education for consumers and colleagues. It is the carrot that encourages customers to respond, so you can make a sale.

■ It's not a surefire way to make the phones ring.

■ It's not an afterthought or opportunity to be taken lightly. It is critical to the image you are building, so be sure to set aside a realistic budget that grows as you do.

Why it's important:

If you don't have a PR and marketing campaign, how will customers—much less reporters—know what you're offering? They won't. So put some time and effort into crafting a clever and memorable strategy, and be realistic about how long it will take to see results. Being pragmatic about your resources and having realistic expectations will keep you from being disappointed or from throwing in the towel when you're actually on track. *Add these to your PR and marketing checklist:*

■ **Face forward.** If you own a small business, you are the face of your firm. Your idea is the reason people walk through the door, so embrace the spotlight.

■ **Budget your money.** As a rule, a company should set aside 10-15 percent of its annual earnings for PR, marketing, and advertising.

■ **Budget your time.** It often takes longer than you think to effectively turn your PR and marketing efforts into sales. Set aside a minimum of 10-15 percent of your week to work on your campaign.

Inkandescent Rule of Thumb: *Consistency, clarity, and strategy are mission-critical. Know why you are doing what you are doing, and be able to measure your return on investment. Time spent should be money earned.*

PLAY WITH IT!

Here's how:

❶ Harness the Power of e-Newsletters

Consistency Counts

■ Send out your newsletter at regular intervals (monthly for professional service firms; weekly for restaurants and other high-touch customer service companies).

■ Create a template that you can use each month. This will help readers to recognize your brand, and if the quality of the content is interesting and inspiring, they'll become loyal followers.

■ Themed newsletters are useful. They tie together common ideas and help distinguish the issues from each other. Pick 12 themes, or topics, that you want to talk about in the coming year and develop a plan to write three articles (an intro, main feature, and sidebar) on each one. More details on specifics are below.

Clarity Matters

■ So does size. Be judicious about the length of your newsletters. It's better to write three useful articles that are short and pithy, rather than one long newsletter with 12 articles that could overwhelm readers.

■ Special offers are helpful—especially if you are a B2C company trying to draw customers into your shop or bistro. Be sure to include an expiration date and an identifier so you can track the effectiveness of each coupon campaign.

■ Assign one person, or a small team of employees, to be responsible for the consistency of the content, and for getting out your newsletter on a regular basis.

A Sound Strategy Can Save You Time, Money, and Face

Monthly newsletters are ideal for most B2B companies. Restaurants and other B2C companies can consider sending out shorter blasts each week. Either way, remember that brevity is your friend; if you pontificate, drone on, or meander off topic, you risk losing your subscribers. Know your audience, and speak to them.

Multi-page newsletters: If you are a school district, law firm, or other professional services provider, and you want to offer a multitude of complex information to your clients, sending them a newsletter that has several pages can be an effective tool. They take longer to create, but show off your expertise in a dynamic way.

Single-page newsletters: As long as these are filled with informative content, they can be the most effective outreach you offer. These should contain:
■ an introduction
■ a main feature story
■ a sidebar that complements the topic featured in the issue.

Grab your markers

Planning Your Newsletter

If you are currently doing a newsletter for your company, take a hard look at it to see if the content interests you! If not, rethink it by answering these questions:

a. The main themes: **What are the big ideas you want share with your customers, potential clients, and reporters? Each issue of your newsletter will be devoted to one of these themes.**

What are the main themes?	

b. The Intro: **What three things have you accomplished this month that your readers should know?**

■ Remember to mention in your monthly newsletter anything that is new and exciting on your website, including any press mentions, TV and radio appearances, and upcoming events.

This month's accomplishments:	

c. **The main article: What feature story can you write about your business or industry that will educate your readers? Consider these ideas:**

Fringe Benefit:
Keeping your website engaging, current, and packed with informative content makes it easier to turn out a great newsletter.

- This article, and all of your outreach efforts, should share the important trends happening in your industry.

  - Professional services firms, especially, have essential information about their area of expertise. It's important to share it with customers, reporters, and the world at large.

  - If you are a restaurant, tell the world about your specials of the day, the next celebration of a holiday or must-attend event, and your catering offerings.

  - Doctors can benefit from this approach, too. Offer medical tips, times to get vaccinations, and other topical information about good health-and-wellness practices.

d. **The sidebar: What can you offer that will complement the feature story? Consider these ideas:**

- Book reviews: Pick books that have been useful to you, as well as others in your industry. You might contact the author to do a Q&A. When you do, be sure to feature their photo, book cover, and link to their website. This is a great way to Pay it Forward (see Step 8, page 109).

- Interviews with other professionals: These include experts in industries related to yours, or those whose opinions provide a value-add to your readers. This is an especially good way to showcase other experts' knowledge about your industry—and show off your stature by featuring the interviews that you conduct.

- Activities: Use your newsletter to spread the word and increase attendance at any events you are hosting, to excite readers about networking opportunities, and generate interest in classes you are offering.

- Interviews in which you are featured in the news: These, and any other press mentions of your company, amplify the reach of the original mention by sharing it with a larger audience. Also be sure to post these press mentions on your social media sites.

Article ideas (Can be ones you use on your website):	Sidebar ideas:

❷ Spread the Word With Social Media Campaigns

This is your most affordable outreach option, in terms of financial investment. But be careful to manage the amount of time you spend on social media sites—and be sure to measure your return on investment. If you are tweeting for an hour each day, be sure you are generating leads and landing clients—and not just more followers. Ditto for Facebook and LinkedIn.

Consistency Counts

■ Just as kids appreciate a regular bedtime (even when they complain), your followers appreciate regular social media postings. Are you going to post daily, weekly, hourly? Have a plan, and stick to it.

■ If you aren't going to be the one doing the posting, assign this task to someone you trust. Remember, the essence of social media is to provide personal insight into you as an entrepreneur, and into your business. If someone is ghosting for you—make sure you share the same sensibility, goals, and "voice." Regularly check what they post to be sure they are on target.

Focus and Clarity Matter

■ Be careful about not being professional—even in this seemingly casual environment. Pictures of you partying after-hours, edgy humor, oversharing, and personal rants should be kept under wraps.

■ Rein in the bragging. Realize that some people are put off by excessive talk about your accomplishments. Don't let that keep you from sharing your big wins—just be aware of your volume and tone. Then craft your messages in a way that won't be likely to offend your competition—or any of your customers/followers.

■ So what should you share—and what should keep to your inner circle? Think about what you want to know about others, including their lessons learned, educational information such as how they accomplished a big goal, and advice for being more successful. That's what they want to know about you. Insights and universal truths are always welcome.

A Sound Strategy Can Save You Time, Money, and Face

■ Twitter is for short informative messages, never sales. Facebook is the friendly option where connections tend to prefer knowing about your personal life rather than your business. LinkedIn is great for findings jobs and employees—and fleshing out your Rolodex with current contacts.

■ You can duplicate the subject matter that you post daily on each site, but tailor the presentation to make it as effective and dynamic as possible on each social media site.

Find inspiration at www.InkandescentNewsletters.com

Bonus Idea
Reach out to the community

Having a presence in the community where you work is a great way to spread the word about what you do. Try these ideas:

■ Host a networking event that puts your business center stage.

■ Sponsor a local team that wears jerseys with your company name and logo.

■ Take a booth at a neighborhood cultural festival—and give out chilled bottles of water with your logo on them.

■ Create a mural project that ties your business to the neighborhood through artwork that features symbols, people, and events that are meaningful to the community.

❸ Make Advertising Work to Your Advantage

Many small-business owners are loath to buy ads—print ads, especially. Why? Their view is often based on the belief that advertising doesn't work—that is, ads don't drive sales. But is that the only measure of success? If the goal of an ad campaign is to have customers come away with a positive view of your brand, products, and services—advertising can be very effective. Consider these factors:

Consistency Counts

■ Does an ad need to appear 20 times before someone will buy your product? Thomas Smith thought so back in 1885. (See "How Many Times Does an Ad Have to Run?" at right.) But realize that if your customers don't need your products or service, and your ads don't entice potential new customers to want them, then seeing an ad 100 times won't result in a sale.

■ According to advertising guru Herbert Krugman, a successful ad campaign requires three levels of exposure: curiosity, recognition, and decision. "There is a myth in the advertising world that viewers will forget your message if you don't repeat your advertising often enough. It is this myth that supports many large advertising expenditures. I would rather say the public comes closer to forgetting nothing they have seen on TV. They just 'put it out of their minds' until and unless it has some use, and then the response to the commercial continues."

■ So what works? Ask yourself what works for *you*. How many times do *you* need to see something before you remember it, and buy it? A good place to start is the Rule of 3s: People need to see your company name three times before they remember it, three more times before they trust it, and three more times before they'll buy what you're selling.

Clarity Matters

■ Know your audience. As the owner of your business, you should know what turns your customers on—and what turns them off. Make sure your design and marketing teams know it, too.

■ Be mindful of brand awareness. Make sure that all of your ads reflect the colors, style, and tone of your other marketing materials—including your logo, website, and other outreach efforts.

■ When customers see your ad, what do you want them to do? Be sure you know, and incorporate that into the design and ad copy—that is, the text or script.

A Sound Strategy Can Save You Time, Money, and Face

■ Whenever buying a print ad, negotiate for the opportunity to also write an article for that publication. And when buying a radio or TV ad, negotiate for the opportunity to appear on that station's news show. This is a powerful one-two punch—and given the ever-changing world of print and broadcast news, most sales teams are now willing to blur the lines between editorial and advertising.

■ Don't be clever just for the fun of it. The content in your ads must reflect your business and be relevant to your customers and potential customers—with the goal of calling them to take action.

■ Remember, the goal of advertising is to attract repeat business, not to simply make a one-time sale. Therefore, get ads in front of the people who are most likely to become loyal customers—and give them a reason to keep coming back for more.

How Many Times Does an Ad Have to Run
Before People Buy the Advertised Product or Service?

In 1885, Thomas Smith wrote *Successful Advertising,* **in which he posits:**

The **first** time people look at any given ad, they don't even see it.

The **second** time, they don't notice it.

The **third** time, they are aware that it is there.

The **fourth** time, they have a fleeting sense that they've seen it somewhere before.

The **fifth** time, they actually read the ad.

The **sixth** time, they thumb their nose at it.

The **seventh** time, they start to get a little irritated with it.

The **eighth** time, they start to think, "Here's that confounded ad again."

The **ninth** time, they start to wonder if they're missing out on something.

The **tenth** time, they ask their friends and neighbors if they've tried it.

The **eleventh** time, they wonder how the company is paying for all these ads.

The **twelfth** time, they start to think that it must be a good product.

The **thirteenth** time, they start to feel the product has value.

The **fourteenth** time, they start to remember wanting a product exactly like this for a long time.

The **fifteenth** time, they start to yearn for it because they can't afford to buy it.

The **sixteenth** time, they accept the fact that they will buy it sometime in the future.

The **seventeenth** time, they make a note to buy the product.

The **eighteenth** time, they curse their poverty for not allowing them to buy this terrific product.

The **nineteenth** time, they count their money very carefully.

The **twentieth** time prospects see the ad, they buy what it is offering.

Become a Columnist
and a Radio Show Host

What it is:

■ A megaphone to tell the world about your area of expertise.

■ The opportunity to reach a larger audience—one you might not otherwise have access to.

■ A way to stretch your entrepreneurial muscles.

What it's not:

■ Your column and radio show are not the spot where you vent, or talk about pet peeves and what's bugging you about the world. Focus on your business. Steer clear of politics and religion, and other potential verbal landmines that can do more harm than good to your reputation.

■ This is not a platform to be completely spontaneous. Preparation is key—especially in terms of hosting a radio podcast. Ditto for when you are interviewed. Keep your sense of humor, for sure. But also know your stuff, and stay on point.

■ This is not a place to be stingy with your ideas. Share your insights freely without worrying you are "giving away the store." Readers and listeners want to learn from your expertise. Be thoughtful and authentic, and you will get more than you give.

Why it's important:

■ Educating customers is essential to building trust and credibility. Columns and podcasts are a great vehicle for this.

■ By writing interesting, informative articles, and creating thoughtful podcast shows, you can control your message—and become the star of your own show.

■ It gives you the opportunity to work *on* your business versus *in* your business. If you are busy doing the daily tasks that keep your business afloat, then writing columns and recording radio shows will force you to step back and be introspective—and to think more broadly about what you are doing, and why you are doing it.

Inkandescent Rule of Thumb: Whether you want to be a columnist in a magazine or host a radio talk show, your success will depend on coming across as a trusted expert and a reliable resource. If you do it well, people will share what you write or say.

PLAY WITH IT!

Here's how:

Remember, there are two reasons to write a column or become a radio host:

1. To become recognized as an expert on whom people rely and turn to repeatedly.

2. To get the word out to a large audience, so that what you say and information about the work you do has the potential to reach even more people.

Look for opportunities to contribute columns in trade publications, hyper-local publications, and industry blogs. With luck, you may be able to work your way up to higher-circulation regional or national publications—newspapers, magazines, or blogs.

How to create a magazine column

Naturally, your column will be about your area of expertise, providing insight and information that will pique the interest of your readers and potential customers. It shouldn't be an ode to you or your company. Be sure to ask someone who has a good feel for content, context, and language to look it over. If done right, your insights will make a lasting impression.

1. Name your column. Each column you write should include your byline, a link to your website, a professional portrait, and a short bio. Make a list of 12 article topics—one per month—that will highlight your expertise. Feel free to use the article topics that you have written about on your website and in your monthly newsletter. This is a great way to leverage the work that you have already done.

12 article topics:

2. Craft a pitch letter. Pick publications in which you'd like to be a columnist. Identify the editor or managing editor for each, so you can reach out by phone and/or email. In your pitch, offer 3 reasons why your column could be a valuable addition to their publication. List those reasons below.

Publications and editors:

3 reasons:

3. Consider buying column space: Sometimes it's worth your while to find a publication that will allow you to buy column space—called an advertorial. Buying advertorial space gives you control of your message and regular exposure to your target audience. Be clever about what you write and strategic about where you place your advertorial.

For examples of great column ideas, visit www.BeInkandescent.com.

Bonus Idea
Turn your columns into a book

Are you ready to write a book? Take your 12 columns and—if you've done your job—you'll have a book sitting at your fingertips. See more details in Step 7 of "The Playbook."

How to host a radio show

By hosting a radio show, you will be seen as an expert. However, the focus shouldn't be on you—but on your guest.

Here's how:

■ Name your show, and write a statement detailing your mission, vision, and goals for the broadcasts, below.

■ On the next page, make a list of 12 show topics, including people you want to interview.

■ Create a list, and include contact info for guests you'd like to have so that you can reach out to them.

■ If you know some great musicians, ask them to create a short piece of theme music for you—then give them credit, and promote them on your website.

Name of your radio show:

Mission, vision, and goals for your show:

Wish list: Topics, and guests—and contact info—you'd love to have on your radio show:	

■ Get the best recording devices you can afford. While most laptops have GarageBand or other recording software built in, the sound quality might not be as good as you'd like.

■ Consider hiring or consulting a radio show producer, as well as an audio engineer, especially if you aren't tech-savvy. The benefit is that they focus on the equipment and recording quality, while you focus on the interview.

■ Before you hit "the studio," be sure you sound like a pro. Practice your intro, run through your script, and get comfortable with the technology you'll be using (a podcaster, microphones, digital recorder, GarageBand, for example).

■ If the person you are interviewing isn't local, you can conduct the interview over the phone using a service such as www.freeconferencecall.com. They take care of the recording.

■ Find a podcast-friendly website to host your show. Sites such as blogtalkradio.com offer affordable options. Alternatively, you can create your own podcast/radio website, like we did with the Inkandescent Radio Network.

■ Write liner notes for each show, and use your social media pages and website to promote each episode after it is recorded and polished.

■ Be sure to have enough bandwidth that you can post mp3 audio files.

For ideas, check out the Inkandescent Radio Network at www.InkandescentRadio.com.

Make a Splash in the News

What it is:

For many entrepreneurs, getting quoted in a magazine or newspaper, or being featured on a broadcast news show, is the cherry on top of their entrepreneurial hot fudge sundae. The reasons are obvious.

■ It's a great way to build credibility. Interviews showcase your knowledge and convince potential customers that you are a trusted source. Ditto for reporters who will continue to call you for quotes, or feature you or your firm in their articles and shows. Being spotlighted in the news is a reflection of your expertise. It's also an indication that you have crafted a sophisticated PR and marketing campaign.

■ It's a prestigious way to gain recognition. What business doesn't benefit from being quoted in the news? Local, regional, and national press attention creates buzz around your business, and increases your visibility. Granted, it's best to be quoted for something positive, and in most cases that's how it plays out, but a little controversy never hurt anyone. Don't shy away from the limelight.

■ It's a powerful way to personalize the services your company provides. You are the face of your business. Being quoted enables you to introduce yourself to the public—and convey not only what your business does, but what sets it apart from other businesses that offer similar products or services.

Caveat emptor: Before you spend oodles of time and money on landing press mentions, know why you want to be quoted, where you would like to be quoted, what you want to say, and what you can reasonably expect to get out of your investment of time and money.

What it's not:

■ It's not a bullet train to overnight success. Clients we've gotten quoted in *The Wall Street Journal*, *The New York Times*, and CBS' "The Early Show" (ourselves included) didn't make millions overnight simply by appearing in the news or on TV.

■ It's not a guaranteed way to land a gazillion clients or customers. While reaching the audience of a publication, radio, or TV news show is valuable, the chances that your appearance will be seen or heard by just the right customer at just the right time can be a matter of luck. That's why it's so important to spread the word whenever you've been in the news. Turn the spotlight into a floodlight.

■ It's not an advertisement. Being featured in the news is part of a broader PR and marketing strategy.

Why it's important:

■ Being a trusted source tells the world that your opinions, and by extension, the company you built, are valuable. Having a reporter toot your horn is a great reason to brag, and another opportunity to build a loyal following and attract the attention of paying customers.

■ Good press is contagious. It's a surefire way to expose your brand and ideas to other reporters. And, when reporters trust your opinion, they are likely to call you back for more insights. That exposure might entice another reporter pick up on your story—and then your stock splits. Now you are in the Rolodex of two or more reporters, with a good possibility of the multiplier effect. That will build your reputation even more.

■ It keeps you on your toes. Not to be Johnny Raincloud, but more often than not, being a media darling is short-lived. Embrace the attention—but don't let it go to your head.

Inkandescent Rule of Thumb: If you have something important to say, say it well and make sure it's heard.

PLAY WITH IT!

Here's how:

Do yourself a favor and don't respond to a query or send a press release to a general news reporter if what you have to say would interest only your employees or people who are already loyal customers. (See page 8 for what 3 of our favorite journalists have to say about getting in the news.)

Hot trends, counter-trends, newsworthy speeches at industry conferences, and newsworthy events are the stuff that newspapers, magazines, and TV and radio shows are made of. It's news that reporters are looking for—so be sure to hit that high note whenever possible, and tailor your media lists so that you are sending your news only to the publications and media outlets that are likely to be interested. There's no need to send a press release to the CBS News desk about a new senior vice president.

1. Respond to queries that reporters post online.

■ Instead of peppering reporters with press releases, cruise through the postings at the reporter-friendly website HARO.com (short for Help A Reporter Out). It has changed the way reporters and PR people play together. The way it works is that reporters looking for sources to interview for their articles post requests for experts. This is an outstanding opportunity for everyone from business owners and authors, to industry analysts and the general public, to get in the news.

■ The key to getting a call back from a reporter is to respond quickly, since reporters are often on short deadlines and receive a lot of responses.

■ It's also important to answer only those queries for which you or your business would obviously be a good source. Taking the time to convey a thoughtful response will give you an advantage when the reporter sifts through the dozens (if not hundreds) of other responses. Using this tool well can generate mentions in outlets ranging from *The Washington Post* to Fox News and Patch.com.

2. Host an event that reporters want to cover.

■ Charitable events and grand openings of new, cutting-edge ventures are likely to attract the media more than galas and networking events.

■ If a celebrity will be keynoting, all the better! Here again, making news is the goal.

■ Try to do something newsworthy at your event. Cut a ribbon, open a time capsule, host a conference, present a check—and have a photographer take photos so you can send them to reporters who miss the event.

3. Write an eye-catching press release.

■ Don't send a reporter a press release about your business unless you can explain why the reporter should care.

■ Use press releases to share information about the work you are doing. Press releases are one way to get the message to reporters in a helpful, non-aggressive manner.

■ Make sure you are telling a good story quickly. On the next page, write about the topics that are of interest to readers—since that is what will hook the reporter. When you educate readers about something they didn't know about the topic, or your business, everyone wins.

Not sure how to write a press release? You won't find a clearer guide than our *"Press Release on How to Write a Great Press Release"* (see sidebar on page 81).

Topics you think reporters would like to know about:

4. Choose wisely where to send your press release.

■ Think like a reporter. Their job is to inform and educate their readers.

■ Below, make a list of publications in which you'd like to be quoted.

■ Write a short letter of introduction about your company and explain the purpose of your pitch. Then attach your press release.

Publications you'd like to be quoted in:

PR RULES: THE PLAYBOOK

5. Rock the social media world: Create your own press buzz.

■ Plan to post one entry daily on each of your social media pages. An easy way to manage multiple social media networks is with a tool like www.hootsuite.com.

■ Massage your message to properly target each audience. Avoid the hard sell on Twitter; be friendly on Facebook; focus on business for LinkedIn, and be artful on Instagram and Pinterest.

■ Below, list five social media outlets that you use (Twitter, Facebook, LinkedIn, for example). Next to each box, customize the message for that outlet.

Today's social media message:

■ Measure the ROI by assessing your time spent (at your hourly rate) against income (or potential income) generated. Be clear on why you are doing what you are doing:

■ Are you driving traffic to your website?

■ Are you offering a special service or coupon that customers can redeem—to measure whether followers are paying attention, and acting on your offers?

■ Are you building your credibility and expanding your network of connections?

6. Ads are also an option.

■ As we discussed in Part 1 in Understanding The PR Playing Field, ads are a great way to get yourself in the news. Just as paying-to-play by investing in a column or radio show can drum up attention to your business, the quickest and easiest way to capture the eyeballs (or eardrums) of a news outlet's audience is to buy ad space in a print publication or broadcast outlet.

■ Ads range in price, of course, so develop a budget—and define what you expect the ROI to be. Like most PR efforts, it's tough to know in advance what the impact of your ad will be. But have a clear idea about what you want. Expect to advertise on a consistent and regular basis for any measurable impact.

Need inspiration? Check out the spots we've gotten our expert clients quoted in by using the techniques we've outlined above at *www.InkandescentNewsmakers.com*.

A PRESS RELEASE ON HOW TO WRITE A GREAT PRESS RELEASE

FOR IMMEDIATE RELEASE

Contact: Hope Katz Gibbs
Inkandescent Public Relations
hope@inkandescentpr.com / 703 346-6975

HOW TO WRITE A GREAT PRESS RELEASE

Tell a great story in a concise and clever manner, add in pithy subheads and easy-to-remember bullet points, and call readers to action.

Washington, DC, Today's Date — "Grabbing the reader's attention, encouraging them to attend an event or learn more about a product or service, and intriguing reporters so they want to learn more is the goal of any good press release," says Inkandescent Public Relations founder Hope Katz Gibbs, a veteran journalist who has written hundreds of press releases that have been picked up by the media.

"My aim is to tell a story that makes readers want to learn more about the topic," she says. "Plus, it's rewarding to write it in a way that reads like a mini-article, since this gives it a greater chance of being picked up by newspapers, magazines, and blogs."

Subheads are a useful way to keep the reader engaged.

The reason is simple. They not only break up the text with quick thoughts that summarize the essence of the release, they provide a useful place to briefly summarize what you're writing about. A fun exercise is to write subheads that are so tight and valuable to the story that if readers scanned only them, they'd understand the purpose of the release.

Bulleted action items serve to draw the reader's eye to key information.
- Bullets should contain short, concise statements that flesh out the critical elements of the press release.
- They reinforce the points that you are trying to make.
- Never provide fewer than three bulleted items—five is ideal, and seven is the maximum.

Keep the release short, filled with authentic keywords, and know what you are hoping to achieve.

Here's why: If it's too long, you risk boring the reader. If the press release is especially heavy on content, additional subheads help to chunk out the important elements of the story you are telling in bite-size pieces. Think of subheads as an abbreviated statement that you are making, followed by the critical details that you want the reader to know.

Length: The ideal length of a press release is one page (350–500 words), depending on the complexity of the topic you are writing about. Some press releases that offer a lot of interesting details can run several pages, but even those should not exceed 1,500 words.

Keywords: While attention should be placed on picking the right keywords to put into any document posted online for maximum search engine optimization, remember that what you are really aiming to do is tell a good story. When you do, the right keywords will naturally find their way into the press release.

Goals: There are three ascending goals for any effective press release, so be sure to keep your eye on the prize.
- **Good:** To post the release on a reputable website where it will be picked up by Internet robots and bump up the organization's search engine rankings;
- **Great:** To have a publication pick it up, and run the release as an article;
- **Ideal:** To have reporters or bloggers be so intrigued by your clever prose that they write an article about your company.

What are some of the best websites on which to post your press release? There are dozens of options to choose from—from free sites to those that charge hundreds per posting. Here are some of our favorites:
- **PR Buzz:** Post an unlimited number of press releases for $299 per year.
- **PRWeb:** Services range from Basic ($89/release) to host the release and have it appear on search engines and news sites; to Financial ($499/release), which promises that your news will appear on top business and financial sites including *Bloomberg* and *WSJ*.
- **PRNewswire:** Its Search Reach package ($129/release) includes posting on *prnewswire.com*; making your release "findable" by Google, Bing, and Yahoo!; driving traffic to your site with "live site preview"; an RSS feed and search-friendly permalink URL; and a social media toolbar. For an extra fee, additional options, such as adding an image, are also available.
- **Dozens of free distribution sites** exist, and free is always nice. But buyer beware. "You get what you pay for" applies here.

Bring it home: To wrap up the press release, be sure to include about 100–150 words of useful, interesting information about your organization. In this case, we'd highlight Inkandescent Public Relations: a full-service PR, marketing, web development, design, and book publishing firm that helps entrepreneurs gain more visibility. Include contact info: visit www.InkandescentPR.com.

Save the date. Announcing an upcoming event? Include the date, time, location, any fees, and a link where the reader can find additional information. This should be clear at the top of the release, and listed again at the bottom to reinforce the point.

END

News You Can Use

For decades, publicists have taken pride in getting their clients quoted in the biggest-circulation and most popular publications possible.

While that's certainly a focus at Inkandescent Public Relations, times have changed. Going hyper-local can be equally effective—because local readers are often your customers—as is having a social media presence.

On these next four pages you'll find 8 reasons to reach out to a reporter, and examples of our clients who have been featured. *See more Inkandescent PR press clippings at www.InkandescentNewsmakers.com.*

NEWS YOU CAN USE: 8 REASONS TO MAKE YOUR VOICE HEARD

1 Feed the Media's Thirst for Entertaining Ideas. Getting on TV can be tricky—unless you have a unique idea that reporters and their audience are hungry to know about.

Case in Point: While tradition is terrific, making a Thanksgiving dish with a twist sounds delicious to many people. Chefs Kim and Edgar Alvarez, owners of the award-winning **Avenida Restaurant** in Philadelphia, shared recipes for Turkey Mole, Roasted Pumpkin Soup with Toasted Pepitas, Chorizo Cornbread Stuffing, and Vanilla Flan with the audience of the **CBS show** in Philadelphia morning show, "Talk Philly."   *See the show: philadelphia.cbslocal.com*

2 Make the Best of Crisis Management Moments. Fortunately, crisis management isn't a regular occurrence for most small-business owners. However, high-profile problems do happen. What's the best way to cope when the proverbial sky starts falling? By telling the truth—in a press release, and by speaking directly to the best reporters working on the story.

Case in Point: Here's how we helped **ACT College President Jeffrey S. Moore** deal with the fallout when he suddenly closed the doors of his Northern Virginia school in the spring of 2012.

The Washington Post

ACT College president defends late aid payments
By Daniel de Vise

The president of ACT College, a for-profit higher education provider shut down last week for alleged federal aid violations, says the institution never intentionally withheld aid dollars from students. The Northern Virginia college closed its three campuses after the US Department of Education revoked its access to federal aid, a deal-breaker for any institution. College President Jeffrey S. Moore defended the institution in a statement and telephone interview Tuesday. "There was never anything intentionally done wrong," Moore said. "We never intended to hold student moneys that should have been paid out to them." *Full article: www.washingtonpost.com*

Be Bold When Bucking a Trend. Journalists often like to write about people who make bold life changes and courageous choices.

Case in Point: Amy Steindler went against the grain when she quit her big Wall Street job to become a life coach. While some considered her crazy, her hometown newspaper, Annapolis, MD's **Capital Gazette,** realized she had done something brave—and something many others fantasize about.

CAPITALGAZETTE.COM

Annapolis woman quits Wall Street to help others
By Shanteé Woodards, Staff Writer

Looking back, Amy Steindler can admit that she knew a finance career wasn't for her, even before the market tanked.

The Annapolis resident had been caught up in the prestige of being a wealth adviser, but knew she wanted to do something more creative. So Steindler quit her job and spent more than a year re-evaluating her life. That led her to discover the work of life coach and *O magazine* columnist Martha Beck. She signed up for Beck's classes and became certified as a life coach, making Steindler one of five to receive certification in the state.

Through her company Insight Out Life, Steindler aims to help clients deal with different aspects of their lives like relationships, careers and health.

"Some (clients) are in a place where they understand that corporate America is not for them, but they're at a loss about figuring out what to do," said Steindler, 52. "It's fun to watch people blossom and say, 'I can live my life in a different way and be fulfilled and happy.'"

To become a Certified Martha Beck Life Coach, participants are required to read Beck's books that deal with self-discovery and apply online to the program. The training requires a written test, an interview with Beck and a series of paid and unpaid coaching hours. Training sessions are offered four times a year and the program's tuition costs $7,000, according to Beck's website.

Steindler doesn't count how many clients she has, and keeps a note on her computer: "I am a talented coach whose clients find me at exactly the right time." When introduced to a prospective client, she'll have a conversation with them and explain her work and they both decide if they will be a good fit. If they hire her, Steindler will send them some paperwork with questions, including one about what they want out of life.   *Full article: www.capitalgazette.com*

 **Share Your Smart Ideas.** Getting great advice from experts in a field you want to work in is welcome information for most job-seekers. Being one of these chosen experts not only increases your visibility, it builds your credibility.

Case in Point: Roxanne Ladd, owner of Behind the Scenes Events, says her business got a boost when *US News & World Report* asked her to offer advice on how to break into the meeting planning business.

Full article: www.money.usnews.com

5 Let reporters know you are the new kid on the block. In most towns, local newspapers report on new businesses. Food section editors are especially eager to write about the best new restaurants in town. It's their job to track the best and brightest.

Case in Point: When **Lyndsey DePalma's House of Steep** opened its doors in 2012, *The Washington Post* Food section sent a reviewer to check out the new digs. The review gave a fabulous boost to her start-up, lauding DePalma's original recipe for delicious tea, sweet treats, and deep relaxation.

The Washington Post
Food

Food: House of Steep in Arlington, VA
By Nevin Martell

Most eateries have a place to sit down while your takeout order is being prepared. It's exceedingly rare that a foot bath is recommended to help pass the time. But that's what happens at **House of Steep**, which opened last September in Arlington. The narrow space offers something of a triple play: teahouse and cafe in the front, "foot sanctuary" in the back. The concept was developed by 31-year-old Arlingtonian Lyndsey DePalma, who says she was inspired by her great-grandmother. "She soaked her feet every day, lived to a ripe old age, was healthy as a horse and had a happy life," DePalma says. "So I thought there might be something to the whole foot-soaking business." *Full article: www.washingtonpost.com/lifestyle/food*

6 Share "How-To" Advice. Getting local press is key when your customer base is local or regional. To interest reporters in a story about your company, explain how what you are doing will help their readers attain their goals—such as making a career change.

Case in Point: Mimi Darmstadter hit the jackpot when **The Washington Post Express** wrote about her career-transition business. To maximize the visibility, she hired Inkandescent PR to write a press release to post on the national wire service about the feature story so it would get even more attention.

Career Transition Coach Mimi Darmstadter: How To Develop a 'Plan B'

Washington DC / PRBuzz / August 16, 2011—Career transition coach Mimi Darmstadter knows the statistics. Since December 2007, 8.8 million people have lost their jobs, according the US Department of Labor.

While devising a plan for an alternative "safety net" career is easier said than done, she told *Washington Post Express* reporter Nevin Martell this week that you can take steps now to find the perfect next career—even if you haven't lost your job.

"Soul-searching is hard," Darmstadter says. "I force people to ask themselves the tough questions."

Full press release on: www.inkandesentpressreleases.com

NEWS YOU CAN USE: 8 REASONS TO MAKE YOUR VOICE HEARD

7. Interpret Trends: We scan more than 300 reporter queries daily at Inkandescent PR, and come across stories that we are qualified to respond to about PR, marketing, and entrepreneurship.

Case in Point: When a reporter from **The Wall Street Journal** was looking for small-business owners to comment on whether there would be a double-dip recession, we were happy to offer insights.

Full article: online.wsj.com

THE WALL STREET JOURNAL.

8. Help a Reporter on a Tight Deadline: Being featured in an article distributed by the **Associated Press**—and other syndicated services—is great, especially if you are hoping to build a national reputation. The reason is simple: news agencies around the country pick up AP stories, from Forbes.com to *The Sacramento Bee*.

Case in Point: When AP reporter **Joyce Rosenberg** was on a deadline before Christmas Day looking for sources to comment on their New Year's resolutions, we were glad to respond. We shared our goal of working smarter so there would be more quality time for family, which she included in an article that appeared in dozens of newspapers on January 1. My husband, kids, and I celebrated the press mention with a special dinner we all made together.

Business owners are making New Year's resolutions [Forbes.com]
By Joyce M. Rosenberg, Associated Press / Forbes

Working on work/life balance

Hope Katz Gibbs wanted to spend less time at work in the new year and more time with her two children. But "instead of dialing things back for a work/life balance, ramping it up seems to be the best strategy at this point," said Gibbs, president of Inkandescent Public Relations. Her Washington-based company, which targets entrepreneurs, expects to have more work as more people start businesses.

So she looked at her family life and realized that overbooking her 14-year-old daughter and 10-year-old son with after-school activities wasn't the answer.   *Full article: www.forbes.com*

Network Wisely

What it is:

■ Networking at its best is "PR on the ground." It's the opportunity to come into contact with potential customers who want to meet you and hear about what you do—and how you can work together. This is PR nirvana.

■ It's an opportunity to introduce your services in person, and put a face on your business.

■ Great networking events also give you the opportunity to find potential suppliers and employees that you'll need as you build your business.

What it's not:

■ A networking event is not a time to over-imbibe, troll for sex, scarf up a free meal—or bring anything but your A-game to the party.

■ It's not a guaranteed way to build your business. Not every event you attend will attract your target audience, leaving you feeling like you wasted your time.

■ Cheap. While some events are free, many cost $50 or more to attend. That may not be a whole lot of money, but it adds up. If you plan on joining several organizations and attending several networking events each month, be sure to calculate the return on investment.

Why it's important:

■ It gets you out of your office. Networking is an essential way to spread the word about what you do. And meeting someone in person is a surefire way to know if you can work together.

■ It helps get you out of your comfort zone. Does networking makes you nervous? Warm up by attending events where you feel most comfortable. For instance, if golf is your passion, take some business associates out for a round. While this is not a novel idea, doing it well takes some finesse. "If you're not close friends with your boss, then a game of golf could be a daunting prospect," admits John Byrne, golf pro and master networker at "Into the Rough," an online source for info on golf, particularly in the United Kingdom. If golf isn't your bag, try bowling, attending a sporting event or an art opening. (See more of Byrne's advice, page 92.)

■ It helps you put your best face forward. Recognize that professional networking opportunities can happen anywhere in day-to-day life—at the grocery store, on a plane, hailing a cab, or on a subway. When you start to be aware of that possibility, you'll find yourself surrounded by potential resources, collaborators, and customers. Start paying attention.

Your Networking ROI

Here's a simple equation to measure your return on investment from the networking events you attend:

Annual membership dues	$ 400
+ 12 events per year at $40 each	$ 480
+ 36 hours at events per year	
(2 hours at each event plus 1 hour of follow-up: Your time, based on $50/hour)	$ 1,800
Total Annual Investment:	$ 2,680

Now calculate the return: New clients, new jobs, new connections. And be sure to consider the value of intangible benefits, such as making new friends, learning something new from a speaker, being inspired, and even being entertained.

Inkandescent Rule of Thumb: Choose interdependence over isolation, and realize the power of cooperation over competition. The key is to break through your comfort zone, maximize your time on the networking playing field, and make yourself memorable.

PLAY WITH IT!

Here's how:

"Networking links people and information to one another for the mutual benefit of everyone involved," says Donna Fisher, author of "Professional Networking for Dummies." "The reason that networking has gotten a bad reputation is that many people are selling in the name of networking. Those who are truly masterful at networking do so in a very quiet, yet powerful manner. You have that personal power within you, and your network is unlimited."

Find the best networking events to attend.

■ Doing your research on events can save you from wasting an evening—and your hard-earned money, because attending a networking event can run you anywhere from $10 to hundreds of dollars.

■ Check out reliable networking websites that list a variety of events for you to consider. You're sure to find some good ones at: www.InkandescentNetworking.com, www.eventbrite.com, local and national Chambers of Commerce, economic development organizations, and professional and trade associations in your industry, among others.

■ Ask colleagues where they network.

Be savvy about meeting new people.

■ It should go without saying, but if you attend a networking event, talk to people you *don't* know!

■ Whether you are an extrovert or introvert, remember why you are there. Approach people at networking events with the idea of offering something of value to them before asking for something in return.

■ Think critically about whether you want to go where your colleagues are—maybe not, or maybe so if they are competitors. Golf courses, and other places where people relax while they work, are ideal locations to meet like-minded folks who will want to do business with you.

Whether you love to network, or hate it but do it anyway—try this:

■ Make a list of five things you love about networking. Tuck it into your pocket, and before you enter an event, pull it out to remind yourself why you are there. Now, go have fun!

5 things you love about networking (copy this list and tuck it into your pocket for future networking events):	

■ List 10 people you have met this year whom you wouldn't have met if you hadn't networked.

10 people you have met through networking:	

■ List five things you hate about networking.

■ Next to each, write two things you can do to ease the pain.

5 things you hate about networking ...		... and what you can do about it:

■ Really hate networking? Connect with a friend and convince them to attend an event with you.

■ Still not comfortable? Read: "Hate Networking? You're Not Doing It Right," in the October 2012 issue of *BeInkandescent.com*.

■ Now get out there and network! You'll find great events to attend in cities around the country: *www.InkandescentNetworking.com*.

The Byrds founder Roger McGuinn

Network Like a Rock Star

WHAT DOES IT TAKE to sustain a career in rock and roll for more than five decades? Networking well, says Roger McGuinn, co-founder of The Byrds.

At 70, the legendary rock star is still going strong. When he performed recently at The Barns at Wolf Trap near Washington, DC, his one-man show wowed the packed house. McGuinn strolled out onto the stage singing "My Back Pages," which was penned by his longtime friend Bob Dylan. For the next hour and a half, the minstrel in the Stetson sat before a beautifully lit ruby backdrop surrounded by his favorite three guitars and a banjo.

Roger McGuinn

As he eloquently shared the history of folk music and told the story of his career, he sang and strummed dozens of the songs that he and The Byrds have made famous. For the finale, he sang "May the Road Rise," an old Irish blessing he turned into a ballad with his wife of more than three decades, business partner—and official roadie—Camilla McGuinn.

April 1, in fact, is the couple's anniversary, and the inspiration for the name of their music label, April First Productions.

The Power of Networking

We counted our lucky stars a few months before the DC gig, when we met the McGuinns while they were on a national tour with The Rock Bottom Remainders, a band made up of best-selling authors. Inkandescent Public Relations was helping promote the DC leg of the band's 2010 Wordstock Tour.

Founded in 1992 by musician and author Kathi Kamen Goldmark, The Rock Bottom Remainders was born when she partnered with her friend Dave Barry and they decided to pull together a handful of literary icons who loved to play music. "We figured it would be a great way to have fun while giving something back and raising money for charity," Kathi told us of the group that includes her husband Sam Barry, and Mitch Albom, Stephen King, Matt Groening, Amy Tan, and Ridley Pearson. That evening, we struck up a friendship with several of the band members, who have become regular contributors to *BeInkandescent magazine*—and this book (see insights from Sam Barry on page 26, and our case study on Ridley Pearson on page 145).

Soon after, we flew down to the McGuinn's home in Florida to interview the down-to-earth couple. Roger picked on his guitar as we talked, and later shared a toast with Camilla's favorite champagne, Veuve Clicquot. "Networking well is all about building relationships," Camilla knows. "You never know who you are going to meet—and that's what makes it so exciting."

It's All About the Hat

Although he didn't wear his signature Stetson during the interview, the humble rock star—who at 13 was inspired to play guitar when he heard Elvis Presley singing on the radio—says it's his hat that the audience notices most. "I learned this adage decades ago, when I was playing with Bobby Darin, and I believe it's true: People hear what they see."

Of course, McGuinn realizes that he didn't get to be inducted into the Rock and Roll Hall of Fame in 1991 without a lot of hard work and determination. "Being good at something requires total dedication. You have to decide that you are passionate about one thing, and that you don't want to do anything else with your life, and you have to practice until you are good at it."

The Byrds—which included David Crosby, Chris Hillman, Gene Clark, and Michael Clarke, then later

Clarence White, Skip Battin, and Gram Parsons—recorded 14 albums, including "Mr. Tambourine Man," "Turn! Turn! Turn!," and "The Ballad of Easy Rider." The group disbanded in 1973.

"We were a ship of pirates; it was every man for himself," shares McGuinn, who released several solo albums after the breakup. He also toured with Bob Dylan's "Rolling Thunder Revue," and played guitar on the track titled, "Ride The Water," on Bo Diddley's "The 20th Anniversary of Rock 'n' Roll" all-star album. In 1978, he again joined forces with former Byrds Gene Clark and Chris Hillman to form "McGuinn, Clark and Hillman." They recorded an album with Capitol Records.

May the Road Rise To Meet You

In fact, 1978 was also the year McGuinn met Camilla. The couple happened to be taking the same acting class in Los Angeles, and were paired as acting partners. While it wasn't quite love at first sight—well, not for Camilla, at least—it soon became clear to both of them that they were destined to be together. "At the time, I was dating a professional actress, who had encouraged me to take the class," says McGuinn, who shared that he was also in debt after the breakup of The Byrds.

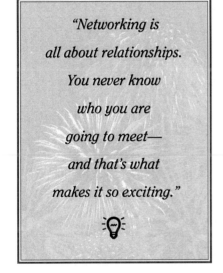

"Networking is all about relationships. You never know who you are going to meet—and that's what makes it so exciting."

Camilla adds, "As for me, I had spent years studying to be an actress, but to support myself had worked as a Playboy Bunny. So I had a car, and $500 in the bank."

"I married her for her money," jokes McGuinn, who on a serious note explains that this was also a time when he was on a quest to get healthy—mentally, physically, and spiritually. "Everyone seemed to have been making out financially, except for the musicians. It's simply very expensive to have a big band on the road. Part of the problem was that we were not getting publishing royalties, and there were other contractual issues. It costs a lot of money to make a giant, live rock show happen. The bottom line was that I owed people money, and I had to figure out a way to pay it back."

By the late 1970s, McGuinn says the life of a troubadour seemed much more appealing than being in a famous band. It didn't take long for him to convince Camilla that taking their act on the road would be a grand adventure.

"We weren't married for two years when it became clear that I'd become the roadie," she says, recalling that when they first began touring the country, they drove from show to show in a Mercedes sedan. They quickly realized that if they needed to sleep in the vehicle, something larger was required. Soon after, they invested in a VW van. "You can put a couch in there, a TV, and a hot plate," Camilla explains. "It's great. We loved the camping life."

While they remember a few cold nights spent sleeping between giant eighteen-wheelers in dark parking lots, those days were also packed with fond memories. One night after a show in New Jersey, they sat on the van's sofa watching their tiny TV as they sipped champagne and dined on lobster tails given to them by the woman who owned the venue where they had just played.

"It doesn't get better than that!" Camilla insists.

Learn more at: www.rogermcguinn.com

TEEING UP SOME GOOD ADVICE

10 Tips for Networking Well on the Golf Course

By John Byrne, golf pro, and founder of Into the Rough

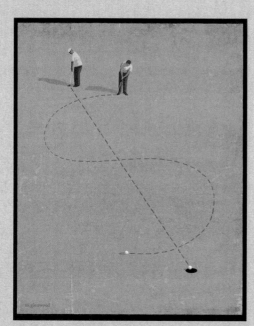

Golf is a great game for networking, and there are many opportunities for success and failure on the course. If you're not close friends with your boss, then playing a round of golf together could be a daunting prospect. Follow our guide to networking and playing with the boss to get ahead, or to avoid getting the sack.

1. Show up on time. Who wants to be waiting around for an idiot who can't turn up on time? It's time they'll never get back—and may never forgive you for.

2. Play competitively. Be civil, but never spare your opponent when the chance is there. After all, this *is* a competition.

3. But never get carried away. If you suffer from "golf rage," then keep a lid on it or don't bother playing at all. No one wants to see a maniac swinging a golf club into the turf.

4. Dress appropriately. Dress according to the golf course you're playing on and the personality you either have, or want to convey. If you're not an exuberant person, then don't come dressed like pro golfer Payne Stewart.

5. Don't spend too much time on lost balls. Balls aren't expensive, time is. And if you are trying to impress people, then their time is even more expensive. So do everyone a favor and hit another.

6. Don't take too long on shots. How many practice swings do you need? You probably don't need more than three so get on with it—before you get left behind.

7. Stay sober. Being drunk during a golf game with work colleagues is generally a bad idea for obvious reasons. However, if your boss is okay with that and encourages you, then stay ahead of the curve and be more sober than he or she is. Using this strategy means you won't have anything to feel guilty about—and you will actually remember what happened.

8. Chat, but don't gossip. No one likes a gossip—and even though many people can't resist gossiping, you don't want a reputation. But you've got to be chatty even if it's not in your makeup. Golf is a social game, so make the round easier by talking through it. Ignore this rule if networking with computer programmers.

9. Offer to pay. Even if you don't intend to and you know your boss or friends won't accept it, offer to pay—be it during the round or afterwards in the bar. Hopefully they'll say no, but by offering you'll have made a good impression.

10. Relax and be yourself. Have fun and let your personality show through. Be natural and all else will follow!

Learn more at www.intotherough.co.uk.

ENSURE YOUR NETWORKING EVITES GRAB ATTENTION

Planning a Networking Event? Start with a Strong Invite

By Robyn Henderson, networking guru, Australia

Robyn Henderson

Reflection is a powerful tool, especially in business. Each month, I ask myself:

- What worked well?
- What didn't work at all?
- What do you wish you had more time for?
- What will you make more time for in the next 12 months?

Yet when it comes to face-to-face networking, if you are waiting a whole year to review your activity, you are potentially missing lots of opportunities. Or even worse, you risk continuing to do something that is not really working.

One thing I know for sure is that master networkers can make decisions quickly and accept or decline potential networking invitations in a heartbeat. So let's look at the decision-making tips that some master networkers use when they receive an invitation and use them as a guide for creating and sending one.

The standard invitation format is via email, Twitter, a forwarded link, Meetup.com, LinkedIn, Facebook, YouTube, or a dedicated website.

Here's a look at the main things that grab attention:

1. Compelling email subject lines. Also good are opening sentence or event titles that capture the imagination. If the sender has targeted their marketing to a specific demographic (that includes you) you will probably move to point 2. If you are not remotely in the target market, the delete button looms.

2. Details. Your interest has been sparked—tell me more! What is the date? Where is it being held? What is the time frame? Some readers will delete the invitation at this point if the location, date, or time does not match their availability. If it does, you will move to point 3.

3. Explaining why this matters. Why should I go, what are the benefits of attending, who else is going? These are all attention-getters, and good copy can clinch the deal here. At the very least, it'll get you to move to the action step—which is point 4.

4. Cost counts. How much does it cost to go? Very quickly we weigh the risk of wasting that amount of money on a bad event versus the potential benefits to be gained by enjoying the event and getting to network with the other attendees.

The definition of what makes a bad event may vary from person to person.

Some may define a bad event as one that is poorly organized, starts late with no real structure, and where everyone is left to their own devices. Sometimes an event has great promise, but lousy delivery.

Yet for others, the informality may be what they like most. Many people have a dollar amount that they are prepared to risk. "Well, it's only $50, so if I don't like it, I can leave—it's not a huge amount of money." Someone else's "dollar meter" might be $1,000; it depends on the demographic, the event, and the potential benefits.

Many people today attend free events knowing full well that although theoretically they are free, there is a big chance of a heavy and very persuasive sell throughout the event for another event or course.

Master networkers consider all of these factors when they receive an invitation, and they take it into account when deciding quickly—yes, no, or maybe.

Learn more at: www.networkingtowin.com.au

Join a Speakers Bureau

What it is:

■ A credibility booster. Speaking to groups of like-minded business folks guarantees that dozens of people, if not more, will learn from your expertise. That builds your credibility as much, if not more, than getting quoted in the news.

■ A way to generate additional clients and customers. The audience may well want to buy what you are saying—literally. In fact, when the industry experts, futurists, and veteran entrepreneurs on our Inkandescent Speakers Bureau are hired to speak, they are often hired to do consulting work or are booked for additional speaking gigs.

■ A means of learning from a captive, relevant audience. This may be one of the most valuable and important reasons to speak! While you may know more about your topic than your audience does, paying close attention to their feedback will help you massage your message so that you can be even more effective.

What it's not:

■ Speaking engagements are not platforms for you to pontificate. The best speakers stay on point and have a message that is engaging and relevant.

■ They are not a place to BS. Authenticity in any speech is critical. So before you embark on this PR and marketing opportunity, be sure of your material, be sure you can speak candidly about your topic, and be willing to share some of your struggles, not just your triumphs.

■ They are not an opportunity to test the waters. Know what you want to say, how you want to say it—and what you want the audience to take away from your speech.

Why it's important:

■ There is probably no better way to find new clients than by speaking at an event where you stand up in front of a room full of people who want to hear what you have to say. Your message is sure to resonate with many in the audience who need your services, and they could be your next customers.

■ Speaking gigs are another potential revenue stream. But be willing to work your way up the speakers bureau food chain. The bigger speakers bureaus take on experts who are already celebrities. Smaller bureaus are more flexible, and are much more likely to take on less-experienced speakers. Be open to starting small.

■ Practice makes perfect. Repeatedly facing your fears can help you overcome them. Glossophobia—fear of public speaking—is one of the most common phobias. Reportedly, as many as 75 percent of adults suffer from it—and many people claim that they prefer death to giving a speech! Comedian Jerry Seinfeld once joked that at a funeral, most people would rather be lying in the casket than delivering the eulogy. If that describes you, find ways to work your way through "speakers block"—or make peace with the fact that this PR tool isn't for you.

Inkandescent Rule of Thumb: If you want to be in the spotlight, go for it!

PLAY WITH IT!

Here's how:

Maybe you want to speak to help sell books, or get more clients for your company. Know why you are playing with this tool, and if it makes sense to move forward, do everything you can to be as successful and engaging as possible. Here are a handful of tips to get you started on your path to the podium.

Practice, practice, practice.

■ Remember what author Ray Bradbury once said: "I know you've heard it a thousand times before. But it's true—hard work pays off. If you want to be good, you have to practice, practice, practice. If you don't love something, then don't do it."

■ The key to being a successful speaker, and landing a spot on a speakers bureau, is having a message that you have perfected and knowing how to deliver it.

■ Being clear, focused, and interesting will get you booked for future speaking gigs.

Know your material.

■ Don't wing it. Going with the flow and being flexible works in some situations—but trusting yourself to be a brilliant speaker in front of an audience without any preparation is something even the pros don't attempt.

■ If an audience member asks you a question that you don't know the answer to, saying, "I don't know" is better than making up something.

■ Practice reading your speech out loud. Then practice your speech with the equipment you are planning to use. Have a couple of back-up plans in place, so that if the equipment fails, your speech won't. The more prepared you are, the more confident you'll be up at the podium.

Speak for free.

■ Giving free speeches lets you get your feet wet on the speakers circuit before the stakes are high. But only accept these initial engagements if you can speak in front of groups of people who will be supportive and genuinely curious about what you have to say.

■ If you are speaking at a conference, attend other sessions specifically to observe which speakers are most effective and engaging, and why.

■ If your public speaking muscle is out of shape, be mindful about improving your speaking technique. Ask for feedback, and be open to critiques.

Turn your vision into reality.

Take out your colored markers, and use them for each step below:

■ With the purple marker, make a list of all the events you dream of speaking at.

■ Use the blue marker to list the topics you can imagine yourself giving a speech about.

   ■ Use the red marker to list the things you need to do to overcome your fears. (Hire a speaking coach or invest in a public speaking course like toastmasters.com or your local community college; invest in a book or DVD dedicated to the topic; practice in front of a mirror, your dog, and small, friendly groups; record yourself speaking and study the recording; practice deep breathing; try yoga; decide this is what you want, and power through it.)

      ■ With green, make a list of the public speaking qualities you shine at. (Have an interesting subject to talk about; have a desire to share your message; be comfortable in front of groups.)

   Fight fear: Expect to be nervous. But be aware of your excitement, too. And don't forget to breathe.

Events you'd like to speak at, and topics you'd like to speak about:	

Giving Presentations May Not Be as Big of a Risk as You Fear

A Q&A with ARTiculate founders Hilary Blair and Robin Miller

Two vivacious communications experts—Hilary Blair and Robin Miller, owners of the communication/presentation company ARTiculate:Real&Clear—help business leaders become good public speakers.

They have their work cut out for them, because after all, it's tough to get up in front of a huge audience—especially if it isn't something you've been trained to do.

"Yes, it's intimidating to stand before a large crowd," admits Blair, an actor and professional voice-over artist with more than 30 years of experience teaching and coaching voice, public speaking, and voice-over skills. "But it's mission-critical. I truly believe that everyone can do it, and do it well. They sometimes just need a little coaching so they are comfortable and clear."

Giving a good presentation involves more than just delivering the message well, though. "It's having an authentic message to deliver that will gain a company more clients," explains Miller, a motivational speaker who has a PhD from the University of North Texas in Musicology, and a Master of Divinity degree from Iliff School of Theology.

On the next page, Blair and Miller discuss some of the reasons so many business owners get hung up when it comes to speaking publicly—and what they can do to take the pain out of making a presentation.

FIGHT YOUR FEAR OF PUBLIC SPEAKING

Your company coaches people to "be how they are," and get out of their own way so they can present their authentic selves when making a presentation. Can anyone learn to do it?

Hilary Blair

Blair: Yes, we believe everyone can learn to present more effectively. The best way to do that is to have them draw on their strengths—not necessarily by fixing their weaknesses. We call it "getting real and getting clear." For us, the joy of working with clients is helping them access their unique qualities. Each person has his or her own individual presentation style, and they often need encouragement to break out of their learned patterns, listen to their internal voice, and communicate it outwardly so that the message they wish to have heard or delivered is, in fact, what is heard and delivered.

Why do you think so many people are petrified to stand up in front of a crowd?

Miller: Most speakers believe the audience is judging them, and rightly so. When we stand up in front of people, they do assess our appearance, our energy, our knowledge, our presentation, etc. But often, we are focused on what people are thinking about us, rather than on what we are giving to them. When a speaker believes his or her message is more important than what people think, then the speaker will present in a manner that is unencumbered—and people will listen.

What are the keys to making a great presentation?

Blair: The first step is to know what your audience needs to hear. Then align your verbal prosody (the rhythm, stress, and intonation of speech) with your nonverbal choices and word choices so that you will achieve the greatest impact.

Those nonverbal choices are important. We often give undue emphasis to the words and tend to undervalue the importance of where/how we stand, what we wear, the look on our face, and other nonverbal cues. How we say it is the final piece needed to connect with audiences. A carefully crafted message makes a difference, but that's not enough. To increase the odds of clearly communicating to our audience, we must be sure that what we are doing and how we are saying what we are saying are aligned.

Is there a difference between making a pitch before a live crowd and recording one for YouTube or a commercial?

Robin Miller

Miller: Yes, indeed! Acting for the stage, film, and voice-over all contain their own nuances. In a nutshell, the meaning for stage acting is conveyed with the full body; film acting concentrates on the use of the eyes, and voice-over is about expressing through the voice. Awareness of these differences can help greatly with nailing successful phone interviews, TV appearances, and live presentations, for instance.

What makes a speech or presentation go south?

Blair: Here is one technique speakers should avoid: Delivering their message from the typed page—head down, reading words not written in a way for being heard aloud, in a monotone.

Liberation occurs when speakers learn to connect with and believe in the message to the point that they can discard their notes, and a real delivery unfolds. We speak in chunks of thought and not in perfect sentences. Papers can create a barrier and a protective boundary to hide behind, and don't always allow for sharing energy and passion. Speakers who choose to present using notes or written scripts must commit to being fully connected to the audience while sharing.

What do you tell people so they are more willing to take the risk of speaking to audiences?

Miller: Anyone can be a great presenter if they present as their authentic self. For example, we trained a CFO of a large investment company who was trying to present like the CEO, who happened to be very charismatic. When the CFO embraced his own quirky personal style and began presenting as himself, he broke through a wall and moved forward successfully.

Learn more at www.articulaterc.com

Write a Book

What it is:

■ An additional boost to your credibility. The key is having something substantial to share with the world in an interesting, articulate, thought-provoking manner. But writing a book is not for everyone. It's an exhausting process (believe us!), and most books aren't best-sellers. But if a book is burning to pop out of you—then write it!

■ A great way to make a splash in the news. Books with heart, depth, and soul that strike a chord with readers also often strike a chord with reporters.

■ Something to talk about as a public speaker. In fact, almost all of the experts we have invited to be on the Inkandescent Speakers Bureau are authors. Not only do they have something to say, they have something more than a speech to sell—and that's good for them and their audience.

What it's not:

■ Writing a book isn't a way to stroke your ego. While many people fantasize about seeing their tome hit the bestseller's list, the odds are against it happening.

■ It's not a million-dollar revenue stream. Even if you do get an advance from a publisher, it will be a long time before you see a royalty check. And since most publishers no longer give advances—is going the traditional route your best option? Self-published books are a great alternative, but expect to spend a minimum of $10,000-$25,000 to publish and promote it. How long will it take you to earn that back?

■ It's not a way to test the waters with a theory or idea you haven't fully researched. Successful business-book authors know their stuff, and are able to flesh it out in a compelling way. They often have services that they are hoping to market through their books. Because books are often loss leaders, know why you are writing the book, and be clear on what you expect to get in return.

Why it's important:

■ Books give you a voice. Despite the odds, the expense, and the time spent—writing a book is an invaluable opportunity to share your thoughts, ideas, and vision with the world. That may be reason enough to write one.

■ Books show off what you know. Heads of companies—large and small—often write books because they want to share the depths of their expertise with clients, potential customers, and reporters. This may be one of the most valuable opportunities you can invest in.

■ A book is a stepping-stone to new possibilities, and a great thing to have on your resumé. Plus, you never know who might pick it up. There are countless stories of the book that sits dormant for years and is then picked up by someone who responds to it and has the power to make your dreams come true. Even if a book isn't a hit with the masses, there may be one person—or more—with whom your thoughts and ideas resonate. Writing a book is a gamble—but so is being an entrepreneur.

Inkandescent Rule of Thumb: *Since writing books isn't a ticket to instant celebrity and wealth, be sure you can afford the investment of time and money required to turn your idea into a published work. And be sure you have the funds to promote and market it so that it gets into readers' hands.*

PLAY WITH IT!

Here's how:

Have a good story to tell.

■ Start with a subject you find fascinating. If you yawn at the thought of spending a few hours reading about the topic, writing a book about it will be torture. Talk to your friends and colleagues about the idea. Does it sound interesting or fun to them? If so, you may be on to something.

■ Your book's purpose may be to inform, engage, entertain, provoke, or persuade. To keep readers involved and demonstrate mastery of your subject, back up your theories and ideas with research, facts, solid interviews with experts, and case studies.

■ Don't sabotage that great story with poor, or even bland, writing. Having a great idea is one thing. Being able to flesh it out so that the message is clear, concise, and interesting to readers is another. Your first draft is exactly that. Even the pros—especially the pros—will tell you that rewriting, editing, rewriting, and editing again are the steps that enabled them to get to a finished book that was worthy of being published. This is not an endeavor for the faint of heart—or those with egos who think editing is what everyone else's writing needs.

Have a game plan.

■ Books take a ridiculously long time to write, longer to get right, and they require a lot of support from professionals—including editors, agents, and designers, to name a few. Be prepared to invest.

■ Find a system that works for you to keep track of your various manuscript versions, your sources, and any holes you need to fill. And back up your work. [See "Back It Up."]

■ Will you use a spreadsheet to track your progress on your book? Hanging file folders? Lists on Google+? Whatever system you choose, make it simple. Be sure you can locate everything—from the phone number of a source you interviewed a year ago, to your initial outline, to the revisions you made yesterday. The system shouldn't become your jailer—it should be your savior to keep you from wasting time or having to redo work already completed.

Grab those markers again and get ready to dream big about that book you have always wanted to write.

■ On the next page, write the title, or several possible titles, in purple.

■ With your blue marker, write a subhead. This should encompass the thing that you want readers to take away from it. Be clever, be pithy, and be short.

■ Using the red marker, create a simple outline of 6 to 10 chapters, with titles, that fleshes out your idea. Let the ideas run through your fingers. You can edit your outline later.

■ Now grab that orange marker and write a sentence that describes what you'll be discussing in each chapter.

■ Cool stuff, right? Now sit back, take a deep breath, and with the yellow marker, highlight the things you have come up with that are the most brilliant things on the page. If the whole page turns yellow, you'll know you have a plan worth pursuing!

Book outline:

Book outline:

Feeling stuck on your outline? Take a break.

■ If you are feeling unsure at any point in the process, use the green marker to jot down your concerns. Put them in the margins, so it doesn't distract from your brainstorming.

■ If it's not flowing, take a deep breath and refocus. If the trickle of thoughts doesn't turn into a waterfall, give yourself some time away from the book you are writing.

■ When you come back, see if your original thoughts stand up, or if you need to rethink or re-work your big ideas. You might need additional paper to finish outlining the book that you're trying to write.

■ Run your ideas past trusted colleagues, and let the process percolate.

■ Writing a book is a big deal, so take your time. But stay with it. If there's a good book in there, with effort it'll find its way to the surface.

■ For more insights, read "8 Secrets to Book Publishing Success," at right.

For information about our three Inkandescent book imprints, and our ghostwriting and publishing opportunities, visit: www.InkandescentPublishing.com.

For advice from some of our clients and author friends about writing a book, see, "25 Publishing Rules of Thumb From Best-Selling Authors," in the February 2012 issue of BeInkandescent.com.

8 Secrets to Book Publishing Success

Writing a book is hard. "Selling a book is even harder," admits broadcasting icon Tom Brokaw, author of seven books, including, "The Time of Our Lives."

As you'll see in the 8 tips below, few authors disagree—even the ones who have sold millions of copies of their books. Certainly, a lot has to do with talent. Even more has to do with having a great story—especially one that is timely, truly memorable, or simply captures the public's imagination.

To find your own recipe for book success, consider the tips below from best-selling authors whom we have had the privilege of interviewing since launching *Belnkandescent magazine* in January 2010. We thank each of them for taking the time to offer their words of book publishing wisdom.

1 **Fall in love with your material.** "Writing a book requires so much energy, dedication, and focus that if you aren't deeply engaged, you will not have the patience to tackle all the challenges of writing, revising, birthing, and taking the work into the world. Be open to the material. It works on you as you work on it, deepening your understanding of what you are saying, inviting you to stand for what you know and have discovered. Writing is a vocation, a calling, a commitment to clarity. As far as the process of putting a book in the world, nothing is impossible. Much is difficult." — *J. Ruth Gendler is a best-selling author, nationally exhibiting artist, and educator who has led writing workshops for adults and children for 25 years. Her "Book of Qualities" has been excerpted widely, used as a classroom exercise in personification and values in school settings from 2nd grade to college English classes, and quoted in sermons and speeches.*

2 **Breathe, touch, and taste the world where your characters live.** "The four-page story about a girl named Velva Jean, which my mother, Penelope Niven, wrote when I was young, always stuck with me. So when I was old enough, I bought the rights for $1, and turned the story into a screenplay. It became an Emmy Award winning movie in 1996, but I couldn't get Velva Jean out of my head. I knew that eventually I wanted to bring her back to life in the form of a book, and I did in 2009. I advise others to do the same: If you can feel fictional characters in your skin, and have a burning desire to know more about who they are and what they do, you know that you have a story that's worth telling." — *Jennifer Niven is the author of "Velva Jean Learns to Drive," which was turned into an Emmy Award winning film. Another of her books, "The Aqua-Net Diaries: Big Hair, Big Dreams, Small Town," was optioned by Warner Brothers as a TV series.*

8 BOOKS

8 Secrets to Book Publishing Success

3 **Ignore the naysayers.** "I knew going in that getting my book published was going to be a long shot. I was not an established author, and I didn't have a ready-built big platform (publisher-speak for folks who follow your work). However, I had an appealing message that I researched thoroughly and wrote about passionately. I decided to take the chance and followed to a 'T' the rules of writing a non-fiction book proposal. And with a little luck, lots of faith and determination, I'm now a published author. It feels great. But most importantly, I got to spread my message to thousands of readers about the magnitude, power, and potential of giving by everyday donors." — **Wendy Smith** is the author of "Give a Little: How Your Small Donations Can Transform Our World." She has worked in the nonprofit sector for 25 years and is now a consultant to organizations around the world, and speaks about the magnitude, power, and potential of citizen donors.

4 **Know that publishing books is a numbers game.** "I tried to get an agent for my first novel by contacting 30 of them. Eight wanted to read the whole manuscript and four wanted to represent it. Sure, these are amazing numbers, but the important number is the 26 agents who rejected it. Same with my 10th novel. After five published novels that sold poorly and three that couldn't find a publisher, I wrote "The Art Forger," which was rejected by a dozen publishers before being published in 2012 by Algonquin Books. But neither my agent nor I ever gave up." — **Barbara Shapiro,** New York Times best-selling author, and winner of the 2013 New England Book Award for Fiction.

5 **Use the meat + salt method.** "To make the people and events in your book spring to life, re-member this simple recipe: Start with a hearty helping of meat, which includes all the facts you'll ever need to know to explain your story properly. And be sure to flavor it with plenty of salt—some juicy bits of humor or a few spicy anecdotes, for example. And one more thing: The facts aren't always pretty. But I strongly believe that as authors, we have to be honest about the good, the bad, and the ugly parts of our past and present." — **Rosalyn Schanzer** *is an author and illustrator of 16 books for young people, including "Witches! The Absolutely True Tale of Disaster in Salem," which won the Gold Medal for Best Illustrated Children's Book of 2011. It was also a 2012 Sibert Honor Book, which is awarded to five distinguished nonfiction books each year.*

8 Secrets to Book Publishing Success

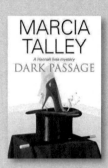

6 **Snag a great editor.** "Your job as an author is to write the best book you possibly can. If the book isn't good, everything else—getting an agent, finding (or keeping) a publisher, striving to hit the best-seller lists—is a moot point. That's why everyone needs a great editor to help them whip their manuscript into shape. If you already have a publisher, then an editor comes with the deal. If you don't, then you need to get your completed manuscript into the hands of a competent editor, preferably someone not related to you, who will give you critical feedback. Market research tells us time and again that the well-written novel, like the proverbial cream, will rise to the top. It isn't rocket science. Write a good book, and it will sell. So get someone to help make sure it's the best book you can turn out." — *Marcia Talley is the Agatha and Anthony award-winning author of 13 mystery novels featuring sleuth Hannah Ives. Talley also participated in two serial novels, "Naked Came the Phoenix," and "I'd Kill for That," which included chapters by 13 famous women mystery authors. Her latest, "Tomorrow's Vengeance," will be released in 2014.*

7 **Research potential agents the way you research your book.** "There is lots of great advice out there about what makes a good agent and how to find one, but one of the most important and often overlooked characteristics in an agent is whether or not the agent is seeking new writers. Keep an eye on the personnel news of websites and e-newsletters like *Publishers Marketplace* and *Publishers Weekly.* Hunt for agents who are new, or who have recently switched agencies, been promoted, or struck out on their own—they are much more likely to be seeking new writers. A new agent at an established agency can give you the best of both worlds: someone young, energetic, and open-minded, but with all the resources of a major agency." — *Jon McGoran is author of the thrillers "Drift," published in 2013, and its sequel, "Deadout," coming in 2014, both from Tor/Forge. He is also the author of three D. H. Dublin forensic mysteries.*

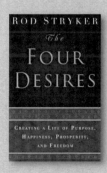

8 **Keep moving forward.** "A great book is the fruit of multiple drafts. However, reworking your writing before you have a completed draft is generally unproductive and even tortuous. In other words, it's an immense waste of your precious time and energy. Only after your manuscript has a beginning, middle, and end, will it be clear what is missing, what doesn't need to be there, and what needs refining. Thus, be good to yourself and avoid the inevitable temptation of trying to rework pages before the draft is done. Make it your daily commitment to forge ahead to the completion of your next—and what will one day be—final draft." — *Rod Stryker is one of the preeminent yoga, tantra, and meditation teachers in the United States. He is the founder of ParaYoga, and the author of, "The Four Desires: Creating a Life of Purpose, Happiness, Prosperity, and Freedom."*

Excerpted from "Publishing Rules: Trade Secrets From Best-Selling Authors," an Inkandescent eBook available on amazon.com.

Pay It Forward

What it is:

■ A great way to share your expertise and experience while helping those in need.

■ A great way to show the world you care, by making a contribution. Donating your time and expertise is as valuable as giving cash.

■ A great way to market your business. When you work with others who are volunteering at the same nonprofit or social business, the synergy of interests will also reflect well on you and your business.

What it's not:

■ It's not a way to boost your ego. There are more than 1.5 million nonprofits in the US, and another 1.2 million around the world. At least one of them, if not several, could use your help. Rather than investing your ego, time, and money in starting up an organization that may, or may not, succeed—pay it forward by joining forces with a group that is already established.

■ It's not an opportunity to sell your wares.

■ Nonprofits are not an easy industry to work in. "The current problem is that in many communities, nonprofits are competing for dollars against other nonprofits that do similar sorts of activities," says Lisa Anne Thompson Taylor, who helps philanthropists and nonprofits through her company, Taylor Strategic Partnerships. "Philanthropists often say to me: 'A lot of organizations who are all doing the same thing ask us for money. Why aren't they working together?'"

Why it's important:

Paying it forward is an opportunity to share your success by helping people who need assistance in ways big or small, so being effective is the challenge—and the goal. We asked the directors of some of our favorite nonprofits why their organizations have been successful. Here's what they said:

■ *Kim Valentini, Smile Network International:* "Every year, thousands of children in developing countries are born with facial deformities—such as cleft lips and cleft palates. These children suffer rejection and social injustices and frequently are hidden away from the mainstream of everyday life. Through global partnerships that enable volunteers to build trust in foreign countries, Smile Network is provided the opportunity to conduct surgical missions and to impart dignity and a better quality of life to individuals whose medical needs may otherwise go untreated." (Learn more at www.smilenetwork.org.)

■ *Steve Gross, Life is good Playmakers:* "Millions of our nation's youngest children have experienced profound trauma in its many forms. It's a silent epidemic. Life can hurt—but play can heal. Our ultimate goal is to help the people who care for the kids who are in the most life-threatening positions find ways to create sacred spaces to let the joy seep out." (Read more about the Playmakers on page 137.)

■ *Charles Best, DonorsChoose.org:* "I knew there were people from all walks of life around the country who would want to improve our public schools." Since 1999, close to 1.4 million citizen philanthropists have donated more than $240 million to fund 455,559 classroom projects posted by 186,044 public school teachers. (Read more on page 38.)

Inkandescent Rule of Thumb: Serve on the board of an organization. Choose one you admire. It could be your alma mater, your kid's school, an arts group, or as the coach of a team.

PLAY WITH IT!

Here's how:

■ **Case in point:** Dr. Alice Waagen, founder of Workforce Learning, has been active for decades in Habitat for Humanity. In addition to sitting on the board of directors of the Northern Virginia chapter, she raises money, gets her friends and colleagues involved, and volunteers to build as many houses as possible. Waagen says it makes her happy to be involved with such a noble organization—and notes that the contacts she's made have helped her build her business. That's the win-win-win scenario in action.

Encourage your employees to volunteer some of their time. Put your money where your mouth is: Give them one day off every year to work for a charitable cause. Make volunteering a team-building experience by having the entire staff volunteer their time to participate in a fundraiser together, such as the Alzheimer's Walk or the Susan B. Komen Race for the Cure, among dozens of other options.

■ **Case in point:** Crews Control, a corporate video-staffing company, takes this a step further. Founder Andrea Keating encourages each employee to find a nonprofit organization they believe in, and a project to help with, and then twice a year the entire staff works together to make it happen.

Not only is this a great team-building opportunity—and a fantastic way to give back—it creates a culture of giving, and that's a gift that has no bounds. In addition, the company matches employees' charitable contributions up to a specified level.

■ **Case in point:** Matt and Judy Curry's automotive service-and-repair company, Curry's Auto Service, makes it a point to sponsor local sports teams around its 10 shops and showrooms—and all the kids on the team get T-shirts featuring Curry's logo. That's a great way to give back, market your brand, and show the world you care about the community, and kids.

Sponsoring a sports team is a great way to pay it forward and spread the word about your brand.

Time out: If you feel there is a cause that is calling *you*—you have two options. You can start your own nonprofit, or team up with an existing one. But, if you're considering starting one, think long and hard, and then follow the four steps below.

Step 1: Research. With the red marker, make a list of the nonprofits around the country that are already addressing the cause that resonates with you, or helping a population that you'd like to assist.

Nonprofits that are already doing this work:	

■ List the leaders of these groups, and their contact information.

Leaders:		Contact info:

■ In orange, list what you could do for the target population if you were inside the fold. This list will become the points you make when you write a letter reaching out to the director to explain why you want to be part of that group.

■ Step back, and with that magical yellow marker, highlight all of the things that you think are most likely to be effective—and you are most likely to be good at.

What you could do to enhance the mission of this organization:	

Step 2: Soul Search. If a nonprofit does not exist or is not doing the work the way you want to do it, and you still think your own nonprofit is needed or is viable—go for it! But remember, you're starting a business, and you need to take all the steps you took when you launched your existing company.

■ Grab the green marker and get realistic. Being as critical as possible, list five reasons that would hinder you from accomplishing your goals—be it insufficient funding, a lack of knowledge of the culture or population, a lack of entree to the decision makers, or even your own lack of follow-through. You know yourself better than anyone!

Five potential roadblocks:	

Step 3: Outline a business plan. In one paragraph, explain the mission of the nonprofit you'd like to start.

■ Ask yourself: What will it accomplish? Whom will it serve?
■ What would you call it? Use the purple marker for this list.

The mission:	

■ With the blue marker, list the 5 things your nonprofit would do to benefit the population you hope to serve.

5 benefits:	

■ List 10 people you could invite to serve on your nonprofit's board of directors.

10 people:	

Step 4: Rock it. Now that you've laid the groundwork, it's time to take the next step. Turn to the next page for inspiration from rock star Michael Franti, on how he created his Do It For The Love Foundation. *For information on potential foundations to work with, check out our Nonprofits column on Be Inkandescent magazine, at www.BeInkandescent.com.*

The Art of Paying It Forward

Rocker Michael Franti Says: "Do It For The Love"

IN HIS BEST-SELLING ALBUM, "All People," American poet, musician, and composer Michael Franti and his band *Spearhead* spread their message of love, peace, and social justice.

In August 2013, Franti took his message to a new level when he founded the Do It For The Love Foundation, a nonprofit wish-granting foundation, bringing people to live concerts who are in the advanced stages of a life-threatening illness, children with severe challenges, and wounded veterans.

"We have partnered with musicians from around the world to create life-changing experiences for their fans and families," says Franti of the network of artists, promoters, producers, and business people

Michael Franti

dedicated to bringing joy, healing, and hope—and an unforgettable experience of celebrating life—to those who need it most.

Since its launch in August 2013, Franti has granted dozens of recipients and caretakers the opportunity to enjoy his shows and share time backstage with him. In addition, performers such as George Straight, Pink, Miley Cyrus—and bands such as Train and Brett Dennen—have jumped on board to work with the Do It For The Love Foundation.

"We look forward to expanding our roster of musicians to include every musician, concert promoter, and genre of music to bring the uplifting gift of music to everyone who really needs it," Franti says.

What inspired the rocker to spread the message of love? Franti's journey began, he believes, when his birth mother gave him up for adoption. She was of Irish, German, and French descent; his father was African-American and Native American. "My birth mother was afraid her family would not accept me," explains Franti, who was adopted by Carole Wisti and Charles Franti, a Finnish-American couple in Oakland with three biological children. While in high school, Franti met a priest who taught him to tell a story on paper, and soon he was writing poetry. He purchased a bass guitar at a pawn shop and started creating music inspired by the hip hop, punk, and reggae he heard on the radio. In 1986, Franti became part of the industrial punk/spoken word band *The Beatings*. The band was chosen by U2 to open for its Zoo TV Tour. In 1994, he founded *Spearhead*, and later founded the record label *Boo Boo Wax*, whose acts have gained a worldwide audience. To commemorate President Obama's inauguration, Franti played at The Green Ball, The Peace Ball, and the Rock the Vote Party.

Franti is also an advocate for peace in the Middle East. His film, "I Know I'm Not Alone," features footage of Iraq, the Palestinian territories, and Israel, and aims to provide a better understanding of the people who live in war-torn countries. "The film came out of my frustration with watching the nightly news and hearing generals, politicians, and pundits explaining the political and economic cost of the war in the Middle East without ever mentioning the human cost," Franti explains. "I wanted to hear about the war by the people more personally affected by it: doctors, nurses, and soldiers, and poets, artists, and musicians." The film struck a chord, and in 2001, Franti received the Domestic Human Rights Award from Global Exchange, for his efforts to end war. In 2006, he was invited by Jenny Macklin, then an Australian Member of Parliament, to show the film at Australia's Parliament House.

Environmentalism rules for Franti. *Spearhead* avoids the use of water bottles on national tours and the tour bus runs on biodiesel. Since his birthday in April 2000, Franti hasn't worn shoes. Why?

"I had been traveling to a lot of countries where people couldn't afford to wear shoes. I would take off my shoes to go play soccer with the kids and I couldn't even take three steps," the rocker explains. "There would be these gravel-filled fields and I just couldn't do it. I went home and wondered how it would feel not be able to afford shoes. So I took off my shoes and have been barefoot since.

Franti partnered with an organization called Soles4Souls.org (see our interview with its CEO, Buddy Teaster, on page 46). "They bring shoes to people all around the world who can't afford them. At our concerts, we collect shoes from our fans and spread the word about the great work they do."

What does Franti suggest that small-business owners do to pay it forward?

In terms of business: In business, it is all about relationships and connecting with people. That doesn't mean doing things because you're hoping to get something in exchange—you do good things because it is the right thing to do. It snowballs, because people will recommend you and call you for service when they need something, because they remember you in a good light and trust you. It also creates community around your business—and that makes your life a lot more fun.

To be a musician for three decades requires an incredible team. It's essential to learn how to collaborate and to delegate responsibilities to people who are better at certain skills than you. At the same time, it also helps you to know every job.

It is also good to have a range of revenue streams so that if one aspect of your business goes awry, another could work out. For example, I own a yoga hotel in Bali called "Soulshine Bali," where we host yoga retreats. I was inspired to open it after I read a book called "The Go-Giver: A little story about a powerful business idea," by Bob Burg and John David Mann. It's about giving back, and making sure that the quality of experience for other people you come into contact with is the best it can be.

In terms of the music industry: It is a fickle field. One week, one artist is huge; the next week it is a new artist, though some artists have been able to maintain it for many years. I think the main thing you need is passion for what you do, and to recognize that not everybody is on stage, singing and holding a guitar. Hundreds of people work behind the scenes to make a show happen— as producers, stage managers, caterers, music producers, videographers, and publicists. If you have a passion for music, follow it, but pay attention to where your nose is taking you. Don't try to force yourself to play a specific role. If it's not working out for you to be a performer, find another way to work in this business.

And once you are in, you have to keep paying it forward. The moment you step out of your hotel room, you are on stage. When you walk into the hotel, if you do not treat the guy picking up your bags with kindness, he will remember that. You want everyone to remember you in a kind way so they want you back. That way, when you go through ups and downs, people are willing to go through them with you. Otherwise, when you go through the downs, people will think you deserve it.

When it comes to making a difference: That's the joy in doing what you love to do. You can sell records and own a beautiful house and car and have everything look perfect on the outside, but when you go back to your house, you should ask yourself, "What did I do today that *really* mattered? What did I make happen for someone else?" Making a difference is about doing what you can.

A woman came up to me in Denver and said that she was a hairdresser, saw my film and was so moved by it, but didn't know what she could possibly do to make a difference in the world. Then one day, a woman who was undergoing chemotherapy walked into her salon; her hair was falling out in clumps, and the hairdresser sat her down in a chair and realized there was nothing she could do with the woman's hair but cut it all off. So the hairdresser talked with this woman, who cried as all of her hair was shaved off. Then, they made her up to look as beautiful as she was—from the inside out. From that experience, these two women decided they should provide this service regularly to others. So now, once a week, she closes down the salon and they invite people going through chemo to come in so the hairdresser can take care of their beauty needs.

There is always something we can do to serve our community. It doesn't have to be "big-letter P" politics, because the "small-letter p" politics can make the bigger difference.

Learn more at www.doitforthelove.org

8 Case Studies
and Inkandescent Insights

Be Inkandescent
Why These 8 Case Studies?

8 ENTREPRENEURS, THEIR STORIES, AND THEIR SAGE ADVICE GRACE THE PAGES OF THIS FINAL SECTION OF OUR PR PLAYBOOK.

You may be wondering how we picked these 8 entrepreneurs from the dozens of cover stories and profiles we've featured on *BeInkandescent.com*.

While it's tough to pick favorites, these leaders clearly stand out as role models in their fields—and, their words resonated particularly well with our online readership.

It's not hard to see why. As you'll see, all 8 of their organizations do more than generate gobs of revenue. They do good by doing well. No matter what challenge they have faced, these leaders have never strayed from their mission to make a difference.

From selling T-shirts that teach the importance of optimism, to getting others to think consciously, globally, and knowing that all change comes from within—these entrepreneurs work hard, work from their hearts, and use common sense to create a win-win-win scenario for everyone they touch.

The result: Their rising tide lifts the boats of everyone around them.

We think you'll learn more than best practices in small business from these 8 case studies. We hope you'll dive a little deeper into defining your purpose as a leader so that you can join their big-thinking, big-hearted ranks—and make a big difference, too. Please take a page from their playbooks.

8

Meet the 8 Featured Entrepreneurs

❶ Be Inspiring: Raj Sisodia, PhD. A founder of the Conscious Capitalism movement, Sisodia is a professor of marketing at Bentley University in Boston. He is the author of seven books, including the best-selling title, "Conscious Capitalism: Liberating the Heroic Spirit of Business," co-authored with Whole Foods CEO John Mackey. Sisodia was named one of the "50 Leading Marketing Thinkers."

❷ Be Insightful: Mansour Javidan, PhD. Director of the Najafi Global Mindset Institute, and the Garvin Distinguished Professor at Thunderbird School of Global Management, Javidan is the past president and chairman of the board of directors of the research project GLOBE—Global Leadership and Organizational Behavior Effectiveness. He also developed the Global Mindset Inventory, an online assessment tool for individual managers and groups of managers, which is featured in his 2013 book, "Developing Your Global Mindset: The Handbook for Successful Global Leaders," which he co-authored with Jennie L. Walker, PhD. He was also involved in facilitating cultural change in TransCanada PipeLine's acquisition of a $15 billion corporation.

❸ Be Introspective: Kristine Carlson. The author of the 2012 best-seller "Don't Sweat the Small Stuff for Moms," as well as "Heartbroken Open," which chronicles how she coped with the 2006 death of her husband, well-known author and speaker Richard Carlson. Together they created the "Don't Sweat the Small Stuff" series—a collection of blockbuster books that topped *The New York Times* best-seller list for years. Carlson is also the creator of the 2013 Mom's Virtual Conference, which featured 50 best-selling authors and speakers, who in a week-long online forum discussed the keys to stressing less and enjoying family life more.

❹ Be Ingenious: Bert Jacobs. Co-founder of the Life is good Company. The $100 million T-shirt company is known for featuring its philosophy of the power of optimism on its soft T-shirts and durable apparel. With his brother John, who created their trademarked character Jake, the duo also founded the Life is good Kids Foundation, which raises money for children facing life-threatening situations. The company has never paid for advertising, for their logo speaks for itself as it spreads good vibes.

❺ Be Interconnected: Dr. Esther Sternberg Author of "Healing Spaces," and "The Balance Within," Sternberg is a former NIH medical researcher credited with helping illuminate the possible underlying mechanism for connections between stress, depression, and autoimmune disease. Since 2012, she has been the research director for the Arizona Center for Integrative Medicine at the University of Arizona, founded by Dr. Andrew Weil.

❻ Be Imaginative: Ridley Pearson. A best-selling author and playwright, Pearson has written more than 30 adult suspense novels and 15 children's adventure novels. He and humorist Dave Barry co-wrote the prequel to Peter Pan, "Peter and the Starcatchers," which became a Broadway sensation, earning five Tony Awards. After opening night, he and the cast and crew waited at a NYC restaurant for the critics' review. Someone handed him a BlackBerry, "and everyone's face was glowing blue in the light of the machine—and when we read the great reviews, we all literally started crying with joy and relief. It was one of those amazing pinch-me moments."

❼ Be Intuitive: Helen Fisher, PhD. Social anthropologist and professor at Rutgers University, Fisher uses fMRI technology to look inside the brains of men and women who said they were madly in love. Her perspectives on love, sexuality, and gender differences have been featured on NPR, NBC, the BBC and CNN. She is the author of five books, including "Why We Love," and her 2010 book, "Why Him? Why Her?" She is also the chief scientific advisor to the Internet dating website, Chemistry.com. Fisher is currently working on a new title about why we choose one partner over another.

❽ Be Innovative: Alan Webber. Co-founder of *Fast Company* magazine in 1995 with Bill Taylor. Webber is a former editor of *Harvard Business Review* and was the *Adweek* Editor of the Year in 1999. He was also a speechwriter for former Secretary of Transportation Neil Goldschmidt under President Carter. He considers himself a Global Detective, and travels the world investigating how things work. In 2009, he published a best-selling business book, "Rules of Thumb: 52 Truths for Winning at Business Without Losing Your Self." The long-time Santa Fe resident ran for governor of New Mexico in 2014.

BE INSPIRING

Raj Sisodia: On Conscious Capitalism

Wᴴᴬᵀ ɪs Cᴏɴsᴄɪᴏᴜs Cᴀᴘɪᴛᴀʟɪsᴍ? Fᴏʀ ᴛʜᴇ ꜰᴜʟʟ sᴛᴏʀʏ, ᴡᴇ ᴡᴇɴᴛ sᴛʀᴀɪɢʜᴛ ᴛᴏ ᴛʜᴇ sᴏᴜʀᴄᴇ: Rᴀᴊ Sɪsᴏᴅɪᴀ, a founder of the Conscious Capitalism movement.

He is also the chairman of the Conscious Capitalism Institute, and the co-author of the best-selling book he wrote with Whole Foods CEO John Mackey, "Conscious Capitalism: Liberating the Heroic Spirit of Business," which was published in 2013 by Harvard Business Review Press.

A professor of marketing at Bentley University, Sisodia has also published seven books and more than 100 academic articles. His work has been featured in *The Wall Street Journal, The New York Times, Fortune, Financial Times, The Washington Post, The Boston Globe,* and on CNBC.

He has been honored with numerous awards as well; he is one of the "50 Leading Marketing Thinkers" and has been named to the "Guru Gallery" by the Chartered Institute of Marketing. Bentley University honored him with the Award for Excellence in Scholarship in 2007 and the Innovation in Teaching Award in 2008. He was named one of the "10 Outstanding Trailblazers of 2010" by Good Business International, and one of the "Top 100 Thought Leaders in Trustworthy Business Behavior" by Trust Across America for 2010 and 2011.

What is Conscious Capitalism?

Raj Sisodia: It is a different way of thinking about business. There has been an attitude out there for 150 years or so about what is business and what is capitalism.

Raj Sisodia, PhD

That attitude has been corrosive and damaging, and was created by outsiders and critics. Economists and Marxists actually defined the terms of what businesses are supposedly about: maximizing profits and serving shareholders. Other stakeholders are just a means to those ends. That narrow, self-serving narrative became the dominant paradigm; that is what is taught in business school. In reality, business is not about that.

What do you think business should be about?

Raj Sisodia: It is about doing something that you have a passion for. It is meeting the needs, real needs, of people. It is about providing a means of elevating your existence beyond a base level. Look at the impact of capitalism. Up until the past 200 years, the average person earned between $400 and $600 per year worldwide for thousands of years. Income really started rising around the year 1800, and now we have reached close to $9,000 per person in real terms. Ninety percent of people used to live on less than a dollar a day. That is now down to about 15 percent. We used to live 30 years on average and now we live about 68 years worldwide. Illiteracy rates have plummeted, and many other indicators of our well-being are way higher than they used to be. A lot of that is because of capitalism. That is one part of the story. The second part is that once we become conscious of what business and capitalism are really about and what they can do, we can amplify the positive impact of businesses to a much higher level. We can actually negate some of the negative side effects of what we have built. It doesn't have to be that businesses can only prosper and make money if they damage the environment, which has a negative impact on people's health and causes a lot of stress. None of that has to be the case. Businesses can have positive side effects, including great financial components.

Conscious Capitalism is the philosophy that business has a higher purpose that goes beyond profit.

Raj Sisodia: Yes. And we have to think of all of the stakeholders as important in their own right, not just a means to an end of making money. We have to create value for all of them. Also, we need leaders who are driven by purpose, service, and the caring that they feel for their stakeholders—not just by power and personal enrichment. Lastly, businesses have unique cultures that are based on trust, caring, transparency, authenticity, and integrity that allow them to continue to operate in this way even though the context around them might change. That is Conscious Capitalism in a nutshell.

How did you meet John Mackey and what inspired you two to collaborate on this book?

Raj Sisodia: I wrote about him and Whole Foods in my 2007 book, "Firms of Endearment: How World-Class Companies Profit From Passion and Purpose." We featured 28 companies—18 public and 10 private—that were loved by all of their stakeholders: customers, suppliers, communities, and investors. We set out to understand what is it that makes that happen.

These companies do have something distinct about them, and that is their passion and purpose. They have different kinds of leaders and they do care about their stakeholders and so on. Whole Foods was one of the companies we featured, though we had not actually interviewed John because he did not grant interviews to book authors then.

While the book was still in a draft form, a colleague with whom I work began discussing it with a fellow passenger while on a flight. That passenger turned out to be a friend of John Mackey's, and said John would like it. So we sent John the draft, and he responded, "This is exactly what I believe in."

We met soon after, and I shared my dream for what I was calling "The Institute for New Capitalism." He said, "Well, I call it Conscious Capitalism." The movement grew from there.

What is your ultimate goal with the Conscious Capitalism movement?

Raj Sisodia: The goal is to get more businesses to start up with this in mind, and also get existing companies and organizations to move in this direction.

Arguably, the transition to Conscious Capitalism is going to happen anyway, because we are living through a period of rapid change. This increases our consciousness.

[See page 124 for the Four Tenets of Conscious Capitalism.]

STICKY QUOTE

A Big Idea to incorporate into your playbook

"Business is good when it creates value, it is ethical because it is based on a voluntary exchange, it is noble because it can elevate our existence, and it is heroic because it lifts people out of poverty and creates prosperity. Free-enterprise capitalism is one of the most powerful ideas humans have ever had."

— John Mackey, CEO, Whole Foods

Try these tips from Raj Sisodia to increase Conscious Capitalism in your company:

1. When you become conscious about how you do business, and you explicitly think about your purpose, ask yourself what your customers would say your purpose is. Sometimes you may find that you haven't articulated your purpose. If you haven't, then come together with your team and come up with a statement defining what you're about and why you exist. That is actually deeply inspiring, as it tends to build on itself. Once you have articulated it, it takes on a life of its own.

2. Think of stakeholders as important in their own right. This becomes easier the more conscious you are. Considering stakeholder needs helps bring about wins for everyone involved in your business—not just the owners and top managers.

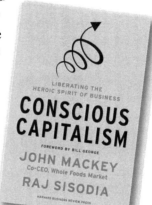

3. Think about how you're creating value for your employees at different levels. When you do this, your employees will regard their work not just as a job or career, but a calling. They will become more deeply invested in the company—emotionally and spiritually.

4. Think about how you are creating value for your suppliers. Many companies have a blind spot when it comes to their suppliers. They think that they can treat everyone else with love and care, but that suppliers don't matter because they are outside the business. Suppliers are incredibly important to businesses. Treat them consciously, like customers. You'll have an advantage in the market.

5. Be conscious about your company's leadership. You need people in roles who have technical skills, as well as emotional and spiritual intelligence. Select employees with those attributes in mind.

6. Pay explicit attention to the culture of your company. There are lots of toxic cultures out there that are averse to change and stand in the way of growing and evolving as a business. Don't let that be how you do business now, or in the future. When we bring our attention to bear on anything, it grows and it flourishes. Even if you are an unconscious conscious capitalist, you have started the process.

Learn more at www.rajsisodia.com

INKANDESCENT INSIGHTS

Takeaways from Raj Sisodia's inspiring playbook:

The big win: The leaders of Conscious Capitalism think globally—in terms of reach and impact. The organization's four tenets (see page 124) center around the philosophy that business has a higher purpose, and that leaders need to be responsible and provide a benefit to myriad stakeholders. This approach to business goes beyond profit, which ultimately benefits the community and the world.

From a PR point of view: This approach enables a company to do more than sell products and services. It provides the company with a larger mission to make a positive difference in the community. This value-centric perspective can be promoted to customers as a reason to develop a new or renewed loyalty to the brand.

THE 8 STEPS IN ACTION

- **Create a stunning website:** The Conscious Capitalism organization, which has been around since 2000, recently expanded its website to enable conference attendees and others to sign up to be part of the movement: *www.consciouscapitalism.org*.

- **Make a splash in the news:** The nation's largest media outlets, including *USA Today* in a cover story on March 26, 2013, picked up on the trend—taking the discussion to a broader audience.

- **Network wisely:** While Sisodia has been hosting Conscious Capitalism Conferences for business leaders around the world for more than a decade, in April 2013 he and co-author John Mackey hosted the 13th Conscious Capitalism Conference in San Francisco. Hundreds of entrepreneurs showed up for two days of lectures, workshops, and networking.

- **Speak:** After their book was published, Sisodia and Mackey hit the road to speak in dozens of cities, including at a huge press conference at the National Press Club in Washington, DC, and they did a Q&A at Gallup headquarters. This gave them the opportunity to take their message to smaller groups, where people had the opportunity to ask the authors thoughtful questions in person.

- **Write a book:** Their book was a game changer for Sisodia and Mackey, and the Conscious Capitalism movement. It sold like gangbusters at Whole Foods, and in bookstores nationwide.

- **Pay it forward:** Sisodia's message is the essence of paying it forward. "The goal of the movement really is to raise consciousness broadly and to get more new businesses to start up this way," he says. "Considering the needs of all stakeholders helps bring about wins for everyone involved in, and with, your business—not just the owners and top managers."

The bottom line: "Free-enterprise capitalism is the most powerful system for social cooperation and human progress ever conceived," says Sisodia. "But we can aspire to something even greater."

Conscious Capitalism's Tenets of Paying It Forward

❶ Higher Purpose. Business has a broad positive impact on the world when it is based on a purpose that goes beyond only generating profits and creating shareholder value. Purpose is the reason a company exists. A compelling sense of higher purpose creates an extraordinary degree of engagement that catalyzes creativity, innovation, and organizational commitment.

❷ Stakeholder Orientation. Stakeholders are the entities that impact or are impacted by business. Conscious businesses recognize that each stakeholder is important and interdependent. Businesses must seek to optimize value creation, and all stakeholders must be motivated by a sense of purpose and core values. When conflicts and trade-offs arise, conscious businesses engage the limitless power of human creativity to create win-win-win-win-win-win situations that transcend those conflicts and create harmony.

❸ Conscious Leadership. Conscious business requires conscious leadership. Conscious leaders are motivated primarily by service to the firm's higher purpose and creating value for all stakeholders. They reject a zero-sum, trade-off-oriented view of business and look for creative, win-win-win approaches.

❹ Conscious Culture and Management. The culture of a conscious business is a source of great strength and stability for the firm, ensuring that its purpose and core values endure over time and through leadership transitions. Conscious cultures naturally evolve from the enterprise's commitments to higher purpose, stakeholder interdependence, and conscious leadership. Traits include: trust, accountability, transparency, integrity, loyalty, egalitarianism, fairness, personal growth, love, and care.

BE INSIGHTFUL

Mansour Javidan: On Thinking Globally

WHEN IT COMES TO THINKING GLOBALLY, MANSOUR JAVIDAN, PhD, IS AN EXPERT. THE DIRECTOR OF THE Najafi Global Mindset Institute, and Garvin Distinguished Professor at Thunderbird School of Global Management, he is also the past president and chairman of the board of directors of the world-renowned research project on executive performance and leadership known simply as GLOBE, an acronym for Global Leadership and Organizational Behavior Effectiveness.

This project's ongoing research involves 825 organizations in 62 countries, documented in three books, including "Strategic Leadership Across Cultures," a book on CEO effectiveness.

Mansour Javidan, PhD

What impact do cultural preferences have on the way the people in each country around the world behave? And what is the best way for businesses to prepare and respond?

To find out, Javidan put the research to the test, taking a four-year sabbatical from his university teaching duties to work with the CEO of TransCanada Pipe-Lines, a multibillion-dollar Canadian energy company. He was instrumental in helping the CEO develop new directions and strategies, and facilitate cultural change within the company and its pipeline business.

And he was directly involved in the company's acquisition of a $15 billion corporation, the largest such merger at the time in Canada, which resulted in the formation of the fourth largest energy services company in the world.

Why don't more people "think globally"?

Mansour Javidan: "Most people figure this can't be rocket science; any good manager can figure it out," he says, noting that it's probably true. "But there's a hard way, and an easy way. The hard way is by parachuting a manager into a global environment without any support or multicultural understanding.

"The manager may have the best technical skills, but if the manager's level of global mindset is low, that person is going to go through a very painful, frustrating experience. And in fact it may jeopardize the company's and the manager's ability to work in that situation"—and result in the company losing business. The easier way, he says, is to be proactive.

That's the goal of his new book, which he wrote with colleague Jennie L. Walker, PhD: "Developing Your Global Mindset: The Handbook for Successful Global Leaders." The book includes a global mindset assessment instrument—called the Global Mindset Inventory, or GMI—that individual managers or groups of managers can take. "By completing this Internet-based questionnaire, managers find out which areas are their strengths and where they need to further develop," Javidan says. "While we have always provided development suggestions during GMI coaching sessions, this handbook takes the support we offer managers to the next level."

Jennie Walker, PhD

Developed in consultation with managers, executives, and some experienced international executive coaches, the book offers advice and ideas on how a manager can improve on all elements of 35 scientifically defined capabilities within the Global Mindset Inventory.

"All of the ideas are very actionable and very specific, and they don't usually take much time to implement," Javidan explained in an interview for Inkandescent Radio. The development tips may be used by individuals or for direct reports, coaches, and teams. In addition to a rich variety of development suggestions, there are engaging narratives throughout the book illustrating the various components of the Global Mindset in action.

The diverse international experiences of the contributing authors bring "Global Mindset" to life through the narratives, as well as seven intriguing case studies at the end of the book. The case studies transport the reader into nuanced, real-world scenarios that cross geographic and cultural borders, says Javidan.

"They push the boundaries of our current global leadership skills to identify ways to successfully influence diverse others while working within the complex and fast-paced world of global business," he says, noting that the case studies may be used for individual development through self-reflection, or in teams, where the discussions will be lively.

Let's talk about "mastering the art of global leadership." What does that mean exactly?

Mansour Javidan: In most industries, growth is increasingly coming through globalization. Companies are looking for new markets in other countries; they're looking for supply-chain partners in other parts of the world, and also talent pools in different parts of the world. It's inescapable that more corporations will be globalizing.

What is the impact of that very simple idea—a company wants to explore global markets—on the day-to-day activities of a typical manager or entrepreneur?

Mansour Javidan: As the company globalizes, a typical manager increasingly will be asked to work effectively with people who are from different parts of the world. It doesn't matter where the manager grew up, as much as where the people with whom the manager is working are from.

That is the crux of the HR challenges that businesses are facing. Think back to your own elementary and high school education, your teachers' advice, and the textbooks you read—did they teach you to live and work with people who are different from you? The answer, when I asked thousands of managers, is, "No."

Most of us have learned how to live and work with people who are "like me." That's what societies do, that's how they educate their kids.

Increasingly, companies are saying to their people, "Yeah, it's good that you can work with people who are like you, but I need you to work with people who are different from you."

Mansour Javidan: Right. And a typical manager is scratching his or her head, saying, "Well, what the hell does that mean? I never trained for that, I was never developed for that." There is a real disconnect between what the companies are very logically asking of their managers and how managers are developed as human beings.

So, is one of the issues of global leadership how to exert your influence?

Mansour Javidan: Yes, leadership is about influence. The question is, how do you influence people who are different from you? Many of us now work with employees in many different countries, and we haven't worked with a single company that would say it has an oversupply of global leaders. Every company we know of tells us it has a shortage of global leaders.

The reason is obvious: People are educated to think locally, and be local leaders, but now their companies are asking them to think globally. Given that fact, the next step is to decide what kind of training, what kind of development, and what kind of support do the corporation and individual need to succeed.

STICKY QUOTE

A Big Idea to incorporate into your playbook

"Most people figure that working globally can't be rocket science; any good manager can figure it out. But there's a hard way, and an easy way. The hard way is by parachuting a manager into a global environment without any support or multicultural understanding. And in fact it may jeopardize the company's and the manager's ability to work in that situation. The easier way is to be proactive."

— Mansour Javidan

Learn more at www.developingglobalmindset.com

INKANDESCENT INSIGHTS

Takeaways from Mansour Javidan's insightful playbook:

The big win: Everyone from solopreneurs to leaders of mega-corporations can benefit from gaining insight into how to expand their thinking about doing business with different cultures. The narratives, as well as seven case studies at the end of the book, transport us into complex, real-world scenarios that cross geographic and cultural borders.

From a PR point of view: Mansour Javidan and Jennie Walker have synthesized their decades of knowledge and understanding into nine sets of concrete advice, breaking each into three smaller bites that are easier to digest. This approach gives them the opportunity to share their advice in a variety of venues—from YouTube to national publications to speeches before international audiences.

How to Supersize Your Small Business

THE 8 STEPS IN ACTION

■ **Create a stunning website:** "Do you pass the Global Mindset airport test?" That's the intriguing headline featured on Mansour Javidan's faculty page on the Thunderbird University website. The Iranian native with a Canadian passport offers insights based on his experience as a frequent flier. True to the thoughtful, academic approach Javidan takes with all of his work, he engages readers by creating an Internet-based questionnaire where managers find out which areas are their strengths and where they need to further develop. For details, go to: *www.developingglobalmindset.com* and click on the Global Mindset Inventory (GMI).

■ **Develop an explosive PR and marketing campaign:** Javidan brings his message to life on YouTube, where you can watch him in action. His passion for the topic of the human impact of globalization, and how the US can become a better world citizen, engages viewers and makes them want to learn more—and get involved. That's the goal of marketing: to create enthusiasm, which leads to sales.

■ **Become a columnist:** Javidan is a regular contributor to business publications, writing articles on thought leadership for *Harvard Business Review*, the *Journal of International Business Studies*, and *Leadership Quarterly*.

■ **Make a splash in the news:** As the former senior editor of the *Journal of World Business*, Javidan has a handle on getting the word out about what he knows. His latest book gives him a hook to snag reporter interest, including *Forbes India* and Ernst & Young's business blog. Their readers are his target audience, which enables him to further spread his message and help companies see the connection between having a global mindset and being successful in the international marketplace.

■ **Network wisely:** His many books and international speaking engagements have put Javidan on the radar of some of the world's largest organizations and companies, where he's made numerous connections. And those networking connections, in turn, have resulted in further business opportunities, including his stint with TransCanada Pipelines.

■ **Speak:** An expert advisor on global leadership at The World Bank, and a US Army senior research fellow, Javidan has made presentations in more than 25 countries around the world. He has also designed and taught a variety of executive development courses, offered and facilitated workshops, and conducted consulting projects. As a public speaker, the professor excels—perhaps because he is incredibly comfortable speaking to an audience.

■ **Write a book:** Mansour Javidan's 2013 book, "Developing Your Global Mindset," has given him a new platform for spreading the information and insights he's gleaned from decades of experience and research. It has the potential to become *the* go-to resource for successfully working globally.

The bottom line: Mansour Javidan's ultimate goal is to make it easier for companies and their employees to work internationally—and thrive.

BE INTROSPECTIVE
Kristine Carlson: On Leading With Love

If YOU'VE EVER HAD YOUR HEART broken, you'll be inspired by the compassion and wisdom of author Kristine Carlson.

Her moving memoir, "Heartbroken Open," was written after the death of her husband and business partner, Richard Carlson—who is remembered for his best-selling "Don't Sweat the Small Stuff" series of books. His sudden death in 2006 forever changed the course of the lives of Kristine and her two teenage daughters.

"His death catapulted me into heartbreak and uncertainty," Carlson writes in the memoir. "It was the end of life as I knew it, and the beginning of a journey through the depths of grief and mourning."

Carlson spoke to *BeInkandescent*

magazine about "Heartbroken Open," how she coped with the death of a loved one, and how others can learn from her experience.

We appreciate your willingness to talk about this incredible experience in your life, one that we are sure is still very painful.

Kristine Carlson

Kristine Carlson: Yes, but talking about it actually does help. And as you know from reading the book, December 13, 2006, was a day that started out like any other day. Richard had stayed at the airport hotel the night before because he was taking a 6 a.m. flight to New York. He did that so that he would be able get in a whole day of work once he got to New York. He always called to talk before he got on a flight, but this time I missed his phone call by five minutes. I overslept, which was unusual for me.

After I got up, I did the breakfast dishes and got my kids to school—both were teenagers in high school, a freshman and a senior. As I pulled into a mall parking space, my phone rang and I saw the New York area code, 212. I thought, "Well that's an odd number. Richard must be calling from his hotel. Maybe his cell battery is out." I answered the call expecting it would be Richard calling to tell me that he had arrived safely. Instead, two strangers were on the line.

A nurse and a doctor began firing questions at me: "Are you related to Richard Carlson?" I was like, "Yeah, I'm his wife. Who are you?" They said, "We are calling from the Jamaica Memorial Hospital in Queens, New York." I was very confused—and then they told me that they had Richard with them.

I started questioning them, saying, "What do you mean? How is Richard with you?"

They said, "We are really sorry to inform you, Mrs. Carlson, but Richard Carlson has expired."

Just that word alone, "expired," threw me. Here we were fully living our lives—I was 43, and Richard was only 45. He didn't have any health problems that we knew of, aside from a little back pain.

Take any day of your life and all of a sudden insert that phone call and that word, "expired," and it just doesn't make sense. You can't even grasp what somebody is telling you in that moment.

I went slightly insane, actually. I felt like I had left my body. I got angry and started yelling at these people as if they were playing a joke on me, and then I realized they weren't, when they started talking about his flight. I knew it was over. I just knew there was no turning back. It was absolutely devastating, and to this day, when I recall hearing the news, the feeling in my body comes back to me.

But what really shocked me was that I didn't know until then that I had been kind of asleep in my life. When I was in the throes of raising kids and being a wife, I didn't realize that I wasn't fully awake to my life. Ironically, Richard's death changed that. As I allowed grief to come into my life, I was deeply rocked. I thought, "Wow, I'm really feeling my life at such a different level now."

So how did you handle that?

Kristine Carlson: It was really hard. The contrast was so dramatic. I would walk outside and all of a sudden see—really see—the trees and the sky. The wind would blow and I would just feel it all at a much deeper level than what I had felt before. I started to realize these things amidst the horrible pain of healing. I came to understand that this awakening was a gift of this terrible experience. Richard and I had lived our whole life by the "don't sweat the small stuff" philosophy—about how to be happy in life. I started to realize that all of those tools I had for being happy and living life well were going to be put to the test. But I knew in my heart I had the wisdom and the strength to go through it.

I kept praying the whole time I was grief-stricken that I would come through on the other side better for it—wiser, deeper, more in my heart. I hoped that one day I could return to joy. Looking back, I can honestly say that after about three years of an up-and-down, roller-coaster kind of living through grief and loss, I finally did. Now my life is about deepening my own life's purpose. In gaining that perspective, I feel I am in a sacred contract with Richard.

When was it that you realized you would be okay?

Kristine Carlson: I remember sitting by myself and having a very strong talk with myself that kind of went like this: "I can't believe this happened to your life. This is really messed up. This sucks. Never anticipated this in a million years, couldn't have seen this coming." Then I remember saying, "You know what, you have had every amazing blessing that life has ever given anyone. Your life has been beyond charmed." I remember feeling that, really noticing that, and realizing what an incredible life Richard and I had together for 25 years. I didn't know how to go on—but also knew that loss is just part of life.

Let's talk about the book "Heartbroken Open," in which you discuss the four aspects of recovery: surrender, trust, accept, and receive.

Kristine Carlson: The book is inspired by the idea that I needed to learn as much as I could from this experience because otherwise, what is the point? Why would we go through that kind of horrible pain and suffering if it wasn't going to transform us into something new? And something better, hopefully. I don't know that I went through stages of grief, which sounds way too orderly for the roller coaster of emotions that I experienced. I tried to allow myself to heal, and give myself permission to befriend my grief. The mantra—surrender, trust, accept, and receive—was something Richard and I lived by from the time we were in our 20s, especially when things were difficult. That mantra gave me tremendous peace, especially when he was gone.

The process of healing seems like it could be endless. When did you start to feel better?

Kristine Carlson: The second year was still pretty messy. I felt a lot more grounded though, and not weighed down as much by grief. I knew I still had a lot of things to learn, and I had to gather the reins on a bunch of stuff—including the business. I was now taking over an international brand that my husband had run. Thank goodness I had been part of so many of his business decisions.

This book is very touching and so honest. I think people who have lost someone they love will benefit from reading "Heartbroken Open."

Kristine Carlson: Yeah, readers tell me that they do, and it means the world to me. I have the benefit of hearing from widows and people who have lost somebody through death. Even people who have gone through divorce, women *and* men, go through the same heartbreak—and they have the same possibilities. I think divorce might be more challenging because it comes with more anger and bitterness than death—but anger and bitterness sometimes come with loss from death, too.

Tell us about "Don't Sweat the Small Stuff for Moms."

Kristine Carlson: My goal is to give mothers tried-and-true advice that will empower them to find greater peace, joy, and harmony within themselves and their homes. It's no small task being a mom today. Both of my girls are out of the nest; they were 14 and 17 when Richard passed away, and going through that was in itself quite a journey.

What is one of your favorite tips from the book?

Kristine Carlson: The fact that there's no such thing as a "perfect" mom. How many times have you carried the burden of thinking you have to live up to some ideal, fairy-tale image of a good mother? One who is unfailingly kind, patient, wise, nurturing, good-tempered, inexhaustibly energetic, a fine cook and homemaker, a multi-tasker—that person few of us have ever actually met who can do it all? That's not to say that, as mothers, we shouldn't strive to be the best examples for our children that we can be, but we do them a disservice when we hide our mistakes, don't allow them to see our flaws, or don't apologize when we have been wrong. We need them to see the world as multidimensional, and that means the people in it, as well. So give yourself permission to be authentic. ⚬

Learn more at www.kristinecarlson.com

I N K A N D E S C E N T   I N S I G H T S

Takeaways from Kristine Carlson's introspective playbook:

The big win: A woman on a journey, Kristine Carlson's power is in her candor as she discusses the process she's experienced since the sudden death in 2006 of her husband and business partner, Richard Carlson. The couple built a business based on being open, honest, and introspective. Critics agree, that is what made the "Don't Sweat the Small Stuff" series one of the top *New York Times* bestsellers in history.

From a PR point of view: Beyond a PR and marketing campaign, Carlson's book, "Heartbroken Open," deeply touches people because it meets them at their most vulnerable points—and acknowledges the difficulty of recovering. By telling readers how she found ways to be courageous and strong despite her grief and confusion, she helps readers transcend their own personal struggles—which fills a need that makes this and her other books consistently big sellers.

How to Supersize Your Small Business

THE 8 STEPS IN ACTION

■ **Create a stunning website:** Since first using the web as a key marketing tool back in 1996 when the "Don't Sweat" series debuted, Kristine Carlson has embraced the power of the Internet. Her latest site includes a blog, a bookstore, and a shop—and most importantly, it is branded to reflect both her softness *and* her strength: *kristinecarlson.com*.

■ **Develop an explosive PR and marketing campaign:** After the death of her husband, Carlson became the face of the "Don't Sweat" brand. Her willingness to talk about her loss has created an even broader audience for her message. She continued the series in 2012 with "Don't Sweat the Small Stuff for Moms," which gave birth to the 2013 Virtual Conference for Moms. It featured 50 best-selling authors and speakers discussing the keys to stressing less and enjoying family life more.

STICKY QUOTE

A Big Idea to incorporate into your playbook

"When you embody your life's purpose and own it, all things you accomplish or do are an extension of that."

— Kristine Carlson

■ **Become a columnist:** In addition to being a featured columnist for various magazines, Carlson uses social media to connect with others. Her columns have appeared in *The Huffington Post, Aspire Magazine,* and *BeInkandescent.com.*

■ **Make a splash in the news:** People are drawn to the inherent drama of a beautiful woman who had it all and lost it through tragedy. But rather than focus on the glamor of her life with Richard, Carlson's introspective look at her loss fuels her authenticity by connecting with readers and viewers as an "Everywoman." She has appeared on "The Oprah Winfrey Show," "Today," "The View," and other national shows, and has been interviewed and featured in numerous radio programs and magazine articles.

■ **Network wisely:** Carlson's online community, DontSweatMoms.com, tries to "Mother the Mothers" by empowering moms. It provides her with a broad networking platform for reaching her core audience on a regular basis. Brilliant!

■ **Speak:** Carlson is a sought-after speaker who focuses on the life lessons we all have struggled to learn. Her speeches include topics featured in her recent book, "Don't Sweat the Small Stuff for Moms," such as: why women need to compromise for themselves, balance as the key to feeling successful, and the importance of recognizing that our children are always changing—and rolling with that change. She created a YouTube video that announced Richard's death to fans. In 2013, she gave a TEDx talk that was a 15-minute tribute to what she has learned. It brought her to tears—and the audience, too.

■ **Write a book:** From "An Hour to Live, An Hour to Love," and "Heartbroken Open," to her most recent, "Don't Sweat the Small Stuff for Moms," Kristine Carlson's books provide a platform for her thoughts and ideas about her key messages: introspection and authenticity.

■ **Pay it forward:** "If you feel like something is missing, maybe it's you," says Carlson on her page of beautiful inspirations called Living the Big Stuff. "I will do most anything if it serves the world community in some way." Sharing her insights freely, she invites readers to check back daily for an introspective quote: www.kristinecarlson.com/inspiration.

The bottom line: From blogs and discussion circles to virtual conferences and books, Carlson's mission is to reach out to the community at large and provide a forum for others to talk about the small stuff of life—and the big stuff, too.

BE INGENIOUS

Bert & John Jacobs: On Life is good

Clad in a t-shirt and jeans, Bert Jacobs comes out to greet us from behind the giant oak desk in his corner office of the Boston headquarters of the Life is good Company.

Located on chichi Newbury Street, the co-founder of the $100 million T-shirt company is anything but pretentious. His infectious smile and down-to-earth demeanor reflect the brand that he and his brother, John, have built since they started selling tees from the back of their VW van in 1987.

"I think that sometimes people look at us and think that we're in la-la land," he says. "Like we're sitting here eating ice cream and throwing Frisbees around on the beach. But we're not."

At least, not always.

"We're competitive people who live in the real world. We wake up and fight like anybody else. But we have a deep-seated belief that it's powerful to be optimistic. And for us, the business is definitely a fulfillment of that philosophy."

Jacobs is also clear that making money isn't the sole goal for his company—and it shouldn't be for any entrepreneur. Consider his thoughts on how you can find success, the *Life is good* way.

Bert Jacobs' 15 Tips for Success

❶ Speak out. I do a lot of public speaking to raise money for our Life is good Kids Foundation, and 100 percent of the fee goes to raise money for children facing life-threatening situations—such as poverty, disease, and a lack of positive influences.

Bert Jacobs

I'm always amazed when I ask the crowds to talk to me about how this negativity has shaped our perceptions of reality. Take the topic of national health care. Ask anyone what the state of our nation's health is, and you'll hear a litany of negativity: Americans are troubled by obesity, the high cost of health care, the number of people who die during surgery, and how limited our access is to the best medical procedures.

The reality is that when Boston was founded in the 1700s, the average lifespan of a Boston resident was 29 years. In 1800, it was in the upper 40s, and today it's 78. Clearly, we must be doing something right. The same is true of our economic system, especially from a global perspective. So, if you take that global view, there is reason for optimism—despite the recent recession and other negative considerations. It just depends on how you look at the world. That's my message, and I love to talk about it. Entrepreneurs simply need to know what they believe in, and then get out there and have good conversations.

2 **Find your audience.** We didn't have anything when we started, except the idea that we wanted to spread the word about optimism. We didn't have the money or the business acumen to grow the concept into a large company. But we knew that it wasn't enough that only we believed in it. There had to be a hunger and a need for optimism. If there wasn't, we would have given up. The first day we put the Life is good shirt featuring Jake on a table for sale, we sold 48 shirts in 45 minutes. We knew we were onto something.

3 **Find good partners who believe in you.** We started out by working with a local screen printer called Midland Graphics, in nearby Marlboro, Mass. Two brothers, Jim and Mike McCarthy, owned it and could relate to what we were trying to do.

That was key, because they essentially financed our operation. We paid them in cash after we sold on the street, and overpaid them a little bit because we knew they needed some things, including more inventory. They began to trust us. We always paid them in a timely fashion, and it was a great relationship. Then, we opened our first warehouse on their property.

We parked a big truck and a container there, and strung up lights because they gave us access to their electricity. It enabled us to hold onto the equity in the beginning, which was important.

4 **Hold onto the equity in your company as long as you can.** There were a few people coming around pretty early on in the business who wanted to invest in us. But we weren't sure they wanted to do it for the right reasons. Although we weren't making much money at the time, we did feel that what we were doing was valuable.

If it wasn't for the McCarthy brothers, I'm not sure we would have been able to do that. If you really have a long-term vision for your concept or organization, it's always best to hold onto the equity. Some people would say it's impossible, but I think there are lots of ways to do things. Maintaining control of our mission was important to us.

5 **Hire and partner with people who share your vision.** I don't think we would have become partners with anyone who didn't agree that business is a powerful tool. We have a deep-seated belief that capitalism can be the most effective way to create positive social change, and so do the other four people who have a financial stake in our company.

We tend to think of nonprofits and government organizations when we think about organizations that do good things, but in truth a lot of the power is with people who know how to make money. If you know how to make money, and have visibility through consumer products, then you can do some pretty amazing things.

6 **Listen to your customers.** Without question, our customers have taught us a lot about what we might be able to do, and it's not always just about making a profit. If it was, I think we would sell the company and go public. But I think we can do a lot of other really interesting things with the brand—like save kids' lives. We get letters from people who have experienced incredible tragedy and loss, and they say that our brand has given them hope. Their testimonials blow us away. We call that fuel.

An 11-year old girl named Lindsey opened our eyes to how others were impacted by our company. She was diagnosed with terminal bone cancer, given less than a year to live, and walked around wearing one of our hats. She told us that even if her life would be a short life, she wanted to appreciate every day.

7 Realize that you don't know as much about your business as you think you do. Thinking you have all the answers is a pitfall. Avoid it when your company starts to grow. There is a lot more you don't know versus what you do know.

8 Know what you are selling. I could bore you with a lot of information about how to make T-shirts—with sourcing strategies and manufacturing details—but we don't really care about those things. To be honest with you, I really don't even care about clothing. My brother doesn't like it when I say that, for fear that it will be misunderstood.

John Jacobs

So let me clarify. What I mean is that the brand provides us a great platform to do good things, and to talk about something more important than T-shirts. That's why we don't want to talk about the stitching on a garment, or the softness of the T-shirts. The tees are soft, and we work really hard to make sure they are. But it's insulting to consumers to tell them that—when they can go into a store and feel the tees for themselves. I'd rather talk about how we can all make a difference in the world.

9 Know that your customers can put you out of business in a minute. Now that we're in the digital era, the power has shifted from the sellers to the buyers. Do you remember the housewife in the Midwest who blogged about the fact that Apple's iPhone battery was too expensive and didn't last long enough? Two weeks later there are 200 letters on Steve Jobs' desk, and he made a change. That housewife changed Apple.

Most entrepreneurs are wising up to the fact that consumers can make your business, or they can rip it down. It's all based on whether or not your business is authentic. I don't think we're overly intelligent about our business, or overly intelligent in general.

We probably made more mistakes than most entrepreneurs, especially in the beginning. One thing that we have done right for the last 17 years is to be consistent and authentic, and we've tried to help people. We've been open-minded, and we've tried not to make the same mistake twice. We are regular people running an organization, and that resonates with people.

10 Think big. A lot of our strategies for future growth are community-based. The people own the Life is good Company. We felt lucky to have gotten to travel in a van, sell and make T-shirts, and see things that we hadn't seen before.

We also believe that optimism creates opportunities, and as we move forward, we envision that a lot of those opportunities will move the organization outside of clothing—maybe into creating healthy and sustainable food products, and even getting into the entertainment industry. We're working on some of those ideas now.

11 Be universal. We hear that Christians think "Life is good" is a Christian message, and we think that's great. But it's also a Jewish message, and very much a Buddhist message. Anybody can associate, and we appreciate that so many groups embrace us. We are very careful not to get involved with any political organization or religious group. To us, the idea that "Life is good" represents all people.

12 Delegate everything—except for two things. You can delegate everything else, but hiring senior staff has to be your decision, and you have to hold on tightly to your vision for the company. Other than that, chances are that others can do almost everything else in your company better than you.

13 Don't white-knuckle it. As a small-business owner, you have to remember to loosen up. I see so many people try to hold onto things so tightly that they white-knuckle it a bit. John was a bit like that early on with drawing Jake. But now we have people who sometimes draw Jake better than he does, and that has opened us up to new options and ideas. That's all good.

❶❹ **Chill out on the prototypes and focus groups.** I know a lot of entrepreneurs who love to create prototypes and host focus groups. Yes, you can sit around in a room and have a dozen people say this is what I like about this and that is what I hate about that.

It has some value. But an even better approach is to get out there and see what sells. We got lucky because the very first day we sold the Jake tees, we got feedback on what is good. When people reach into their pockets and get out "dough, re, mi," that's enlightening.

That told us that more than anything else they could buy on the street, they wanted Jake. Here's my advice: Don't quit your day job. Make something and see if it sells. That's how you know if you have a viable business.

❶❺ **Start from the end.** Don't think about how you can get to the next step, or where you'd like to be next year. Ask yourself this question: When you are old and gray, what do you want to look back on and say that you have accomplished? Once you know the answer, go ahead and do it.

People don't do that enough. They are realistic, sure. But I encourage everyone to be idealistic. As the poet Mary Oliver asked, "Tell me, what is it you plan to do with your one wild and precious life?"

That's the only question you need to answer when you are starting a business, picking a major in college, or plowing through a midlife crisis. We weren't created for business, it was created for us. Your business should serve your life's purpose.

Learn more at www.lifeisgood.com

INKANDESCENT INSIGHTS

Takeaways from the Life is good Company's ingenious playbook:

The big win: Brothers Bert and John Jacobs shared their personal view of the world because they wanted others to focus on the positive aspects of life—not just because they wanted to make money. "I think that people look at us and think that we're in la-la land, like we're sitting here eating ice cream and throwing Frisbees, but we're not," says Bert Jacobs. At least, not always. "We're competitive people who live in the real world. We fight like anybody else. But we have a deep-seated belief that it's powerful to be optimistic. And for us, the business is definitely a fulfillment of that philosophy."

From a PR point of view: Bert and John Jacobs' ambition was to create a fun, playful, heartfelt and iconic logo that touched people. The logo character, who goes by the name of "Jake," has come to epitomize the notion that "life is good," and customers have come to equate the logo with the personality of the company itself—believing the Life is good Company is fun, playful, and genuine. Another ingenious strategy the brothers Jacob used was to vary the logo. Rather than keep their uber-successful logo static, Bert, John, and their team of clever artists have come up with zillions of variations on their theme—from yoga moms and coffee drinkers to soccer aficionados and BBQ-grilling dads—thereby opening up their brand to more people. As a result, no advertising has ever been necessary. Instead, fans across the country are walking billboards for the Life is good brand. Talk about an ingenious marketing campaign.

Chief Playmaker

Steve Gross: On the Importance of Play

"**P**LAY IS SERIOUS BUSINESS," SAYS Steve Gross, the chief Playmaker at the Life is good Kids Foundation, whose mission is to help kids overcome life-threatening challenges.

"Millions of our nation's youngest children have experienced profound trauma in its many forms, including domestic violence, abuse, neglect, natural disasters, and severe poverty," explains Gross. "It's a silent epidemic. Life can hurt—but play can heal."

Studies show that when children don't play, their brains and bodies don't develop properly. They are at much greater risk for mental and physical diseases, including anxiety and depression, obesity, heart disease, and cancer. And too often, they have trouble being productive members of society.

"Play teaches us how to manage and transform our 'negative' emotions and experiences. It supercharges learning, helps us relieve stress, and connects us to others and to the world around us. Play can also make work more productive and pleasurable."

In 2011, Gross and his band of Playmakers jumped into their lime-green cars and traveled 1,200 miles in 30 days to spread the power of joy and optimism to thousands of kids.

Steve Gross

In cities including Boston, New York, Philadelphia, Baltimore, DC, Tuscaloosa, and New Orleans, they provided certification training and gave play equipment to childcare workers, preschool teachers, and health care professionals.

"We're not the smartest people on the 'play' block; after all, some brilliant educators and academics have spent their entire careers studying the topic," Gross realizes. "What we're trying to bring to the party is a way to get to the heart and soul of what play and playfulness is all about."

And he believes from the top of his favorite beret to the tips of his flip flops that play isn't what you do—it's how you do it. "Some kids are playing when they are mowing the lawn, raking leaves, or taking out the trash," he says. "The key is to find the joy in whatever you do. Playing, and being playful, doesn't just mean getting a group of kids together for an organized soccer game."

In fact, Gross suggests that the Playmakers movement isn't about play at all. The core of his organization, he insists, focuses on how children are treated in our society. "When you treat kids in a joyful, empowering, inspiring way, you give them guidelines for how to be joyful, empowered, and inspiring themselves," he shares. "So our ultimate goal is to help the people who care for the kids who are in the most life-threatening positions find ways to create sacred spaces to let the joy seep out." ꑃ

THE 8 STEPS IN ACTION

■ **Create a stunning website:** Like the rest of the Life is good creations, its website draws you in and makes you want to spread the optimism. It does a great job of reflecting the company philosophy by looking and feeling upbeat. In addition to buying its products, you can access info about its annual Playmakers Festival, held each September near Boston. *www.lifeisgood.com*

■ **Develop an explosive PR and marketing campaign:** You can't get much more explosive than having thousands of people wearing shirts with your message emblazoned across the chest. While the products speak for themselves, one of the keys to the company's success has been the "shop local" approach to marketing. It sells a variety of apparel, pet products, a stationery line, and footballs, Frisbees, and other recreational products in about 30 countries and 5,000 retailers in the United States, including 100 dedicated Life is good stores.

■ **Make a splash in the news:** From the *Huffington Post* and *Entrepreneur* magazine to *Inc.* and "ABC News Nightline," Bert and John are a reporter's dream: Savvy rags-to-riches entrepreneurs with a great story to tell. Plus, they continue to invent clever concepts (like the annual Playmakers Festival) that stay true to the brand, engage customers, and garner press attention.

■ **Network wisely:** Not only are the Jacobs' master networkers—they provide opportunities for other like-minded folks to network with each other at their Playmakers Festival, which raises about $1 million each year and features fun activities, artist meet-and-greets, and some of the top bands in the nation.

■ **Speak:** From a keynote addresses at Bentley University, to a speech to the Leaders of Philanthropy Awards luncheon, audiences around the country are eager to hear the "stay positive" message that Bert and John Jacobs deliver.

■ **Write a book:** "Life is good: Simple words from Jake and Rocket," is the 2007 book that doesn't age. The 187-page hardback features the creative designs and simple, positive messages that have made the company into a $100-million property.

■ **"Play" it forward:** "Play is the way," says Steve Gross, who runs the Life is good Kids Foundation and has penned articles on the importance of play at an early age. Kids are engaging in droves. For a recent Life is good Festival fundraiser, 11-year-old Lily had a backyard festival of her own and collected more than $400 in donations because she wanted to help other children. "Kids are so clever and always want to have fun. Whether they are throwing a party, running a race, or have a unique idea for a fundraiser—encourage them to get involved and help kids in need."

The bottom line: "One thing that we've done right for the last 17 years is to be consistent and authentic, and we've tried to help people," Bert Jacobs says. That they make a product that people like is also a winning business strategy. Quality is the key to the Life is good products—from the words-to-live-by messages to super soft T-shirts that wash well. It's rare that a company will be true to its brand in such a multi-layered manner.

> **STICKY QUOTE**
>
>
>
> **A Big Idea to incorporate into your playbook**
>
> "We tend to think of nonprofits and government organizations when we think about organizations that do good things, but in truth a lot of the power is with people who know how to make money. If you know how to make money, and you have visibility through consumer products, then you can do some pretty amazing things."
>
> — Bert Jacobs

RULE

BE INTERCONNECTED

Dr. Esther Sternberg: On Healing Yourself

DOES THE WORLD MAKE YOU SICK? If the distractions and distortions around you, the jarring colors and sounds, can shake up the healing chemistry of your mind enough to make you sick, can other aspects of your environment—ones that are more pleasing to your senses—have the power to heal you?

Esther Sternberg, MD, is credited with helping illuminate the possible underlying mechanisms for connections between stress, depression, and auto-immune disease, which she wrote about in her 2010 book, "Healing Spaces."

A former NIH medical researcher, she is currently the research director of the Arizona Center for Integrative Medicine at the University of Arizona at Tucson, founded by Dr. Andrew Weil.

You had a personal experience with healing when you developed arthritis shortly after caring for your mother when she was dying from breast cancer. Can you tell us more about what you learned from your own bout with illness, and how it deepened your understanding of the mind-body connection?

Dr. Esther Sternberg

Esther Sternberg: I went through a period of extreme stress at that time, and soon after my mother died I developed inflammatory arthritis. It involved my shoulders, elbows, and wrists. Based on my research, I attributed the illness to the emotional pain I had lived through. And suddenly, I understood the mind-body connection in a very personal way—and at a level far deeper than when I was looking it from an academic, scientific perspective. I came to realize exactly what it meant to be ill, and to try to heal yourself.

Around the same time, I moved into a new house, and my neighbors were Greek. They came over to introduce themselves and saw that I was writing what was to become my first book, "The Balance Within." They told me they had always wanted a writer to stay in their cottage in Crete, and asked if I wanted to accompany them there. I did, of course, and it was a life-altering experience. Their home is located in a village along the south coast, and it was so relaxing. I was there for only a little more than a week, but day by day, I could palpably feel myself healing. It was then that I began to realize the importance of "place" in healing.

At first I was tired and didn't really want to do anything but sit around or sleep. I was afraid to walk very much, because my knees felt unstable. But the couple's daughter changed all that. She was about 20, and asked me if I'd accompany her to the beach. I was hesitant at first, because that would require quite a long walk along uneven ground.

Then she told me that she was blind in one eye, and needed help getting to the beach. So cheesy as it sounds, we agreed that she'd be my legs and I'd be her eyes. Like in the story, "Heidi," that young woman gave me the courage to walk—slowly at first, but every day we made our way to the beach together, and it was the first step in my healing process.

Another wonderful experience came soon after when I met an elderly Greek man who I learned was in the advanced stages of prostate cancer. Despite that, every single day he'd climb a steep hill to get to our little cottage, which was on his way to his ultimate destination—the chapel that was built on top of the ruins of a temple to Asclepius, the Greek god of healing. And every day of my stay, on his way up to that chapel, he'd stop by to give me a grapefruit or an orange.

After a few days of watching him do this, I figured that if he could make the climb, surely I could do it, too. And that got me going. I'd climb to the steps of that chapel where I'd sit and contemplate. I listened to the sound of the sheep and goats and the wind, and the scritch-scratch of the gardener tending the grounds. I didn't realize I was meditating, but I was—feeling a deep state of calm as I was present in the moment, aware of nature, and the places and beautiful sights around me.

The love and kindness I experienced there is also an example of the power of being surrounded by altruistic friends, and how that is so connected to our healing. That, plus the walking every day, swimming in the ocean, listening to music, and eating the healthy Mediterranean diet, are activities that can really help you heal.

Making those healthy changes in your life did help you heal, yes?

Esther Sternberg: They did! My aha! moment came at the end of my stay, when it was clear that if I continued on the road I was on at home—working 24-7, eating cheeseburgers and fries, and not exercising, I'd never get well. I knew I had to make a change, and since my return from Greece all those years ago, I have made dramatic changes and am much better for them.

What does your day look like today?

Esther Sternberg: I start off quietly, sitting on my patio. I take time to contemplate my day, and my life, as I did sitting at the chapel in Crete. I also swim almost every day, and if I can't, I make an effort to walk for about 30 minutes—which has been shown to reduce the effects of chronic stress on the body, and to improve one's mood.

I eat a healthy Mediterranean diet, which I wasn't doing before I got sick. This type of diet includes foods high in Omega-3, such as salmon, shrimp, scallops, tuna, and halibut, sardines, soybeans, tofu, flaxseed, and walnuts. I also eat Greek yogurt, lots of salads, and fresh vegetables and fruit.

Plus, pretty much the only fat I really consume is olive oil, because researchers—including my colleague and friend Dr. Gary Beauchamp—are discovering that its link to an ibuprofen-like chemical may be one of the reasons that the Mediterranean diet is so good for you. (See Dr. Sternberg's Q&A with Dr. Beauchamp on that topic in the June 2012 issue of *www.BeInkandescent.com.*)

In the PBS documentary based on your book, "The Science of Healing," you examine the role the brain plays in healing, and address some critical questions, such as: What is healing? Is there a mind-body connection? What happens in the brain when healing occurs? What role does emotion play? Tell us the most shocking or enlightening thing that you discovered in your research.

Esther Sternberg: One of the biggest misconceptions most people have is that they equate healing with curing. In truth, curing an illness or ailment is something that is very different from healing.

That said, it's clear that healing means different things to different people. In fact, the experts in the healing community say you can die healed. So to me, healing really is a state of mind. It's being at peace with yourself and your illness, and accepting it for what it is.

Once you find this emotional completeness of being healed, it's all the more possible to be cured. But that also depends on the illness. If you have terminal cancer, a cure may not be possible.

Nonetheless, people who are dying will often say they feel healed. I had a healing myself, when finally

I understood in a personal, tangible way the difference between going on with my day-to-day routine of taking anti-inflammatory pills and dragging myself around, versus actually healing myself and making changes in my life. What I have come to know is that healing is an emotional connection to yourself, your loved ones, and the world around you. It gives you a sense of peace that's very Buddhist. It's an acceptance—but not a giving up.

Your first book, "The Balance Within," examines the science connecting health and emotions. In the final chapter, "Prometheus Unbound," you note that this connection "may sound like utopia, and perhaps be too much to expect from science. If this new science accomplishes a single thing, it will help physicians speak the language of their patients, and listen to them." Clearly, this was a problem when you published the book in 2001. Since then, have you found that doctors are more open to the idea of the mind-body connection, and the role of "place" in well-being?

Esther Sternberg: Some biomedical scientists are still coming around to this idea, but many professionals in other fields—environmentalists, landscape architects, green building designers, urban planners—have long known about the importance of creating beautiful spaces to enhance our well-being.

Scientists, however, have been looking for evidence—empirical evidence—to prove that our surroundings are essential for good physical health. Although these notions have been around for a long time, there wasn't one central place to go to prove it.

In my books, I have tried to bridge the gap by gathering evidence from the fields of neuroscience, sensory neuroscience, immunology, and environmental psychology to show how different environmental features are extremely important in providing a positive—or negative—environment for healing.

In your 2009 book, "Healing Spaces," you again tackle the mind-body connection when you talk about how your surroundings can impact not only well-being, but healing, as well. You write: "Does the world make you sick? If the distractions and distortions around you, the jarring colors and sounds, could shake up the healing chemistry of your mind enough to make you sick—might your surroundings also have the power to heal you?" What are the ideal settings for healing?

Esther Sternberg: Soothing places. Because places with lots of noise, too much light, too little light, and so forth, can further harm an ill patient by triggering the stress response.

By and large, we in the scientific medical community have begun to embrace the idea of the mind-body connection. The data has been out there for years, but the studies weren't designed to investigate *how* the environment heals. Our challenge now is to bring that understanding to our patients in more profound ways, and initiate what we now call integrative medicine in our medical practices, and at clinics, hospice centers, and hospitals. It's not an alternative, but how medicine should be done—by integrating mind-body with conventional medicine, taking into account people's emotions, and finding ways to enhance their senses and awareness of place. It's a very exciting time in medicine.

The bottom line about healing yourself is that we all have the wonderful opportunity to find our own healing spaces everywhere in the world. I have recreated a little piece of Greece in my home. But your healing space might be in a garden at your church, at a special spot near where you work, or under a tree in your backyard. What's wonderful is that we all benefit, because increasingly, healing gardens and artful spaces are being built in public places—in parks and hospitals, schools, hotels, and office complexes. The magic of a healing space is that it makes you feel at peace. It's where you can sit, relax, and get in touch with the natural world that surrounds you.

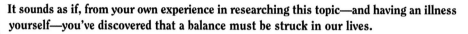

It sounds as if, from your own experience in researching this topic—and having an illness yourself—you've discovered that a balance must be struck in our lives.

Esther Sternberg: Most definitely. And I can tell you that I am fortunate in that when I got sick, I was able to plug myself into an NIH program that tested my genes. I also had a knee biopsy, which revealed that I have a gene that predisposes me to mild to moderate inflammatory arthritis.

Fortunately I also found out that I don't have a lot of genes that predispose me to severe autoimmune disease.

I know from experience that lifestyle can change the balance in terms of whether you get sick or not—and how sick you get depending on the illness you develop. In my case, the load of genes that I have is manageable, so long as I take care of myself. When I feel myself overdoing it and getting really stressed, I know it's time to change my direction—I now know what will trigger me into a relapse, and I can pull myself back from the brink.

One thing I want to make clear to everyone is that if you can't do it—if you can't heal yourself—don't feel guilty. It could be that you carry too large of a load of bad genes, and that you simply can't heal without medication.

Indeed, that's why we have medication—and that's why we call it integrative medicine. There are various approaches that couple healing strategies with advances in pharmacological care, and the combination of those two essential tools is the key to healing more people. ☼

Learn more at www.esthersternberg.com

INKANDESCENT INSIGHTS

Takeaways from Esther Sternberg's interconnected playbook:

The big win: "There is a turning point in the course of healing when you go from the dark side to the light, when your interest in the world revives, and despair gives way to hope," writes Dr. Esther Sternberg in "Healing Spaces," the book that led to the creation of the PBS special, "The Science of Healing." Internationally recognized for her discoveries of the science of the mind-body interaction, Dr. Sternberg has become a force in collaborative initiatives on the inter-relationships of mind, body, stress, wellness, and environment. Her two books are informative and scientifically based, and have inspired doctors and laypeople alike.

From a PR point of view: Dr. Sternberg's disclosure of her intense personal experience with illness—the stress of caring for her terminally ill mother and her own resulting inflammatory arthritis—doesn't just generate sympathy, it gives her credibility, and it shows off the compassionate side of this authoritative scientist. Plus, it empowers people by showing them simple ways to not only heal themselves from illness, but feel better every day. That's information everyone can use—and great public relations.

Dr. Esther Sternberg's Favorite Ways to Heal Yourself

❶ Stimulate your five senses.

What gives your senses pleasure? Is it a bouquet of flowers? Is it a beautiful view? Is it pictures of your family?

There is a physician in Ireland, professor Shaun McCann at Trinity College in Dublin, who brought bone-marrow transplants to his country. In treating his patients, he realized that to truly heal, they needed to be comfortable and calm. So he created a project called "Open Window." He set up webcams and worked with artists, art curators, and art historians to develop a menu of images that patients said they would like to look at. In addition to modern and ancient art, patients told him they wanted to see images of their family, or of nature—of animals grazing, such as cows and horses.

They also liked pictures of canoes floating down a stream with the landscape passing by. These scenes are hypnotic and relaxing, and he made viewing them possible.

Do your own self-interview, and ask yourself: "What would I like to look at, taste, touch, smell, and hear?" Then surround yourself with all of those beautiful things.

❷ Go offline and escape from your daily grind.

Go snorkeling or hiking, or take a walk in your favorite park. Or, like me, sit by a window or on your patio each morning. Start with a simple mindfulness meditation three days a week. Sit in a beautiful place, calm yourself down, and breathe. Do it for five minutes for a week, then add additional minutes in week two. Believe it or not, it'll become a great way to spend a bit of time each day.

❸ Begin a healthy diet and exercise program.

Eat all the things you know you should—fresh fruits and vegetables, fish, a little meat, and use olive oil. It's easier than you think. And once a day, swim, walk, run, or ride a bike (even if it's an exercise bike indoors.) Just move your body, and you'll see the benefits of a calmer mind, and a healthier body, in a very short period of time.

❹ Surround yourself with the people whom you love—and the people who love you.

Friends and family members are great healers, so don't be afraid to reach out and ask for help. Odds are good that even if you don't ask, those who love you will show up when you need them to. This is especially important if you are a chronic caregiver; surround yourself with others who can help take the burden off. Remember, you don't want to run yourself into the ground, or you won't be there to help your loved ones.

> STICKY QUOTE
>
>
>
> **A Big Idea on healing to incorporate into your playbook**
>
> "As you lie in bed, you suddenly notice the dappled sunlight on the blinds and you no longer shield your eyes. You become aware of birdsong outside, and the soothing whir of the ventilation system down the hall. You no longer dread the effort needed to get up, but take your first cautious steps, like a child, to explore the newfound space around you.
>
> "This is the point when the destructive forces of illness give way to healing. In every sense, it is a turning point—a turning of your mind's awareness from a focus on your inner self to a focus on the outer world."
>
> — Dr. Esther Sternberg

How to Supersize Your Small Business

THE 8 STEPS IN ACTION

■ **Create a stunning website:** In addition to putting her books center stage on her website, www.esthersternberg.com, the homepage reflects Dr. Sternberg's impressive academic background while giving readers insight into her speaking tour, PBS specials, and her successful medical career: *www.esthersternberg.com.*

■ **Develop an explosive PR and marketing campaign:** Just as her research guides her theories, Dr. Sternberg promotes her work by sticking to the academic facts—and also engaging us emotionally—thereby making her message accessible to everyone. Her engaging books have become an effective marketing campaign in themselves. Case in point: they inspired the PBS special, "The Science of Healing." Today, her position as the head of research at the Arizona Center for Integrative Medicine gives her more visibility and influence in a growing field.

■ **Become a columnist:** She is a regular contributor to *Science* magazine's column, "Books et al;" she's also a regular columnist for *Arthritis Today.*

■ **Make a splash in the news:** Dr. Sternberg has been featured on numerous radio and television programs, including the PBS shows "The New Medicine," and "Life Part II," and NPR's "Speaking of Faith," and "On Being." Famous for her ability to translate complex scientific subjects for lay audiences, Sternberg has testified before Congress and advised the World Health Organization. In December 2012, she gave a speech at the Vatican and met Pope Benedict. Both events made a splash in the news and raised her profile.

■ **Speak:** A dynamic public speaker who is recognized by her peers as a spokesperson for the field, Dr. Sternberg lectures nationally and internationally to both lay and scientific audiences. She is often interviewed on radio, television, and in print media on subjects including the mind-body connection, stress and illness, spirituality, love, health, and place and well-being.

■ **Write a book:** Trained as a rheumatologist, she is adept at translating complex scientific subjects into highly accessible prose, with a combination of academic credibility, passion for science, and compassion for those who are ill. Dr. Sternberg has been able to share her message internationally through her popular books, "Healing Spaces: The Science of Place and Well-Being" and "The Balance Within: The Science Connecting Health & Emotion."

■ **Pay it forward:** Dr. Sternberg has been recognized by the National Library of Medicine as one of 300 women physicians who have changed the face of medicine. She has given hope to and helped thousands deal with chronic illness and pain through her research and her books, PBS special, and numerous speaking engagements. Before moving to Arizona, Dr. Sternberg was section chief of Neuroendocrine Immunology and Behavior at the National Institute of Mental Health; director of the Integrative Neural Immune Program; and co-chair of the NIH Intramural Program on Research on Women's Health.

The bottom line: While it can be difficult to make medical research interesting to the general public, Dr. Sternberg has found a way to bridge the gap. "I was very much grounded in the conventional scientific method, and almost serendipitously discovered that the brain's stress response is important in autoimmune diseases like arthritis," she explains. "When you discover that, and can prove it on a molecular, neurobiological, and hormonal basis in animals, then it's possible to step back and consider what it is about the brain and emotions that can help us heal."

BE IMAGINATIVE
Author Ridley Pearson: On Living Your Dream

WHO DOESN'T WANT TO FLY TO THE "SECOND STAR TO THE right, and straight on till morning" to find themselves on the island of Neverland?

"Certainly no one I've ever met," says best-selling author Ridley Pearson, whose novels cover a lot of ground, from the paranormal to the Peter Pan prequels, which he co-authored with humorist Dave Barry. Pearson is perhaps best known for his crime and suspense novels, which have been translated into 22 languages and sell in 70 countries.

What makes Pearson's novels so engaging, critics agree, is his ability to pull in readers in the first paragraph—and keep them hanging on until the last page.

Consider the opening of "Peter and the Starcatchers":

Ridley Pearson

"The tired old carriage, pulled by two tired old horses, rumbled onto the wharf, its creaky wheels bumpety-bumping on the uneven planks, waking Peter from his restless slumber. The carriage interior, hot and stuffy, smelled of five smallish boys and one largish man, none of whom was keen on bathing."

In the ensuing 450 paperback pages, we learn that Peter is the leader of the boys—because he was the oldest. Or so he said. This charismatic leader who dresses in tights and has a flying fairy for a best friend can't help but capture your heart and imagination. Readers are sucked into the fast-paced adventure that takes place on the high seas as Peter and his new gal-pal Molly (a character created in the image of the strong young women that Pearson and Barry were raising) overcome pirates and thieves in their quest to keep the world safe from evil.

Despite his gift as a wordsmith, Pearson's first love wasn't books. It was music.
"I always wanted to grow up to be the leader of a band," says the Connecticut native. He attended boarding school before heading off to Kansas University with his best bud, Otis Read. When Read was diagnosed with cancer during their sophomore year, however, it was a game changer for both men.

"He asked me to help him through the treatments, and how could I refuse?" asks Pearson, who was also tempted by Read's offer to start a band. "When Otis recovered, we started playing music together, Hall & Oates style, and it was a dream come true."

Somewhere around year five of the band, he realized what a difficult life it was to be a full-time musician.

"We were young and determined, and so we persevered," says Pearson, who with Read spent the next 11 years going from gig to gig. They put together a variety of other bands during that period, and had a ball traveling the country and scraping by.

"We knew when we were in our late 20s that we didn't want to be earning little money and lugging tons of equipment around in our converted school bus when we were 40," he recalls.

After one barely profitable night playing at a coffeehouse in Bend, Oregon, the band decided to call it quits. "It was one of the saddest days of my life," Pearson shares, "but it had to be done."

One dream begets another

But Pearson never gave up on his dream of being a storyteller. During the last few years of his music career, he had begun writing manuscripts and books.

"I went into the writing business naively, which proved to be a benefit. I wasn't aware of the odds, but even if I was, it would have seemed like a better opportunity than the hard-knocks music business."

Fortunately, tenacity is Pearson's friend, because he wrote for more than eight years before selling a single thing.

"I started writing on-spec scripts for TV shows like 'Columbo,' because I loved the genre," he said, admitting that he never sold one. "But I was really fortunate during that time to find some guys who were willing to mentor me. Their advice, and my trial and error, got me to the point where I could finally sell something. Then I got an agent—and I got lucky."

His first published novel, "Never Look Back," was published in 1984.

"Getting the hardcover book in the mail was one of the highlights of my life," Pearson shares. "At the time, I was living in a house that my parents had built in Idaho, and I remember clearly the UPS man handing me the package. Before I even signed for it, I tore it open, and there it was—my novel. It was a breathless moment. I went running into the backyard, jumping around and screaming with delight. It was an out-of-body experience."

Never, never, never give up

To achieve those spectacular moments, take Winston Churchill's advice following the German Blitz in World War II: "Never, never, never give up."

INKANDESCENT INSIGHTS

Takeaways from Ridley Pearson's imaginative playbook:

The big win: Following his second dream (the one that came after he got to be leader of a band) has paid off handsomely for Ridley Pearson. He's created a series of best-selling books—in addition to writing a Tony Award winning Broadway show. But the author notes that his writing success came only after he spent many years trying to make a living in the music business. One key to his success is that he didn't give up writing, even though it took him eight years to get published.

From a PR point of view: Though there are some surprising exceptions, generally writers have to write well to be successful at it. But it's having a sense of humor on top of great storytelling ability that can knock PR campaigns such as Pearson's out of the park. Plus, he has demonstrated expertise in writing fiction for adults, for children, and for Broadway. That versatility gives him an advantage over many other authors—and best of all, the audience benefits from his good writing. Talk about a win-win-win.

"The thing about success is that if you are doing something you love, you can't make yourself give up on the dream," he insists. "I have had umpteen zillion part-time jobs to support myself so that I could do what I loved, and I'd still be doing whatever it took to tell stories and play music. Even if I was working in a corporation to support my family," he says, "I'd be writing and playing music in my spare time. It's who I am. I am a storyteller."

Though his career as an author was taking off by the 1990s, he couldn't give up his passion for music. And that's when he met Dave Barry, and the other founding members of the Rock Bottom Remainders, a band founded in 1992 by Kathi Kamen Goldmark.

"The arts are for sharks," Pearson likes to say. "You have to keep swimming. You can't rest—or you will sink or get eaten."

The power of collaboration

Pearson says he never stops studying, learning, creating, and working with other creative people. "And every day, I think I'm a little better at what I do for what I read, the movies I watch—and just being in the world and listening. It makes the sentences better, the plots deeper, and the stories richer."

That desire to work with other creative people is what led Pearson and Dave Barry to collaborate in 2002.

"We had been friends for years and one day decided that it would be fun to work together," Pearson explains. "We got to thinking about Peter Pan, and what his life was like before he made his way into the Darlings' house.

"Either of us could have probably written the series alone, but we knew that if we came together, the story would be more powerful."

The "Peter and the Starcatchers" series has "sold more copies than paper napkins," Pearson jokes.

The book became a hit Broadway show that was lauded by critics and has won five Tony awards.

Pearson adds that a highlight of his life was the night that he, Barry, and the cast and crew were waiting for critic Ben Brantley's review while at a bar called Phoebe's in NoHo.

"It was like a scene from one of those old movies, where the cast and crew are all dressed up and drinking cocktails, waiting for the verdict to arrive."

This being the digital era, the review came across as a text. Fortunately, someone had a BlackBerry and handed it to Pearson.

"Everyone's face was glowing blue in the light of the device as we read the great review," he recalls. "We all started crying with joy and relief. It was another one of those amazing pinch-me moments."

Learn more at www.ridleypearson.com

THE 8 STEPS IN ACTION

■ **Create a stunning website:** Simple but comprehensive, Pearson's website features a homepage navigation that sends readers to his suspense novels, his adventure books, and his bio page, entitled, "Ridley Who?" The home page is short, sweet, and effective. The website is user-friendly, too; visitors can quickly go toward either the adult suspense novels or the young reader adventure books: *www.ridleypearson.com.*

■ **Develop an explosive PR and marketing campaign:** Pearson uses his website as an effective marketing tool. Pages have info on his books, information on his upcoming appearances, and interesting news bits. You can join his mailing list for information about upcoming books. To keep young readers engaged, he runs a tally of high scores from the "Kingdom Keepers Expert Quest," and features photos from his speaking engagements.

■ **Make a splash in the news:** Pearson has appeared on the "Today" show, "Good Morning America," "Craig Ferguson," CNN, the BBC, NPR, and he has been reviewed in major newspapers around the world. The Broadway adaptation of "Peter and the Starcatchers" won five Tony Awards. The media comes to this celebrity. But early in his career, Pearson struggled as a musician for 11 years, and then for eight more years as a writer before making a splash in the news.

■ **Network wisely:** While working as a chauffeur for authors on book tours, networking maven Kathi Kamen Goldmark was instrumental in bringing together musically talented authors to form The Rock Bottom Remainders, '60s-style rock 'n roll band that included Pearson and Dave Barry. That led to their collaboration on "Peter and the Starcatchers." Early in his career, he was also successful at connecting with people willing to mentor him; following their advice helped jump-start his writing career.

■ **Speak:** With so much success, Pearson is a sought-after speaker. He has appeared at the South Florida Gifted & Talented Symposium, the Largest Book Party–First Book St. Louis, and Walt Disney World Radio Cruise. "Disney schedules my appearances based on the sales of the books," he explains, so Pearson does what he can to help spread the word about his books to keep sales up.

■ **Write a book:** Pearson has penned 30 adult suspense novels and more than 15 children's adventure novels published in 22 languages. He admits the process isn't pretty. "I rewrite every novel no fewer than four times, sometimes as many as nine times," he says. "You can't believe how many hours that consumes. It's *endless.* You have to be patient to be a published writer, and you have to practice humility, because the editor (or teacher) is nearly always right."

■ **Pay it forward:** Pearson's crime novels emphasize dazzling investigative detail, and, all too often, imitate life. His novels have helped solve two homicides and settle an environmental lawsuit. Hoping to raise awareness of the illegal use of child labor to produce rugs in Amsterdam sweatshops, he wrote "Choke Point." "Every year, there are 800,000 human trafficking victims worldwide," he notes, "and the average age is 11-14, with 80 percent of victims being female. I hope to bring these matters to people's attention as part the effort to stop this criminal activity."

The bottom line: "Don't give up—if you are doing something you love, you can't make yourself give up," he insists. "But change the plan if it's not working."

STICKY QUOTE

A Big Idea to incorporate into your playbook

"Thirty years ago, when I was researching my early novels, I would need to spend two to three weeks touring a city with local experts. Now that same intimacy is available via technology. This new world order is somewhat shocking to me, but it works, so why fight it?" Advice for beginning writers: "Stay in the chair and write. Pick an amount of time each day—30 minutes, one hour—and sit down and DO IT."

—Ridley Pearson

BE INTUITIVE

Helen Fisher: On the Science of Love

W HAT IS LOVE? AND WHY DO WE PICK THE people we choose to love, hire, and befriend? Is there really love at first sight? How did love evolve?

To answer these eternal questions, Rutgers University professor and anthropologist Helen Fisher, PhD, has traveled from the desert outback of East Africa, to Tokyo and Iran, and back home to New York City, to determine if one culture perceives love differently than another.

She then used fMRI technology to look inside the brains of 50 men and women who said they were madly in love.

Her perspectives on love, sexuality, and gender differences have been featured in *TIME* magazine, and on NPR, NBC, the BBC, and CNN. She has also authored five books: "The Sex Contract," "Anatomy of Love," "The First Sex," "Why We Love," and her 2010 book, "Why Him? Why Her?" Fisher is currently working on a new title about why we choose one partner over another.

In "Why We Love," Fisher explains that everywhere in the world, people fall into romantic love. "Like the craving for food and water and the maternal instinct, passion is a fundamental human drive," she says. "Courting and winning a particular mate is one of our most profound urges."

Helen Fisher, PhD

Fisher took the question to another level in her next book, "Why Him? Why Her?," and analyzed how people can find real love by understanding their personality type. The research for that book became the basis of the Chemistry.com questionnaire that matches people with compatible brain chemistry.

We begin our discussion with Fisher by talking about that eternal question of why humans love. Fisher says there are three basic mating drives that inhabit our brains:

■ **Lust:** The craving for sexual gratification emerged to motivate our ancestors to seek sexual union with almost any partner.

■ **Romantic Love:** The elation and obsession of being in love with a mate enabled the ancients to focus their attention on a single individual at a time, and to conserve time and energy.

■ **Attachment:** The sense of peace and security one feels toward a long-time mate motivated our ancestors to stay together long enough to rear their young.

Although Fisher admits the magic of love cannot be underestimated, she is convinced that the need to procreate is the primary motivator.

"If you have four children, and I have no children, your genes are going to live on," she says. "So we

all know deep down inside that our sexual behavior is going to have important consequences."

What, exactly, is going on in the brain when we experience those feelings of lust, romantic love, and attachment?

Fisher had initially hypothesized that romantic love was associated with elevated levels of dopamine and/or norepinephrine, two key neurotransmitters. After interviewing dozens of men and women, and using high-tech tools to analyze their brain activity, her theory was confirmed when the fMRI showed activity in the region of the brain that is part of the reward system.

"That part of the brain—called the reptilian brain—evolved long before mammals proliferated some 65 million years ago," says Fisher, noting, "This result was what I was looking for."

The reason is that the nerve cells in this portion of the brain distribute dopamine to many parts of the brain. "It produces focused attention, as well as fierce energy, concentrated motivation to attain a reward, and feelings of elation, even mania—the core feelings of romantic love," she says.

As a result, Fisher was able to observe chemical changes in the brain as her subjects looked at the photos of their loved ones, giving her an insider's view of some of the chemical underpinnings of love.

After these findings were published, Fisher was asked to become the scientific advisor to Match.com's sister site, Chemistry.com. Using her research, she crafted the "Chemistry Profile," a personality assessment and matching system that includes dozens of questions ranging from, "Is your sock drawer ready for public inspection?" to "Are your friends the social crowd, intellectuals, adventurers, or activists?"

Other questions ask the test taker to identify a mate's ideal body type, fitness regime, favorite Friday night date, and religious preferences. While the questions may seem straightforward, the answers identify the chemicals dominant in the brain: dopamine, serotonin, testosterone, and/or estrogen.

■ **Dopamine-Driven Explorers:** People with naturally high levels of dopamine tend to be risk takers, novelty seekers, artistic, creative, and curious. Fisher found that 26 percent of the 40,000 men and women she polled fell into this category.

■ **Serotonin-Driven Builders:** Those with a lot of serotonin tend to gravitate toward the traditional. They are calm, social, popular, loyal, conscientious, and tend to be organized and enjoy rules. Often, they are pillars of society and good in business. This includes about 29 percent of the population.

INKANDESCENT INSIGHTS

Takeaways from Helen Fisher's intuitive playbook:

The big win: Helen Fisher's success is rooted in taking a topic full of mystery—love—and translating it into information people want: the reasons for the romantic choices they make. It's a surefire attention-getter. Who doesn't want to know the answers to such questions as: Why do we pick the people we choose to love, hire, and befriend? Is there really love at first sight? How did love evolve?

From a PR point of view: Her research and credentials take the topic of love above and beyond the tabloid. She has traveled extensively to determine if one culture perceives love differently than another. She also has used fMRI technology to look inside the brains of 50 men and women who said they were madly in love. This is the stuff that great stories are made of. Add to that the fact that Fisher's research is the basis of the Chemistry.com questionnaire, and she's a publicist's dream.

■ **Testosterone-Driven Directors:** This group is direct, and skilled at understanding rule-based systems. They are highly analytical, logical, emotionally contained, bold, and ambitious—and account for about 16 percent of the population.

■ **Estrogen-Driven Negotiators:** Those with high amounts of estrogen have good people skills, an active imagination, are altruistic, idealistic, and nurturing. They tend to see the "big picture," but are not very detail oriented. Approximately 25 percent of people fit into this category.

"Everyone has a combination of chemicals, but one or two tend to dominate," Fisher explains. "Consistently, though, dopamine-driven Explorers go for each other, as do serotonin-driven Builders. Testosterone-driven Directors and estrogen-driven Negotiators are happiest when they mate with each other."

Fisher's research leads her to a few forecasts about the future of love and relationships.

"Since women started returning to the workforce a few decades ago, the balance of power between the sexes has shifted," she notes, explaining that for centuries in hunting and gathering societies, women were on an equal footing with men, going out to gather the evening meal and being equally responsible for the survival of the family and community.

"But with the invention of farming tools that required physical strength, women were relegated to seemingly secondary roles of keeping house and rearing children. Arranged marriages dominated, and mating became more of an economic and sometimes political agreement between families."

Fisher expects this shift to gain strength as more women graduate from college—and earn almost as many PhDs as men. Their economic and political power will continue to grow, and Fisher forecasts that women will return to the place of power they held before the plow was invented.

"Men are now being pressured to please a woman—or she won't have them back," Fisher insists. "Going forward, men are definitely going to have to work a little harder to get and keep a mate."

Fisher also believes that the pursuit of romantic love later in life will increase.

As more baby boomers hit 50—and realize they could live another 40-50 years—many will be looking around for someone new to "light their fire," she forecasts. "Romantic love is deeply threaded into our human spirit. If we don't have that in our lives, we feel like we are missing something. And we are."

Trusting your intuition

Intuition is another fascinating topic in Fisher's wheelhouse.

"While intuition may seem to arise from some mysterious inner source, it's actually a form of unconscious reasoning," she says. "It's rooted in the way our brains collect and store information. As you accumulate knowledge—whether it's about which books your spouse likes or how to play chess—you begin to recognize patterns."

Here's how:

1. Your brain unconsciously organizes these patterns into blocks of information, a process the late social scientist Herbert Simon, PhD, called "chunking."

2. Over time, your brain chunks and links more and more patterns, then stores these clusters of knowledge in your long-term memory. When you see a tiny detail of a familiar pattern, you instantly recognize the larger composition—and that's what we regard as a flash of intuition.

3. This elaborate brain circuitry likely evolved so that our forebears could quickly size up a person or a situation. Our female ancestors, in particular, needed this skill: They had to tune in to their infants to enable them to survive. And this helps explain why women today have an edge when it comes to reading people.

So listen to your gut feelings instead of brushing them aside.

"There are times to trust your intuition and times to let your head take the lead. Still, your intuition may not always steer you right, but it can be a useful first step in decision-making." ⋰💡⋱

Learn more at www.helenfisher.com

How to Supersize Your Small Business

THE 8 STEPS IN ACTION

■ **Create a stunning website:** Beautifully presented on www.helenfisher.com is her extensive research on the future of human sex, love, marriage, gender differences in the brain, and how your personality type shapes who you love. The TEDx talk she gave is spotlighted—enabling her to dynamically show audiences what she knows. Her website also includes free, interactive quizzes for visitors to find out about their own personality and what types of people they are compatible with: *www.helenfisher.com.*

■ **Develop an explosive PR and marketing campaign:** Fisher spreads her message through videos on YouTube, her blog on Chemistry.com, and speeches around the world, including at Davos in 2009. It's Fisher's research on love and sex that keeps us coming back for more.

■ **Become a columnist:** Fisher's articles have appeared in dozens of publications including, *Psychology Today, Journal of Neurophysiology, O Magazine, Elle,* and *More.*

■ **Make a splash in the news:** Fisher has appeared on many US and international TV and radio shows, including "20/20," "Today," "Nightline," "The Colbert Report," "The View," and "Oprah."

■ **Network wisely:** Fisher's accomplishments have led to new opportunities, allowing her to expand her networks. Since 1983, she has served as an anthropological commentator and consultant for businesses and the media. From there, she began working with Match.com and Chemistry.com, which led to her column in *Reader's Digest,* as well as work with Oprah's Harpo Productions, VISA, and other companies.

■ **Speak:** To hear Helen Fisher speak is truly a treat. She exudes passion for her topic. Audiences worldwide have been the beneficiaries of her lectures, which include speeches at The World Economic Forum (Davos), the International meeting of the G20, TED conferences, the International Monetary Fund, The Aspen Institute, the United Nations, USA Today/Gannett, and the Harvard Kennedy School of Government.

■ **Write a book:** A researcher who has shared her work with the world, Fisher has authored five books: "The Sex Contract," "Anatomy of Love," "The First Sex," "Why We Love," and "Why Him? Why Her?" She is currently working on a new book about why we choose one partner over another.

> STICKY QUOTE
>
>
>
> **A Big Idea to incorporate into your playbook**
>
> "Eighty-nine percent of men and 94 percent of women regarded it as important that a date be able to laugh at themselves—an essential ingredient in a long-term partnership."
>
> — Dr. Helen Fisher
>
> (Wouldn't colleagues and customers alike find this trait appealing?)

The bottom line: As Fisher proves, you don't need to have an unusual topic to be memorable. You need an unusual take on it, and the expertise to back it up.

BE INNOVATIVE

Alan Webber: On Being a Global Detective

WHILE ALAN WEBBER'S NAME MAY NOT BE FAMILIAR TO YOU, odds are good that you have read the publication he founded in November 1995 with Bill Taylor—*Fast Company* magazine.

Both men were former *Harvard Business Review* editors, and their publication was founded on a single premise: A global revolution was changing business, and business was changing the world. "Discarding the old rules of business, *Fast Company* set out to chronicle how changing companies create and compete, to highlight new business practices, and to showcase the teams and individuals who are inventing the future and reinventing business," Webber explains, adding that they were proud to have been named *Adweek's* Editor of the Year in 1999.

Prior to his successful foray into publishing, Webber was a political speechwriter focusing on innovative policy initiatives. Today, he continues exploring reinvention, and considers himself a "global detective"—one who travels the world speaking at innovation and foresight conferences, and investigating how things work. To that end, in 2009 he published a best-selling business book, "Rules of Thumb: 52 Truths for Winning at Business Without Losing Your Self."

You and Bill Taylor were both at *Harvard Business Review* when you came up with the idea to create *Fast Company*. Tell us about what inspired you.

Alan Webber: One of the big inspirations was a fellowship I got from the Japan Society of New York to spend three months in Japan at the end of the 1980s—back when that country was thriving, and the US was fretting over national economic competitiveness. Harvard gave me a sabbatical, and off I went to interview "the next generation of Japanese

leaders" in business, government, and the bureaucracy—across the board. It was a huge opportunity to see the future as it was emerging. When I got back from that trip, I had four themes that I was sure were going to change the way we all worked, and the way business was done:

■ A generational shift, as baby boomers replaced the World War II generation, and brought different values and sensibilities to the workplace;

■ The rise of globalization, erasing geographic boundaries from the way companies operated;

Alan Webber

■ The rise of diversity, replacing the old notion that leaders had to be white men with particular pedigrees in order to make it to the top; and

■ The emergence of digital technology, creating a world in which almost everything is portable, personal, and digital.

Of course, having that kind of epiphany didn't immediately turn into a magazine. It took Bill's relentless focus on implementation and a lot of work to develop a business plan that would turn our ideas into the kind of architecture that every great magazine needs. Then we had to find a group of backers who were willing to give us a first round of investment so we could put out a "beta" issue; and after that, we made a deal with Mort Zuckerman and Fred Drasner, who owned *US News & World Report* and *The Daily News*.

It was easily the hardest thing I've ever done, and the most rewarding. Magazine-ing is a real team sport, and we built a championship team made up of young, smart, energetic, fun people who wanted to create a new kind of business magazine.

Some of the thought leaders we have profiled in *BeInkandescent magazine*, including Dan Pink and Barry Lynn, also spent time in a Japan Society fellowship program. They also told us that this experience changed their personal and professional lives. What was it about Japan that intrigued you most?

Alan Webber: I fell in love with the aesthetics of Japan, the care with which the Japanese do everything, the exquisite art of presentation that goes into Japanese culture and business. And I met some amazing people and made some wonderful, lifelong friends on that trip, including Dan and Barry. That fellowship, and the sabbatical that Harvard gave me, were amazing gifts that have made a huge difference in my life.

Share with us some of the details of your years as a speechwriter for former Secretary of Transportation Neil Goldschmidt. What inspired you to get into the speechwriting business, and what is your fondest memory from those days?

Alan Webber: Starting in 5th grade, I entered a public speaking contest that my school held every year. You had to pick something to memorize, and then deliver it in front of the school. I fell in love with the spoken word, with the idea that speeches could not only convey ideas, but also genuinely move people's emotions.

When I went to work for Neil in the 1970s—first when he was a city commissioner in Oregon, and then when he was the mayor of Portland—it felt completely natural that I would write speeches for him. Back in those days, we didn't have computers, so speeches had to be typed out on IBM Selectric typewriters equipped with a special type ball that put everything in uppercase letters, which made it easier to read. One year, as the mayor was giving his "state of the city" address, I was back at the office making last-minute changes to his speech; an aide would then run the new copy over to the venue where he was speaking. That was "just in time" speechwriting!

My speechwriting duties continued when Neil became Secretary of Transportation under President Jimmy Carter in 1979. In that role, I even had the opportunity to make suggestions for the State of the Union address, and write a talk for one of the president's advisors to give in Detroit.

Then there was the time that officials at the White House asked Neil to nominate President Carter for re-election at the Democratic Convention in New York. That was the year Ted Kennedy was challenging Carter for the nomination.

I was asked to write Neil's speech. Very exciting, right?—a speech to be delivered at a nationally televised political convention! But the Kennedy delegates assembled in front of the podium as soon as Neil got up to speak, and started chanting, "Time's up!" The TV networks cut away from Neil in order to talk with their pundits—so nobody heard or saw the speech. Win some, lose some.

In addition to "Rules of Thumb," you have written "Going Global," which looks at the techniques and tactics needed to succeed in the global economy; and "Changing Alliances," which reports on a Harvard Business School study of competitiveness in the US auto industry. How has your experience as an author differed from your work as a magazine editor?

Alan Webber: In some ways, it's easier to be a magazine editor than an author. As an editor, your job is to be the reader's best friend. You want to make every article you work on as clear, concise, engaging, and compelling as possible. At *Fast Company*, we always believed that any article could be cut by 50 percent and it wouldn't hurt the article—in fact, it might help it! And as an editor, it's usually easy to ask the right questions that can help the article become clearer, crisper, more focused: What are you really trying to say here? What's the point of this piece? Where's your logic flow? Where's the argument for what you're presenting? Editors get to give their authors tough love.

When you're the author, however, the whole game changes. You get to have your own voice, present your own thinking, give your own point of view—and that's fun and rewarding. But suddenly, your perspective about cutting the piece by 50 percent changes—hey, those are good words! I wrote them!

All that stuff about asking hard questions? It's hard to ask yourself tough questions! It's hard to be objective about your own writing. What writing and editing have in common is that the real work of writing is in the re-writing. So if you've spent a lot of time as an editor, it will make you a better writer, and a better author.

Your newest title is an e-book, "The Global Detective."

Alan Webber: It is! A few years ago I found myself at the art museum in Salzburg, Austria. There was an amazing work of art on display, "The Black Box," a piece created by the brilliant South African artist William Kentridge. It was a multimedia presentation that dramatizes a horrific act of genocide committed against the Herero tribe in Namibia in 1906.

In the middle of this powerful work of art, a slide appears that says "Global Detective." When I saw it, I knew immediately that was my new job title. As a global detective, my job is to travel around the world, looking at what's going on, collecting clues, trying to solve the mysteries of our time: What's going on and why?

So, when I took off for Europe not long ago, I described my adventures in a travelog/blog/narrative. The e-book that's out now covers the part of the trip that took me to Germany and Austria. I'm working on Part 2, which continues the work of the global detective when I went on to Denmark and Finland.

Now that you are a global detective, do you have any insights into the solution to the world's global economic problems? No pressure.

Alan Webber: Thanks for asking! I do have a few clues that I've been gathering and trying to connect. Not long ago I was in New Zealand and China, back to back. In both places I asked the people I met, "What's the biggest problem in your country?" In both places, they told me that it's "the growing gap between the rich and the poor."

Then I went to Wales to the Do Lectures. I asked the people there, "What is the biggest problem in the UK?" The answer: "The growing gap between the rich and the poor." It's true almost everywhere I go—and recognition of that problem is certainly what's behind the Occupy Wall Street movement.

If you look at the data, the United States has the largest gap between the rich and the poor of any advanced, industrialized nation in the world.

And the gap is getting larger. From that gap comes a stream of social problems that are the issues that keep us all awake at night: the failures of public education, the health care crisis, and problems of unemployment and crime—the fraying of the social fabric in ways large and small.

In my role as a global detective, I'm now looking for solutions that work in addressing these social problems. If we can identify those solutions, find out not just how they work but why they work, and what they have in common, then we can develop a new approach to creating positive change. We can work at the grassroots level to solve problems; and in the process, we may be able to develop ways to close the gap between the rich and the poor.

Given a few years of perspective, do your "Rules of Thumb" still stand up? Are there any rules you'd delete? What would you add in?

Alan Webber: Every once in a while I take out "Rules of Thumb" and read through it. It's a little like the "I Ching"—depending on how I feel or what's going on in my life, different rules jump out at me, speak to me—or don't speak to me. Which I think is the real strength of the book. It doesn't try to give you a "one size fits all" set of ideas or practices. Instead, it presents 52 working precepts that you can read and use as you need them. There are some that come up more often than others—at least for me. There's the rule that says, "Change is a math formula."

The formula is, "Change happens when the cost of the status quo is greater than the risk of change." Another one that seems to fit the moment is, "If you want to see with fresh eyes, re-frame the picture."

This speaks to the art of re-framing, something that organizations all over the world are struggling to do, as they seek to cope with change. And of course there are new rules that present themselves all the time, if you're paying attention.

The other day, for example, I went to a terrific display at the San Francisco Museum of Modern Art, showing the work of Dieter Rams, whose designs have influenced several generations of designers, up to and including much of the work that has come out of Apple. His rules of thumb for design were posted on the walls at the show—and I wrote them all down. It was a great example of Rule #52 in my book, which says: "Stay alert! There are teachers everywhere." That may be the most important rule of all.

You are working with the Center for Social Value Creation at the University of Maryland's Robert H. Smith School of Business. What can we expect to see there in the coming years?

Alan Webber: Go back to what I said about the growing gap between the rich and the poor and my own search for solutions that work for problems that matter. Increasingly, I'd say, this question of social equity and economic justice is at the heart of a growing conversation about business, work, the economy, and society. Scholars are writing about it; financial analysts are proposing new metrics to change how we measure and what we measure; political leaders are offering their approaches.

It is a conversation the world is having right now—and needs to have. And young people are eager to participate in the discussion.

It's all about the future—it's all about their future. Even if we don't yet know the answers, at least we're asking the right questions—and that is the role of education, whether in a business school or in a magazine. So I'm enormously hopeful that centers like this one at the University of Maryland can be important nodes where this conversation can flourish.

INKANDESCENT INSIGHTS

Takeaways from Alan Webber's innovative playbook:

The big win: An award-winning, nationally recognized editor, author, and columnist, Webber has become a go-to guy for small-business insights. In 1995, he launched *Fast Company* magazine, which became the fastest growing, most successful business magazine in history. Webber was named *Adweek's* Editor of the Year in 1999, along with co-founding editor William Taylor.

From a PR point of view: Business savvy pours from Webber's books, blog, and website. While it's easy to see why he's so successful as a leader, it's Webber's down-to-earth, no-nonsense approach to work and life that makes him so appealing. He's a publicist's dream because not only is he easygoing, his thought-provoking ideas are gobbled up by readers and the press. Clearly, Webber is leading by example, and that's the best PR campaign there is.

At 65, as a long-time Santa Fe resident, you are running for governor of New Mexico. Why did you decide get into politics?

Alan Webber: The reason why is simple. I wasn't presenting myself as a candidate. I was presenting myself as somebody with a lot of experience in business, economic development, and issues like public education. I heard the same thing from people everywhere, whether it was Las Cruces or Pecos, and that is, the state's not doing very well. The state's in real trouble. The state's at a standstill. I heard that more than once. And we've got to do something to get New Mexico moving again. I looked around at the Democratic slate and I felt very candidly that I was the one who could actually do the best job presenting a better vision for the state and could win the election for the governor's office.

You didn't grow up in New Mexico, and you are getting some flack about that.

Alan Webber: It's true. I'm constantly asked: How long have you lived in New Mexico? Who are your people? How well do you know us? The flip side of that is so many of the people I met while I was exploring the idea [of running] were incredibly supportive. They didn't ask me, "Who are you to be interested in New Mexico's future?" They said, "We're really interested in New Mexico's future, too, and if you are, welcome to the conversation." I'm not surprised it came up. I have to tell you, when I lived in Boston, people were really concerned that I didn't come over on the Mayflower. ⌀

Learn more at www.alanwebber.com

Alan Webber's ③ Favorite Rules of Thumb

The dominant themes are change and leadership.

❶ Focus on the signal-to-noise ratio. Leaders today don't just make decisions; they make sense. Get outside of the United States and you'll be struck by how much noise there is in our system. People are screaming at each other: talk radio, news-as-entertainment TV, and the blogosphere. We have too much noise, but not enough signal. What real leaders have to offer is more signal and less noise.

❷ If you want to think big, start small. The leaders I admire most are the ones who have had the courage to take an idea they believe in and test it out at the grassroots level. Make it a petri dish sized experiment. See if it works. See if it doesn't work. See how it could work better. Silicon Valley likes to brag, "Go big or go home." When I look at change in the world, it's almost always the opposite: Start small and see if it works. Then keep trying until you find out what actually does work.

❸ Ask the last question first. The last question is, "What's the point of the exercise? What's your definition of victory?" When I look at the disconnects that afflict so many companies, institutions, and organizations, what they have in common is that they've lost track of why they are doing what they are doing.

Wall Street used to exist to provide capital for companies to grow; now it exists to make money on money. So in the case of Wall Street, what's the point of the exercise? Just to make more money? CEOs used to feel they were charged with building great organizations, creating great places for people to work, producing exceptional products and services. Now they focus on driving up the company's share price, on creating shareholder value.

As change comes more unexpectedly and as demands on all of us grow, being able to answer, "What's the point of the exercise?" is a great source of personal comfort, power, and influence. It's what makes for real leaders—and successful entrepreneurs.

How to Supersize Your Small Business

THE
8
STEPS IN
ACTION

■ **Create a stunning website:** Easy to navigate and chock full of ideas, Webber's website, www.alanwebber.com, is actually a news portal for business trends. His articles and blog postings are evergreen—that is, they are perpetually relevant, sustainable and lasting—including "The New Geography of Jobs," and "The Leadership Lessons of Steve Jobs." In his bid for governor of New Mexico in 2014, he openly used his campaign website to gather Facebook contact information from visitors.

■ **Develop an explosive PR and marketing campaign:** The co-founder of *Fast Company* magazine, and a Harvard Business School grad, Webber is a marketing genius. So it's no surprise that everything he's touched in the years since has turned to gold, such as adopting the role—and moniker—of "global detective." You can do the same. Leverage your message so that it appeals to your target audience. And take a page from Webber's playbook: Become effective in business—and in life. That's the power of public relations.

■ **Network wisely:** For Webber, social media is the platform that keeps him in touch with thousands of fans. On Twitter alone he has nearly 5,000 followers. But his personal network of media, political, and international business connections are what continue to help him leverage his brand.

■ **Speak:** This expert on change and innovation in the knowledge economy works with the Leigh Bureau, known as the world's longest-established premium speakers bureau. Founded in 1929, the bureau's previous speakers have included Eleanor Roosevelt and Boris Yeltsin. Clearly, Webber is in good company, and he takes his message around the country as well as around the world, which is what you'd expect for someone who describes himself as a global detective.

■ **Write a book:** "Rules of Thumb" is an encyclopedia of great ideas—one that takes a while to digest. To truly absorb its wisdom you need to read it over time—one rule at a time. What's fantastic about the book is that you can come back to it again and again, and gain fresh insights. That kind of wisdom keeps the book on the shelf for years. It has been on mine since 2009.

■ **Pay it forward:** Webber's 52 truths are the stuff that gets an entrepreneur up in the morning. It's the purpose behind the work, and the philosophy behind the ideas that drive the meaning of the business. He pays it forward by sharing the big ideas he's learned over a stellar career in business. Every rule ends with a section called, "So What?" "It's a tool for observing your own work and life and coming up with rules that can help you work smarter, grow faster, and succeed sooner."

The bottom line: Webber uses all he's learned to understand and predict future trends—with an eye toward creating "a global dialog to develop a new operating manual with rules of thumb from around the world—rules designed to make the world a better place and the future the way we want it."

> STICKY QUOTE
>
>
>
> **A Big Idea to incorporate into your playbook**
>
> "All work is teamwork. If you want to create intangible value—and then keep on doing it—create a culture and a working environment where trustworthy, creative, courageous people bring their best ideas and best effort to work every day, and where they work well together."
>
> — Alan Webber

*"Only those who will risk going **too far** can possibly find out*
how
far
one
can
go."

— T. S. Eli

INKANDESCENT PUBLISHING COMPANY
THE INKANDESCENT GROUP, LLC

Inkandescent Publishing is the book publishing division of The Inkandescent Group, LLC, a public relations, content marketing, website development, graphic design, and publishing company that helps small businesses get more visibility and increase their market share. Having worked with hundreds of entrepreneurs since incorporating in 2008, the company uses its *8 Steps to PR Success* to put successful growth strategies into play using PR, marketing, advertising, and social media tools: www.TheInkandescentGroup.com.

**Founder & President
The Inkandescent Group**

HOPE KATZ GIBBS

Journalist, publicist, author, and entrepreneur Hope Katz Gibbs started her career as a newspaper reporter after graduating from the University of Pennsylvania in 1986. In the years since, she has won awards for feature and column writing for articles that have appeared in *The Washington Post, USA Today, The Miami Herald, Costco Connection*, and dozens of other business, education, and general interest magazines, newsletters, and blogs. Read her clips at www.hopegibbs.com.

Hope got into the PR business in 2001, when she put her graduate studies in educational leadership at The George Washington University to work and became the director of communications for the City of Fairfax Schools in Northern Virginia. Soon after, her PR client list expanded to include the international futurist think tank, Social Technologies, which was based in her stomping ground of Washington, DC.

In 2008, Hope incorporated The Inkandescent Group, LLC, and since then has helped hundreds of entrepreneurs, educators, authors, and small-business owners increase their visibility through the company's PR and book publishing services. "PR Rules: The Playbook," is the first book published through the Inkandescent Publishing Company. Learn more at www.InkandescentPR.com.

Senior VP

KATHLEEN MCCARTHY

The managing editor and senior VP of The Inkandescent Group, Kathleen has been a freelance editor and writer for more than two decades. She enjoys riding the publication arc—the beginning of every issue is a fresh start, and the end of every issue brings a completed publication. A deadline fanatic, Kathleen is zealous about the virtues of the serial comma and admires writers who can translate dense topics into artful prose.

As the managing editor of *Be Inkandescent magazine*, Kathleen edits 25 articles per month, and also makes sure all of the Inkandescent books, newsletters, press releases, and other materials are eloquent, filled with content, and grammatically correct.

Kathleen's writing expertise is in the mental health and nonprofit fields, having worked as a writer and editor for the American Psychological Association, the National Association of College and University Business Officers, and the American Society for Engineering Education. She also handles the editing, design, and layout for the monthly online newsletter of the American Mental Health Counselors Association. Past freelance clients include the Centers for Disease Control, GE Information Services, and the University of Mary Washington.

Art Director

MICHAEL GLENWOOD GIBBS

A freelance illustrator and designer since attending Pratt Institute as a photography and illustration major, Michael's award-winning artwork has appeared in *Newsweek, Time, The New York Times, The Washington Post, The Wall Street Journal, Fortune Magazine, New Republic, Harvard Business Review*, and publications for United Airlines, Verizon, American Airlines, Boston Consulting Group, Johns Hopkins, Vanderbilt, and American University.

Michael has also illustrated book covers, as well as poster campaigns for the Pittsburgh Opera, The Virginia Opera, Harvard University, and other orchestra and theater groups.

His illustrations have consistently been recognized by peer-reviewed art organizations such as The Society of Illustrators, Communication Arts Illustration Annual, 3×3 Annual of International Illustration, Creative Quarterly, Print, and Spectrum. His work has been exhibited at museums and galleries including the Society of Illustrator's Museum of American Illustration in New York City, the Billy Shire Fine Arts Gallery in Los Angeles, the Neptune Gallery in Los Angeles, and in the Washington area at the Corcoran Museum of Art, the Sumner School Museum, The Ratner Museum, The Edison Place Gallery, The Cafritz Foundation Gallery, and the University of Maryland Gallery. View Michael's portfolios at www.michaelgibbs.com and www.mglenwood.com.

Photo credits:

Steve Barrett Photography *ix*, 9, 10, 11, 17,
    18, 19, 28, 29, 50, 51, 59, 85, 161
Anna Paige Gibbs, 141
Robert Walker/ICU2 Sports Photography 110

All illustrations by Michael Glenwood Gibbs,
©1990-2014 Michael Glenwood Gibbs

Sharon Armstrong, author, "The Essential HR Handbook," www.theessentialhrhandbook.com
"Although most small-business owners know they need good public relations, many aren't sure exactly what it is or how to get it. Gibbs and McCarthy break the PR process down into simple, easy-to-follow steps designed to create favorable publicity for your company, enhance your reputation in the marketplace, and ultimately get more customers in the door. This is an excellent resource for any entrepreneur—clear, concise, and actionable, and a must-read for small-business owners."

Andrea Arroyo, international fine artist, www.andreaarroyo.com
"I found Hope Katz Gibbs' book to be a comprehensive public relations guide. Hope is truly an expert in her field, and this book is a must-read for all entrepreneurs."

Jim Barnes, editor and IPPY Book Awards director, www.independentpublisher.com
"I have a couple of new authors ask me every day, 'How do I get my book out into the marketplace?' and now I have the perfect tool to recommend. This book is filled with great advice, well organized and concise with a lively design that makes it fun and easy to read. Anyone who wants to improve the way they promote their products, businesses, or themselves should read this book."

Bryan Beatty, CFP®, partner, Egan, Berger & Weiner, LLC, www.ebwfinancialnews.com
"You need a game plan on how to stand out and get noticed. 'PR Rules' will help you understand the new world of PR. It is a must-read for any aspiring business owner."

Stephanie Bhonslay, owner, GardenU, www.gardenugardening.com
"'PR Rules' provides the absolutely essential information required for small businesses to grow in the 21st century."

Chef Kim Alvarez, owner, Avenida Restaurant, www.avenidarestaurant.com
"'When it comes to understanding PR, there's no greater source than 'PR Rules,' which offers practical advice that every entrepreneur can immediately put to use. We have worked with The Inkandescent Group for years, and know from experience how valuable it is to hire a savvy, insightful team that is creative, fun to work with, and really knows their stuff."

Chris Carbone, futurist, on Twitter @cwcarbone
"'PR Rules' is part practical workbook and part inspirational guide. With it, Hope Gibbs and her team have created a rare thing—a business book that you can get fired up about. They help you turn your big business ideas from what's possible into actionable items. I know from experience working with Hope that her 8 Steps to PR Success is a strategy that works."

Kristine Carlson, author, "Don't Sweat the Small Stuff for Moms," www.kristinecarlson.com
"When it comes to not sweating the small stuff, Hope Gibbs' 'PR Rules' provides an easy-to-navigate primer that takes the guesswork out of public relations. Indeed, having good PR is critical for any small business. And having PR advisors you can trust is equally important. This guidebook does the trick. I highly recommend it."

Rita Cheng, CFP®, CEO, Blue Ocean Global Wealth; author, www.wealthmanagementrules.com
"Hope Katz Gibbs and Kathleen McCarthy have put together an innovative, powerful playbook that is indispensable because it offers practical, easy-to-implement advice. It's not just a roadmap to PR success—but to business success. You will truly benefit from the tactics and strategies. The editing work they did with my book, "Wealth Management Rules," is proof."

Meg Cox, reporter, *The Wall Street Journal*, www.megcox.com
"Hope Gibbs really knows the PR business. This book taps top experts and is an extremely practical and accessible guide."

Ana Dutra, CEO, Mandala Global Advisors; former CEO, Korn/Ferry Leadership and Talent Consulting
"In 'PR Rules,' Hope Katz Gibbs delivers an extraordinary PR and marketing playbook in a pragmatic, clear, and humorous way. Hope's advice and experience will help not only entrepreneurs and small-business owners but any executive who wants to leverage PR, social media, and marketing in a laser-focused and effective way. She removes the clutter and confusion from PR, helping readers to craft a PR strategy that centers on what really matters for each individual and company."

WHAT PEOPLE ARE SAYING ABOUT "PR RULES: THE PLAYBOOK"

Lisa DuBois Farrell, account executive, Washington, DC
"'PR Rules' takes the guessing out of the public relations equation. I bought copies for all of my clients!"

Lou Ferrante, author, Mob Rules, www.louisferrante.com
"Best how-to book ever written on PR! Hope Katz Gibbs is an expert in the field and her book should be mandatory reading for every small-business owner, who by nature are do-it-yourselfers. And yet, many spend tens of thousands on PR. Hope's do-it-yourself book is the last investment you should make in PR. A must-read!"

Sonya Gavankar, broadcast journalist, "Face of the Newseum," Miss DC 1997, www.sonyagavankar.com
"The publicity game has changed, and this guide will easily become the playbook for the new phase of the public relations industry. Hope's 'PR Rules' is *the* guide for the businessperson searching for the spotlight, and the entrepreneur needing focus as they create a business plan. Hope leverages her career and personal experience in one easy-to-navigate place."

Michael Glenwood Gibbs, illustrator and designer, www.michaelgibbs.com and www.mglenwood.com
"As the author's husband (and the book's designer), you might expect that, well *of course* he'll give 'PR Rules' a five-star review. But as I read it, over the course of designing it, a 💡 went off over my head time after time as I discovered useful information, profound insight, and let's-get-going inspiration on every page. (So *that's* what she's been doing all this time!) It's a treasure trove of information and insight, and already I'm putting the book's advice to work in my own business."

Robyn Henderson, networking strategist, www.networkingtowin.com.au
"'PR Rules: The Playbook' is filled with practical, affordable ideas to fast-track PR, media exposure, and results. Every chapter is brimming with stacks of really useful tips and tactics. Well done."

Eileen Hull, "The Queen of Crafts," and creator, #PaperTrail Teaching Tour, www.eileenhull.com
"I did not want to stop reading 'PR Rules.' It's full of practical tips on using PR to build your brand and take it to the next level. Why re-invent the wheel? Gibbs and McCarthy have your back. Buy the book, take notes, and turn them into actionable next steps for your business. It's an excellent resource that every entrepreneur should keep close at hand."

Caroline Leavitt, *New York Times* best-selling author, "Is This Tomorrow," www.carolineleavitt.com
"Great PR can help a book find and grow an audience. I know personally how much Hope Katz Gibbs has done for me, and this book is going to stay on my desk!"

Janice Miller, School Board chairman, City of Fairfax Schools, www.cityoffairfaxschools.org
"Message is essential, and hiring the right person to get your message out is equally important. Hope Katz Gibbs served our schools extremely well as the director of communications. She's hard-working, smart, savvy, clever, and creative—all in one classy package. Her 'just right' public relations moves put our schools on the right track."

Jeff Moore, former owner, ACT College
"The crisis management expertise, thoroughness, and dedication that Inkandescent PR provided during the unexpected and very difficult closure of our school was a tremendous asset! When it seemed the world was against me, Hope Gibbs listened to me, believed in me, and helped me tell the story from my point of view. I am truly grateful for her help."

Peter J. Noonan, EdD, superintendent, City of Fairfax Schools, on Twitter @peternoonan
"Sometimes in leadership positions, we become so focused on the mission that we forget the importance of communicating effectively. 'PR Rules' offers practical ideas that I've been incorporating into my work since I started working with Hope Gibbs in 2002. Her guidebook will help many others because they now have the benefit of learning from her expertise."

Lisa Rueff, executive director, Do It For The Love Foundation, www.doitforthelove.org
"Hope Katz Gibbs has created a must-read—an extensive and excellent resource for all business owners. So much thought, care, and attention to detail have gone into this book. Every business owner should read it. Their business will thrive as a result. Thank you, Hope, for your dedication and guidance."

WHAT PEOPLE ARE SAYING ABOUT "PR RULES: THE PLAYBOOK"

Gina Schaefer, founder, Ace Hardware DC, www.acehardwaredc.com
"I have really enjoyed reading 'PR Rules' and have dog-eared most of it! Hope gives us bite-size chunks of good advice. Each of the profiles offers practical advice, real-life experiences, and great information for business owners in all industries and at all levels. As the owner of nine Ace Hardware stores in Washington, DC, and Baltimore, I am already putting the advice in this book to use. I highly recommend it."

David Bruce Smith, author and publisher, David Bruce Smith Publications, creator, The Grateful American™ Series, www.davidbrucesmith.com
"If you want to learn how to have significant success, you must read this book."

Dr. Esther Sternberg, author and research director, Arizona Center for Integrative Medicine at the University of Arizona at Tucson, www.esthersternberg.com
"This engagingly written and practical book combines biographical sketches and personal narratives with bulleted pointers gleaned from the individual experiences of the subjects interviewed. I especially enjoyed the 8 Steps in Action section in Part 3 of the book, in which Hope distills common themes for success that can be applied by anyone seeking to expand a business."

Buddy Teaster, president and CEO, www.Soles4Souls.org
"Hope comes at life and business with a powerful combination of head and heart. She understands that it takes both elements to get the most out of whatever you're doing, including PR. Excellent roadmap to engaging your audience from all perspectives!"

Janet Terry, writer/producer, WUSA9, Washington, DC, www.wusa9.com
"Hope Katz Gibbs is a master of public relations. If anyone can help you understand the rules of PR and help your business benefit, it is Hope. I've known her for years. She is smart, bold, and innovative and stands out in a very competitive field."

Jennie L. Walker, PhD, PHR, director of Global Learning & Market Development at the Najafi Global Mindset Institute, Thunderbird School of Global Management, globalmindset.thunderbird.edu
"'PR Rules: The Playbook' brings public relations in the digital age to life through examples, narratives, and case studies that engage and inspire. Hope Katz Gibbs has created more than just a 'how-to' book; she has captured voices of experience and wisdom in the field for the benefit of those who want to pump up their PR strategies."

Alan Webber, co-founder, *Fast Company* magazine; 2014 candidate for governor of New Mexico, www.alanwebber.com
"Back when I wrote 'Rules of Thumb,' Hope interviewed me for the cover of her business magazine and did a great job. Now she's written the Rules of Thumb for PR—and it is an absolute winner! This book is a must-read for every small-business owner. Buy it, read it, and do what it says!"

Gene Weingarten, *Washington Post* columnist, www.washingtonpost.com
"Hope Katz Gibbs is far less pathetic, incompetent, and shameless than most PR people. Her book actually contains some smart advice, not that any of those clueless frauds in PR will take it." *[See "Flack Yourself," page ix.]*

Lee Woodruff, veteran PR expert, contributor to "CBS This Morning," best-selling author, www.leewoodruff.com
"In a digital age where the rules seem to be broken or changed every week, 'PR Rules' offers concise, clear, and usable information from industry experts on how to move forward in an ever-changing marketing terrain. Even a PR veteran like myself can learn something from this book by Hope Katz Gibbs and her team."